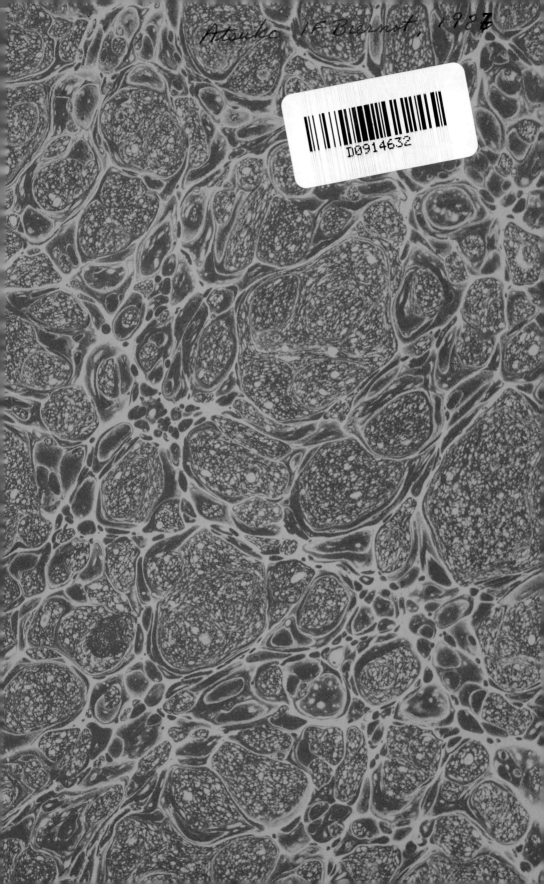

The
National Archives
and
Foreign Relations Research

NATIONAL ARCHIVES CONFERENCES / VOLUME 4

*Papers and Proceedings of the Conference on*
*The National Archives and Foreign Relations Research*

Sponsored by the National Archives and Records Service
June 16–17, 1969 / The National Archives Building / Washington, D.C.

# The
# National Archives
# and
# Foreign Relations
# Research

EDITED BY

## Milton O. Gustafson

OHIO UNIVERSITY PRESS
*Athens, Ohio*

# Contents

## PUBLICATION OF RECORDS ON UNITED STATES FOREIGN RELATIONS

## ADMINISTRATIVE HISTORY OF THE DEPARTMENT OF STATE

## DOMESTIC INFLUENCES ON UNITED STATES FOREIGN POLICY

## THE DIPLOMACY OF WAR AND PEACE

# UNITED STATES RELATIONS WITH EUROPE

# UNITED STATES RELATIONS WITH LATIN AMERICA

# UNITED STATES RELATIONS WITH EAST ASIA

# UNITED STATES RELATIONS WITH THE
# MIDDLE EAST AND AFRICA

# HISTORY AND FOREIGN POLICY

# Foreword

The National Archives and Records Service has inaugurated a series of conferences for the exchange of ideas and information between archivists and researchers. These conferences are designed both to inform scholars about the wealth of useful research materials available in the National Archives and Records Service and to provide an opportunity for researchers to suggest ways in which their use of these records could be facilitated.

The National Archives and Records Service, a part of the General Services Administration, administers the permanently valuable, noncurrent records of the federal government. These archival holdings date from the days of the Continental Congresses to the present.

Among the approximately one million cubic feet of records now constituting the National Archives of the United States are such hallowed documents as the Declaration of Independence, the Constitution, and the Bill of Rights. However, most of the archives, whether in the National Archives Building, the regional archives branches, or the presidential libraries, are less dramatic. They are preserved because of their continuing practical utility for the ordinary processes of government, for the establishment and protection of individual rights, and for their value in documenting our nation's history.

One goal of the National Archives staff is to explore and make more widely known these historical records. It is hoped that these conferences will be a positive act in that direction. The papers of each conference will be published, in the belief that this lively exchange of ideas and information should be preserved and made available in printed form.

ARTHUR F. SAMPSON
Administrator of General Services

# Preface

The National Archives conference series was established in 1967 to increase contacts and improve relations between the scholarly community and the National Archives. Through the exchange of ideas at these conferences many benefits result. We at the National Archives seek new and better ways to serve the research needs of scholars, and we want scholars to learn as much as they can about the great variety of research resources available in the National Archives. In order for us to aid agencies in devising record-keeping systems, to judge what should be permanently preserved and what should be destroyed, to decide what finding aids to prepare and what records to microfilm—in short, in order to do our job effectively—we must keep up to date on the changing research requirements of scholars. On the other hand, scholars should become more acquainted with our programs and problems. Our programs need public support, and we need an informed constituency to help us resolve some of our problems. These conferences therefore are designed to foster a two-way communication between the academic community and the National Archives.

The Conference on the Archives of United States Foreign Relations, held on June 16 and 17, 1969, was the fourth semiannual National Archives conference. Because records of the Department of State have always been one of the most heavily used research resources in the National Archives, shortly after the conference series began it was decided to recognize this interest of historians and other scholars by conducting a conference devoted to American foreign policy.

Milton O. Gustafson was selected as conference director and is the editor of this volume. Before joining the National Archives staff in July 1967 as a diplomatic records specialist, he had used records and papers in the National Archives and in the presidential libraries for his own dissertation research; thus he was uniquely capable of bringing together archivists, historians, and other scholars to focus on the general subject of the archives of United States foreign relations. In 1971 Dr. Gustafson became chief of the Diplomatic Branch.

The idea of focusing on American foreign policy was of personal interest to me since my first administrative position at the National Archives was as chief of the Foreign Affairs Branch in 1960. I once sat in the office Dr. Gustafson now occupies, supervised many of the people still on his staff, and came to know many of the people who participated in this conference.

I therefore realize as he does the values and the limitations for research of the records of the Department of State in the National Archives. The papers presented in this volume describe archival and other sources for research and will, I hope, serve as a stimulus and a guide for coming generations of scholars working on topics in the field of American foreign relations.

JAMES B. RHOADS
Archivist of the United States

# Introduction

In planning the Conference on the Archives of United States Foreign Relations, the National Archives staff decided to focus on the problems of the researcher—the problem of finding a relevant topic and the resources needed to study that topic. The conference was designed around separate sessions that focused on United States relations with specific countries and areas, the two major wars of this century, domestic influences on foreign policy, administrative history, the publication of diplomatic documents, and the archival sources relevant to each of these topics. During the two days of the conference the speakers delivered twenty-three formal papers in ten different sessions, some of them held concurrently. This volume consists of both those papers and the discussions by the distinguished participants and the speakers that followed each session.

The first seven papers in the volume were delivered at a panel session on resources of the National Archives and Records Service relating to the study of United States foreign relations. My own paper described the State Department's different filing systems, the different record groups for State Department records in the National Archives, and National Archives accessioning and microfilming policies. Garry D. Ryan discussed the records of the War Department that relate to foreign policy. Dr. Ryan has specialized in military records since he joined the National Archives staff in 1956, and he is currently chief of the Modern Military Branch. Robert Krauskopf, who has also specialized in military records since he joined the National Archives staff in 1948, discussed Navy Department records and the role of the navy in American foreign policy. Dr. Krauskopf is now chief of the Old Military Branch.

Robert Wolfe, the National Archives specialist on records captured from Germany after World War II, is chief of the Captured Records Branch. He described the unique availability in the National Archives of records, on microfilm, of the German, Italian, and Japanese governments that relate to foreign policy. Wolfe, who did his graduate work and taught at Brooklyn

College, began working with German records in 1960 on the American Historical Association microfilming project, and he joined the National Archives staff in 1961.

Daniel J. Reed, assistant archivist for Presidential Libraries, discussed the resources of the Hoover, Roosevelt, Truman, and Eisenhower presidential libraries that relate to foreign policy. Dr. Reed had previously served as director of libraries at the University of Detroit, assistant chief of the Manuscript Division in the Library of Congress, and principal historian in the Smithsonian Institution's National Portrait Gallery before joining the National Archives staff in 1969.

A. Philip Muntz was director of the Special Records Division in charge of cartographic and audiovisual records before he resigned from the National Archives in 1972. Dr. Muntz's paper not only called attention to the obvious fact that maps and photographs are needed to embellish books but also showed how cartographic and audiovisual records are valuable for other research purposes. Meyer H. Fishbein, who joined the staff of the National Archives in 1940, was chief of the Business Economics Branch before becoming director of the Records Appraisal Division. His paper discussed some neglected sources, the records of federal agencies—other than the State or Defense departments—that relate to American foreign policy.

William M. Franklin and Albert H. Leisinger, Jr., were the two speakers during the session on the publication of diplomatic documents. Leisinger, who joined the National Archives staff in 1941 and is now the deputy assistant archivist for the National Archives, not only knows more about the National Archives microfilm publication program than anyone else, but through his book, *Microphotography for Archives,* has acquired a world-wide reputation on the subject. Leisinger described the history of the program that he directed for many years when he was in charge of exhibits and publications, how records are selected for microfilming, and what records are available on microfilm.

Franklin, who has been director of the Historical Office since 1962, discussed the history of the *Foreign Relations* series as well as its future. Franklin served as principal editor of three volumes in the *Foreign Relations* series—those that relate to the wartime conferences at Washington, 1941–42; Casablanca, Cairo, and Tehran, 1943; and Malta and Yalta, 1945. Dr. Franklin has also published several articles on World War II diplomacy.

A separate session devoted to the administrative history of the Department of State featured a paper by Elmer Plischke of the Department of Government and Politics at the University of Maryland. Prof. Plischke has written four textbooks, including *Conduct of American Diplomacy,* thirteen other books, including *Personal Diplomacy of the President of the United States,* and over fifty articles and essays on American diplomacy. Plischke emphasized the importance of studying the institutions and processes of American diplomacy in order to better understand substantive policy matters.

One of the afternoon sessions on the first day of the conference was devoted to domestic influences on American foreign policy and featured papers by two distinguished diplomatic historians. Alexander DeConde has written a diplomatic history textbook, *A History of American Foreign Policy,* and numerous other works, including *Entangling Alliance: Politics and Diplomacy under George Washington,* and the *Quasi-War: The Politics and Diplomacy of the Undeclared War with France, 1797–1801.* DeConde, professor of history at the University of California at Santa Barbara, focused on the necessity of understanding the complete range of cultural influences on foreign policy in the nineteenth century.

Wayne S. Cole is professor of history at the University of Maryland. He is also the author of a textbook, *An Interpretive History of American Foreign Relations,* and numerous other publications, including *America First: The Battle against Intervention, 1940–1941,* and *Senator Gerald P. Nye and American Foreign Relations.* Prof. Cole discussed domestic influences on United States foreign policy in the twentieth century, and both his and DeConde's papers provided the framework for an extended discussion.

Another afternoon session on the first day of the conference was devoted to an analysis of the diplomacy of war and peace. Prof. Lawrence Gelfand of the University of Iowa discussed American involvement in World War I. Gelfand is the author of *The Inquiry: American Preparations for Peace, 1917–1919.* Gaddis Smith, professor of history at Yale University, noted the effect of the Vietnam war on the history of the World War II period and suggested that much more research and writing needs to be done. His own works, *American Diplomacy during the Second World War* and a volume on Dean Acheson in the *American Secretaries of State and Their Diplomacy* series, are valuable additions to the literature on this subject.

On the second day of the conference there were four afternoon sessions, each devoted to an analysis of United States relations with a particular area of the world. Norman Graebner and Robert Ferrell discussed American relations with Europe in the nineteenth and twentieth centuries. Graebner, the Edward R. Stettinius Professor in modern American hisotry at the University of Virginia, is the author of numerous publications, including *Empire on the Pacific, The New Isolationism, Cold War Diplomacy,* and *Ideas and Diplomacy,* Robert Ferrell's publications include *Peace in Their Time, American Diplomacy in the Great Depression,* and a textbook titled

*American Diplomacy*. Ferrell, professor of history at Indiana University, has succeeded the late Samuel Flagg Bemis as editor of the new volumes in the *American Secretaries of State and Their Diplomacy* series.

Another professor of history at Indiana University, David M. Pletcher, shared a session on United States-Latin American relations with Robert Freeman Smith. Pletcher has specialized in nineteenth-century relations, as his books illustrate—*Rails, Mines, and Progress: Seven American Promoters in Mexico, 1867–1911; The Awkward Years: American Foreign Relations under Garfield and Arthur;* and *The Diplomacy of Annexation.* Smith, now at the University of Toledo, has published numerous articles and essays on the Latin American policy of the United States in the twentieth century, and his books include *The United States and Cuba: Business and Diplomacy, 1917–1960, Background to Revolution: The Development of Modern Cuba,* and *The United States and Revolutionary Nationalism in Mexico, 1916–1932.*

The session on American-East Asian relations featured papers by Warren I. Cohen of Michigan State University on United States relations with China and Waldo Heinrichs of the University of Illinois on United States relations with Japan. Cohen has written *America's Response to China,* and Heinrichs is the author of *American Ambassador: Joseph C. Grew and the Development of the U.S. Diplomatic Tradition.*

The final afternoon session was devoted to papers on United States relations with the Middle East and with Africa. John A. DeNovo, professor of history at the University of Wisconsin, both discussed the historical literature of American relations with the Middle East and suggested topics for future inquiry. DeNovo's paper was not in its final form at the time of the conference, and he revised it in 1970 to include recently published items. Morris Rieger, who before his retirement in 1972 was special assistant to the Archivist for International Relations, described the sources in the National Archives relating to the study of United States relations with Africa.

Since the purpose of this conference was to bring together the records keepers and the records users to facilitate better understanding of the problems of each, it was appropriate to have a keynote address by someone who was responsible for creating records. Foy D. Kohler, professor in the Center for Advanced International Studies at the University of Miami, created many State Department records in his thirty-six-year career in the Foreign Service before he retired in 1967. He served as assistant chief in the Division of Near Eastern Affairs, assistant secretary for European affairs, and deputy undersecretary of state for political affairs in the Department of State. Abroad, he served in United States diplomatic missions in Rumania, Yugoslavia, Greece, Egypt, the United Kingdom, Turkey, and—the highlight of his career—in the Soviet Union as ambassador from 1962 to 1966. In 1970 Kohler wrote *Understanding the Russians: A Citizen's Primer.*

Kohler discussed the influence of history upon the diplomat, the diplomat's method of keeping records and thereby influencing the writing of history, and historical revisionism on the origins of the cold war. Stimulated by the conviviality of the evening reception, many participants contributed to the provocative discussion that followed.

The papers and the discussion have not been revised to take account of the changes since the summer of 1969. Many books, articles, and doctoral dissertations have been written since then, and it would be impossible to mention all of them and how they have affected the suggestions and conclusions of the speakers.

A major area of change since the conference has been in the area of access to records. During the discussion following the first panel in this volume the general problem of access to security-classified records received the most attention. In that discussion Dr. William M. Franklin of the State Department's Historical Office described the only two methods of declassification: the first is to have teams of people knowledgeable in history and records go through the documents and pass a judgment—such a program was begun in 1972 with the establishment of the Declassification Division in the National Archives. The second method of declassifying documents is to allow time to elapse. The records of the State Department, which were generally open only through 1941 at the time of the conference, are today open through 1947. It is expected that records for later years will be opened after the *Foreign Relations* volumes for each year have been published. In addition, the program of allowing limited access to certain records of the State Department has been eliminated. That policy required that a scholar apply for access to the records and submit his notes for review. Also, many office or "lot" files of the World War II period and the central files through 1949 have been transferred to the National Archives since the time of the conference.

Many of the records in presidential libraries that Daniel Reed described as restricted at the time of the conference have since been declassified or otherwise made available for research; the Kennedy and Johnson libraries have also been opened for research; and all of the presidential libraries have continued to accession additional papers—most notably the papers that Harry S Truman had retained in his office.

Because time was limited, no discussions were held at two of the conference sessions. The text of the discussion printed in this volume has been edited to eliminate repetition, confusion, or irrelevance. The order of the sessions has also been slightly rearranged to provide a more coherent framework for the volume.

There are many people to whom I am indebted. Dr. Frank B. Evans, who was director of the Diplomatic, Legal, and Fiscal Records Division, suggested the theme of this conference and recommended me as director. Even though I had been on the National Archives staff less than nine months, the Archivist of the United States, Dr. James B. Rhoads, not only agreed with that recommendation, but allowed me freedom to plan and execute all the details. Because that task was too great for one person, I requested and received assistance from Dr. E. G. Campbell, assistant archivist for the National Archives; Mark G. Eckhoff, who succeeded Dr. Evans as director of the Diplomatic, Legal, and Fiscal Records Division; and from Dr. Rhoads.

Each session was chaired by a member of the National Archives staff, and I also wish to thank them: Herbert E. Angel, Oliver W. Holmes, W. Neil Franklin, Mark G. Eckhoff, Ronald L. Heise, Robert Wolfe, George S. Ulibarri, James W. Moore, and Harold T. Pinkett. The chairman for the evening session was the Administrator of General Services, Robert L. Kunzig.

Many of the participants in the conference have told me how pleased they were with the physical arrangements that enriched their two days at the National Archives Building—especially the luncheons and the evening reception. Credit for arrangements should go to Newman Jeffrey and Steven Lee Carson of the Educational Programs staff. For the editing of this volume, credit should go to Dr. Frank G. Burke, assistant archivist for Educational Programs, and the editors of the Conference Papers staff. I especially want to thank Kathleen Mach for putting everything together and prodding me to complete this introduction. Secretarial and administrative assistance was provided by Sandra Barksdale, Patricia Perkins, Teresa Foster, Kenneth Harris, and especially Patricia G. Dowling. Most of all, I want to thank those who presented papers at the conference.

MILTON O. GUSTAFSON
Conference Director

# National Archives Records on United States Foreign Relations

# National Archives Records on United States Foreign Relations: State Department

MILTON O. GUSTAFSON

Almost everyone who has done research on United States foreign relations has used records of the Department of State—either the documents published in *Foreign Relations,* the microfilm publications of the National Archives, the unpublished original files, or all three. Even though they use these records, however, too few scholars understand them from the point of view of the archivist. Some experienced researchers, of course, do recognize the importance of analyzing filing systems and record practices. And they realize that to better understand a historical event, one should also try to understand the documents that were created to record that event.

Archival terminology is one problem. A scholar once admitted to me that after a year of research he had just figured out the difference between the decimal file and Record Group 59. The difference, of course, is that the decimal file was the State Department's filing system from 1910 to 1963, and that the record group is the system used by the National Archives to keep control over its accessioned records. Most records of the State Department are in the General Records of the Department of State, Record Group 59. There are, however, eleven other record groups for records of the State Department, separate from Record Group 59 because of the unique way in which the records were created or maintained, or because of the unique activities they document. In this paper I shall first describe the major files in Record Group 59 and then briefly survey the other eleven State Department record groups.

## RECORD GROUP 59

### CENTRAL FILE RECORDS

The 17,000 cubic feet of records in Record Group 59 are divided into two large subgroups called central file records and non-central file records. The central file records are the most used by diplomatic historians. Selection of topics for research, especially for master's theses, is facilitated if one understands that the records are divided into three different time periods—1789 to 1906, 1906 to 1910, and 1910 to 1944—because of the nature of the filing system.

For the records of the pre-1906 period the department kept separate correspondence series in three major groupings—diplomatic, consular, and miscellaneous letters. Within each grouping are letters received and copies of letters sent, filed by country when possible, and thereunder filed chronologically. It is obviously difficult to do research on a specific incident like the *Baltimore* affair with Chile in 1891. To locate all relevant State Department documents, one would have to examine the separate series of diplomatic despatches from the United States minister in Chile, the diplomatic instructions to him from the department, the notes to the Chilean minister in Washington, notes from him to the department, perhaps the consular despatches from the United States consul in Valparaiso, instructions to the consul, and the Miscellaneous Letters Received and the Domestic Letters Sent series for the State Department's correspondence with the president, the Navy Department, Congress, and private citizens.

In 1906 Secretary of State Elihu Root ordered a switch to a subject system for classifying and filing records. All of the letters in the separate series of diplomatic, consular, and miscellaneous correspondence, as well as the internal memorandums of the department, were filed together in one main series—the numerical file—according to subject. As new subjects arôse they were given a case file number (6436, for example) and subsequent documents filed on the same subject were given subordinate enclosure numbers (such as 6436/1 and 6436/2).

The numerical file, perhaps the simplest kind of subject file, lasted less than five years. The disadvantage of the file was that there was no real standard for determining when a new case file should be started; some files became extremely large, while others consisted of only one document. As the number of case files approached 29,000, the State Department changed in 1910 to a more comprehensive subject filing system—the decimal file.

The decimal file is a subject file like the numerical file, but with the subjects predetermined according to a decimal code. The first digit represents the primary subject class: 0 for general and miscellaneous matters, 1 for administration, 2 for extradition, 3 for protection of interests, 4 for claims, 5 for international meetings, 6 for commercial relations, 7 for treaty and political relations, and 8 for matters relating to the internal affairs of states. Within each primary class subjects are further defined and identified by a decimal classification, and country numbers are used to identify subjects relating to that country. Thus, 763.72119 means political relations (7) between Austria-Hungary (63) and Serbia (72), which became the World War I file, and 119 relates to the termination of the war; 862.20212 means military activities (202) of Germany (62) in Mexico (12); and 393.1163 means protection (3) of American (11) religious missions (63) in China (93). Each subject is listed in the filing manual, which is available as a National Archives microfilm publication.

Following the decimal file subject number is a slash mark ( / ) and the document number. Documents in each subject file are numbered consecutively from the year 1906 through June 30, 1944; for documents filed after that date, the document numbers represent the date of the document. For example, 840.48/7-644 is for a document dated July 6, 1944, in the subject file for internal affairs (8) of Europe (40) relating to relief (48); since there are many documents with that date in that file, some additional information, such as a telegram number, is needed for exact identification.

RECORDS NOT IN THE CENTRAL FILE

Although over 82 percent of the records in Record Group 59 are part of the central file, the preliminary inventory for this record group takes three times as many pages to describe the non-central file records. Many of the series of non-central file records were created by the administrative or service offices of the department, such as the Bureau of Accounts or the Passport Division; other series relate to special activities such as the publishing of the laws, or special subjects such as the War of 1812 and the Civil War. I would like to mention briefly only a few of these series of non-central file records that relate to United States foreign relations, particularly those containing documents at the division level which help to show how a policy was developed.

In his memoirs George Kennan describes the sudden decision to abolish the Division of Eastern European Affairs (known as the Russian Division) in 1936. The division's library on Soviet affairs, the "best in the United States," was to go to the Library of Congress, and its "elaborate and voluminous files," which Soviet Ambassador Litvinov admitted were more complete than the records of the Soviet Foreign Office itself, were to be destroyed. Kennan reports that he and Charles Bohlen saved many of the books by hiding them in the State Department attic. Fifteen boxes and twenty-nine binders of records eventually were transferred to the National Archives. These records describe Soviet developments from 1917 to 1941, and they also reflect the bureaucratic disagreement about American policy toward the Soviet Union—a disagreement which Kennan claims was the real reason for abolishing the division.

Similar records of the Division of Latin American Affairs for the 1905–44 period fill fifteen boxes. These records include original correspondence and memorandums created or received by Sumner Welles when he was the division chief; copies of his memorandums when he was undersecretary for the 1937–43 period, some of which are missing from the central file; and original correspondence of Laurence Duggan relating to Vice President Henry Wallace's tour of South America in 1943. The division also maintained a "Confidential Book File," a series of studies and reports on boundary disputes, the Platt amendment, and other political and economic problems relating to Latin America. Another unique series relating to Latin America is the Francis White file, forty-two boxes of records created or received by White from 1921 to 1933, when he dealt with Latin American affairs as division chief and as assistant secretary of state.

The Leo Pasvolsky files relate to lend-lease and other financial assistance programs, postwar planning proposals, and other matters of interest to Pasvolsky, one of Cordell Hull's top assistants in the 1938–45 period. Besides original memorandums of conversations and correspondence that never reached the central file, there are memorandums received by Pasvolsky, often including attached chits or explanatory notes by other department officials.

The studies and surveys of the Research and Analysis Branch of the Office of Strategic Services, 1941–45, and the State Department from 1945 to 1961, fill 324 boxes. Although copies of these reports were widely distributed throughout the government, the State Department's set is the most complete.

## OTHER STATE DEPARTMENT RECORD GROUPS

Of the eleven other record groups for State Department records relating to foreign policy, which are used less frequently than Record Group 59, the most important are the Records of the Foreign Service Posts of the Department of State, Record Group 84. These are the records created, received, and filed at the United States embassies, legations, and consulates all over the world. Most searchers prefer to use State Department records for correspondence between the department and the post, but sometimes the department's file copy of instructions only lists the enclosures; the actual enclosures, of course, are filed with the post records. The records of the diplomatic missions include some unique documents—the notes to and from the host country's foreign office. The most valuable part of consular post records is the miscellaneous correspondence—correspondence with American businessmen or local officials, not otherwise referred to Washington.

Research in the post records can be a problem. Records from many posts have been lost or disarranged, and record-keeping practices were not uniform. Before 1912 the records are arranged by series, similar to the department's pre-1906 filing system. After 1912 the posts used the same decimal filing system as the State Department, but the files were broken yearly.

Time permits only brief mention of the other ten record groups. The treaty files are in Record Group 11; perhaps someday someone will continue David Hunter Miller's scholarly analysis of these documents, complete now only through 1863. Records of United States participation in international conferences are in Record Group 43; for the most part these are conference documents, and related background documents are in the central file. Records of boundary and claims commissions and arbitrations are in Record Group 76. Records relating to foreign affairs during the period of the Continental and Confederation Congresses are in Record Group 360.

Two record groups contain records of the World War I period: Records of the War Trade Board and Records of the American Commission to Negotiate Peace, including the records of the Inquiry. During World War II, the Office of War Information, the Office of Inter-American Affairs, and the Foreign Economic Administration created records that are in separate record groups. Another record group is for interdepartmental and intradepartmental committees, such as the records of the State-War-Navy Coordinating Committee of the 1944–47 period.

## PROBLEMS IN ACCESSIONING AND MICROFILMING RECORDS

After this brief description of State Department records from the archivist's point of view, let me briefly note some of our problems relating to accessioning and microfilming of records. Because we cannot do everything we want to do immediately, we have to establish priorities in planning our future work programs. Top priority will be given to those projects that help us provide better reference service for our scholarly users. We welcome your advice.

When should we accession the next bloc of decimal file records, those of the 1945–49 period? Space is available for those records, but why should we accession records that are restricted or closed for research? Providing reference service on such records is a headache for us, especially so because these records are still heavily used by the State Department.

Perhaps we should concentrate on accessioning lot files of the World War II period. Lot files, for the most part, are decentralized office files like Dean Acheson's files for the 1941–46 period; the Freeman Matthews–John Hickerson files, 1941–47, relating to Western European affairs; the John Carter Vincent–Joseph Ballantine files, 1941–47, relating to Far Eastern affairs; and an administrative file for the 1945 San Francisco Conference that contains official documents, memorandums, miscellaneous correspondence, and a five-volume history of the conference by Bernadotte Schmitt. These lot files would supplement the central file records.

What should we do with the Foreign Service Post records? We already have over twenty-five thousand cubic feet for the 1789–1935 period. The post records for the 1936–48 period, now in the Washington National Records Center, amount to about another twelve thousand cubic feet. You can guess at the total that has accumulated since 1948. Should the taxpayer be forced to pay for boxing these records, shipping them to the United States, and preserving them in this ornate building in the heart of Washington, especially when many of the records are duplicated in the central file of the department? It has been suggested that they be destroyed at the post.

Turning to our microfilm publication program, where do we stand and what do we want to do? So far we have filmed almost all of the records of the pre-1906 period and 87 percent of the records in classes seven and eight of the decimal file for the 1910–29 period. Other files of the 1910–29 period should be filmed, simply on the basis of use, such as the 500A2a file, the files of the Washington Conference of 1921–22, and the 462.00R296 file, German reparations and the Dawes and Young Plans. During the coming year we intend to film all of the records in the numerical file for the 1906–10 period, the Paris Peace Commission records, and selected files from the 1930–39 period. We hope that you who have used these records and those who want microfilm will advise us on priorities, procedures, and what information should go into the accompanying descriptive pamphlets. You have to let us know.

# National Archives Records on United States Foreign Relations: War Department

GARRY D. RYAN

Until 1898 the interests of the United States Army and of the War Department were largely internal. What contact the military had with the governments and peoples of other countries was limited almost exclusively to periods of war or crises and to the areas contiguous with the United States: British Canada, Spanish Florida, and the Republics of Texas and Mexico. The War Department's involvement in the affairs of other nations increased greatly between 1898 and 1939, a forty-year period that witnessed the dispatch of expeditionary forces to the Philippines, France, North Russia, and Siberia; the maintenance of occupation forces in Cuba, Mexico, China, and Germany; and the assignment of military attachés to the capital cities of most of the nations of the world. With the advent of World War II, the War Department's involvement in the affairs of other nations became truly global, and a large part of the War Department's activities became foreign relations.

The records of the War Department in the National Archives reflect this chronological tripartition to such a degree that I have organized my paper on this basis and shall now discuss the records of each of these three time periods in turn.

By far the best source of War Department records relating to United States foreign relations in the nineteenth century is the records of the Office of the Adjutant General (AGO). The Adjutant General was the principal records keeper of the War Department until the end of World War II. So voluminous are the permanently valuable records created by this single office that the National Archives found it necessary to split them chronologically at 1917: the records antedating that year are in Record Group 94, and the post-1917 records comprise Record Group 407. Together they total more than sixty thousand cubic feet of records.

The main series of letters received by the Adjutant General's Office during the nineteenth century include files relating to such topics as the occupation of East Florida in 1812; Andrew Jackson's capture of Saint Mark's and Pensacola in 1818; the disturbances along the northeast boundary and the Niagara frontier during Van Buren's administration; the 1859 American military occupation of San Juan Island; the activities of the Irish-American Fenian Brotherhood along the Canadian border after the close of the Civil War; and the capture and occupation of Bagdad, Mexico, in 1866 by American freebooters. Another huge file titled "Mexican Border Troubles, 1875–84" has been described as containing an "exceptionally full and vivid picture of the social, economic, and political turbulence along the lower Rio Grande During the 1870s."

I have taken the above description from the *Guide to Materials on Latin America in the National Archives,* which is available from the Publication Sales Branch of the National Archives. This guide contains detailed descriptions of the contents of many War, State, Navy, and Treasury Department files relating to Latin America. Dr. George Ulibarri, a staff member, is preparing a revision that will extend coverage to recent accessions and other records not included in the original volume.

In addition to the main series of letters received, the records of the Adjutant General's Office contain a number of small series of field records relating to the Mexican War. The correspondence of Zachary Taylor and the records of the civil and military governments in those sections of Mexico occupied by American troops document the relations between the American troops and the Mexican citizenry, the establishment of peace between the two countries, and the administration of the American civil and military governments at Tampico, along the Jalapa-Pueblo route between Veracruz and Mexico City, and in and about the Federal District itself.

No other record group of War Department records even remotely approaches Record Group 94 in the richness of its documentation relating to American foreign affairs in the nineteenth century. Particularly disappointing in this regard are the Records of the Office of the Secretary of War, Record Group 107. Beginning with the creation of the bureau system in the War Department during the years when John C. Calhoun served as Monroe's secretary of war, much of the important correspondence received in the Office of the Secretary was referred to one of the bureaus for action, and the original correspondence was filed in the bureau responsible for acting along with the record of the action taken. This trend became more pronounced with the passage of time, and it accounts for the fact that most of the important War Department correspondence relating to foreign affairs is not to be found in Record Group 107.

Between 1898 and 1939, the United States was involved in a series of foreign wars and adventures, most of which resulted in the creation of United States Army overseas commands. The records of these commands, although they offer exciting research possibilities to students of American foreign relations, have not been used extensively by other than military historians. One of the few diplomatic historians who made good use of these records, George F. Kennan, examined the files created by the American Forces in North Russia and the American Forces in Siberia for his study of *Soviet-American Relations, 1917–1920*, volume 2, *The Decision to Intervene* (Princeton: Princeton University Press, 1958).

Historians interested in our relations with China might find much of value among the records of the 1900–1901 China Relief Expedition and of the post-World War I American Forces in China. The records of these two China commands and of the American Forces in Siberia form part of Records of United States Army Overseas Commands, 1898–1942, Record Group 395. For Latin American specialists, this same record group includes the records of the Army of Cuban Pacification and of the 1916–17 Mexican Punitive Expedition.

A record group of prime importance for research in the field of United States foreign relations is Records of the American Expeditionary Forces (World War I), 1917–23, Record Group 120. Most of the series in the record group relate to purely military matters, but the group does contain the files of the American representative on several important international bodies: the Supreme War Council, the Military Board of Allied Supply, the Permanent International Armistice Commission, the Inter-Allied Rhineland High Commission, and the Inter-Allied Railroad Commission.

In addition, Record Group 120 includes the records of the American Forces in North Russia, the American Military Mission to Italy, the American-Polish Relief Expedition of 1919–20, and the records of the postwar occupation army (the American Forces in Germany [AFG]). I know of only one searcher who has made extensive use of these AFG files. This is unfortunate because they contain a great deal of information about the surprising uses to which the AFG was put and the attitudes of the American troops toward the Germans and vice versa. Perhaps someday some enterprising historian will compare the AFG experience with the post–World War II American occupation—on all levels of contact between the Americans and Germans and not just at the top echelons.

So far, I have mentioned only field records of the 1898–39 period. The more important records created abroad and received in Washington by the War Department ended in the Adjutant General's Office and in one or another of the divisions of the War Department General Staff, which had been created in 1903. Those seeking policy-making documentation relating to the American intervention in Cuba in 1906 or in Mexico in 1914 and 1916–17 should begin with the general correspondence file of the Adjutant General's Office. During and after World War I, the War Department carried on by cable much of its important correspondence with its far-flung commands at Chaumont, London, Archangel, Vladivostok, Coblenz, Manila, and Tientsen by cable. The resulting voluminous series of cablegrams sent and received by the Cable Section of the AGO deal with almost every possible relationship that might occur between a foreign army and the people and government among which it was stationed.

To conclude the discussion of the 1898 to 1939 period and to begin the third and final section of this paper, I should like to mention several large series of records of the War Department General and Special Staffs, Record Group 165, which have proved valuable to the historians of American foreign relations of the first half of the twentieth century.

The records of G-2, Military Intelligence Division, include thousands of military attaché reports originating from almost every part of the world, as well as copies of reports received from foreign agents of the Office of Naval Intelligence, and Departments of State and Commerce, and other sources. Although most of the reports deal exclusively with the internal affairs of the country in which they originated, enough of them relate to such topics as pro- or anti-American feelings, economic penetrations, and the maintenance of military missions to make them of interest to historians of foreign affairs. These series of reports are virtually complete from 1917 to 1945, but, as researchers have discovered much to their chagrin, in 1925 the Military Intelligence Division destroyed a good many of the pre-1914 military attaché reports—because they lacked permanent value!

An examination of the detailed bibliographies in the foreign relations volumes that are included in the multivolume series entitled *The United States Army in World War II* reveals that the historians of the Office of the Chief of Military History (who wrote, for example, *Rearming the French; The Framework of Hemisphere Defense; The Persian Corridor and Aid to Russia; Stillwell's Mission to China;* and *Military Relations between the United States and Canada: 1939–1945*) are generally agreed that the records of the Operations Division (OPD) and those of its predecessor, the War Plans Division, comprise the most important single collection of World War II War Department records relating to policy and strategy. In addition to the series of general correspondence files, which cover the period 1921 to 1945, the records of the OPD include the army's set of Joint Chiefs of Staff and Combined Chiefs of Staff papers; the original papers have not yet been transferred to the National Archives. Another series of important

OPD records consists of nearly forty feet of top-secret correspondence relating to the leasing of Atlantic bases located in British possessions and to Allied military conferences of World War II.

A second important War Department record group for the study of foreign relations in World War II is Records of Headquarters Army Service Forces, Record Group 160. The thirteen feet of correspondence of General Sommervell, who commanded ASF, are enclosed in folders bearing such laconic titles as "British," "Russian," "Pan-American Highway," "Ledo Road," and "Potsdam Conference." The titles may not arouse much interest; the contents will.

A key office under General Sommervell's command was the International Division, which shared with its counterpart in Headquarters Army Ground Forces the army's interest in the lend-lease program for supplying anti-Axis governments with material and equipment and in the reciprocal aid program. The International Division reviewed foreign requests for ASF-procured materiel, represented ASF viewpoints on foreign aid before the proper subcommittees of the Munitions Assignments Board and the President's Soviet Protocol Committee, and kept records of ASF-procured materiel transferred to foreign countries. All of these functions are well documented among the division's records.

This discussion of War Department records relating to United States foreign relations during World War II could continue indefinitely. I hope I have been able to provide a general idea of the possibilities for research in the field, but my presentation should not be considered exhaustive—of necessity it has been highly selective. For those who are interested in War Department records of this period, I recommend the National Archives publications entitled *Federal Records of World War II,* vol. 2, *Military Agencies,* which describes the records of a much greater number of War Department agencies.

# National Archives Records on United States Foreign Relations: Navy Department

## ROBERT W. KRAUSKOPF

Since the earliest days of our history, naval affairs and foreign affairs have impinged upon each other in many ways. Examples of these interrelationships are well known to students of diplomatic history.

On one level this naval-diplomatic collaboration has been of a personal character. There are abundant instances in our history of the selection of naval officers to carry out or to participate in important diplomatic missions for the government. One has only to recall the negotiations of Commodore Preble with the rulers of the Barbary States during Jefferson's administration; Decatur's mission to Algiers; Commodore Biddle's abortive mission to Japan in 1845; Perry's successful treaty with the Japanese in the following decade; Commodore Shufeldt's Korean treaty of 1882; and in more recent times, Admiral Mahan's assignment as a member of the American delegation to the first Hague Conference and the appointment by President Roosevelt in World War II of Admirals Standley and Leahy to serve as ambassadors to Russia and France, respectively.

At another level—the policy level—the United States has consistently and continuously employed its naval strength to support its foreign policy objectives. Over the years these have always included the protection of United States political and economic interests throughout the world and the protection of American citizens abroad. In the Western Hemisphere it was the navy, when it became powerful enough, that was relied upon as our chief instrument for enforcement of the Monroe Doctrine. From time to time our foreign policy objectives have also included instances of cooperation with the navies of other countries, as in the supression of piracy and the slave trade.

How remarkably consistent we have been in this area of our policy is strikingly exemplified by a comparison of the language of two official statements issued 145 years apart. In 1801 President Jefferson, in announcing the decision to send an American naval squadron to the Mediterranean, said: "We have found it expedient to detach a squadron of observation into the Mediterranean Sea, to superintend the safety of our commerce there, and to exercise the seamen in nautical duties." In 1946, when the wheel had turned full circle and the United States had decided again to keep an important naval force in the Mediterranean, Secretary Forrestal described the step in words that had very much the same ring: "Units of the American fleet have been in the Mediterranean and will continue to be there in the future to (1) support American forces in Europe, (2) carry out American policy and diplomacy, and (3) for purposes of experience, morale, and education of personnel of the fleet."

During the period between World War I and World War II, the navy played still another significant role in American foreign relations. These two decades saw the success of international efforts to impose control over the growth of naval armaments; and the United States, as one of the leading naval powers, was deeply involved in the negotiations at Washington, Geneva, and London that achieved and maintained this equilibrium.

Since it is impossible on this occasion to give an exhaustive picture of the naval records holdings of the National Archives, I will attempt to mention the specific record groups in our care that seem to be especially valuable for their research potentialities to the diplomatic historian. Unquestionably, the most significant of these is the Naval Records Collection of the Office of Naval Records and Library, Record Group 45. As its title indicates, this is a collection of documentary materials assembled by the Office of Naval Records and Library from the official files of many offices of the Navy Department, an effort that began in the 1880s and extended into the 1920s. In effect, it represents an attempt by the Navy Department, long before the establishment of any federal archival agency that could care for them, to bring together all of its own historically valuable documents. The result is somewhat of an archival potpourri, a highly variegated mixture. The constituent elements of the record group represent a number of different provenances; their original arrangement has been entirely transformed by the organizers of the collection, and the official materials have been supplemented by private journals and other papers obtained through gift or purchase from sources outside the Navy Department.

The greater part of the collection consists of records that originated in the Office of the Secretary of the Navy, including nearly all of the bound volumes of letters sent and received by that office before 1886 and many individual papers removed from files of the secretary's office dating as late as 1927. It also comprises most of the records of the Board of Navy Commissioners, which functioned from 1815 to 1842. The collection focuses upon the nineteenth century, but there is also very substantial coverage of the First World War.

Although the removal of many of the documents from their original context somewhat impairs its research usefulness, the relative value of the collection is nevertheless very high because its component items were consciously selected for their significance, the less important materials being discarded or left in their original locations. For research into all aspects of nineteenth- and early twentieth-century naval history, Record Group 45 is indispensable.

Next in importance to Record Group 45 are the General Records of the Department of the Navy, Record Group 80. This contains the official files of the Office of the Secretary of the Navy from 1885 to 1946, with the exception, as we have seen, of individual papers that may have been withdrawn by the Office of Naval Records and Library and are now to be found in Record Group 45. Correspondence of the Office of the Chief of Naval Operations, from the time of its establishment in 1915 until 1942, is interfiled with the secretary's correspondence. From 1917 onwards, separate security-classified files exist along with the unclassified files. Other records included in this record group are those of such subordinate units of the secretary's office as the assistant and undersecretaries' offices and records of certain boards and commissions established by the secretary for special purposes. As is true of Record Group 45, the material in Record Group 80, within its administrative and chronological limits, is of the highest value for the study of the foreign affairs aspects of naval policy.

Complementing Record Groups 45 and 80 is the third naval record group of importance, Records of the Office of the Chief of Naval Operations, Record Group 38. The principal material of interest allocated to this record group are the general files of the Office of the Chief of Naval Operations from 1942, when they began to be separately maintained, until 1946. Also in this record group are the correspondence and reports received from naval attachés from about 1882 to 1922 and the records of the Military Government of Santo Domingo, which was a responsibility of the Navy Department from 1916 to 1924.

Frequently involved in American contacts with foreign powers, whether in major incidents or routine matters, were the marines. In Records of the United States Marine Corps, Record Group 127, we have available for research most of the correspondence of the Office of the Commandant of the Corps, beginning with 1798 and extending to 1950. There are also some field records of the corps, including those of marine detachments that served in Haiti, 1915–34, and in Nicaragua, 1928–32.

Finally, I should mention briefly the Records of the Bureau of Naval Personnel, Record Group 24. Among the responsibilities of this bureau and its predecessor, the Bureau of Navigation, is the duty of collecting and preserving logs of naval vessels. The records of the bureau in our custody now contain about seventy-two thousand individual ships' logs, ranging in date from 1801 to 1946. Each logbook records, on a daily basis, the position and course of the ship, other navigational data, and remarks about such events as engagements with the enemy, visits of foreign dignitaries, or ceremonies held aboard ship. These entries are often of value for establishing and verifying specific historical points. Some contain observations of special interest and significance, but in general they are, because of the format of the logbook, quite brief. They can supplement, but not replace, the formal reports of commanding officers about the events concerned.

In addition to these five groups, there are of course numerous other record groups among our holdings of naval records that would be concerned, though less directly, with diplomatic relations. Among them would be records of the Hydrographic Office, the Bureau of Yards and Docks, the Bureau of Aeronautics, the Naval Observatory, Naval Districts and Shore Establishments, and Naval Operating Forces.

The connection of our naval records with possible topics in the field of foreign relations presents endless possibilities. It would be hard, for example, to envisage any thorough scholarly study of United States relations with China or Japan that did not consider their naval aspects and make use of naval sources; the same would be true of a consideration of our relations with Australia and New Zealand in the twentieth century; or of our relations with any part of Latin America—especially Mexico, Panama, and Cuba; or of our relations with the Middle East, the North African nations, Russia in the twentieth century, or Liberia.

In conclusion, I would like to say a few words about restrictions upon access to the records, since these are always crucial to researchers working in the more recent periods of our history. In general, the type of restriction that most affects materials of interest to diplomatic historians is that involving security classification. Most secret and confidential naval and military records dated before January 1, 1946, with the exception of a few subject categories, have been declassified by the Department of Defense. In instances, however, where a scholar's research requires access to records that cannot yet be declassified, the Navy Department will, upon application, give the individual the necessary security clearance subject to the usual conditions of review of the research notes and the completed manuscript.

The National Archives is actively involved in microfilming, as a form of publication, selected segments of its holdings that have high research value.

The naval records that have so far been affected by this program are mostly drawn from the Naval Records Collection of the Office of Naval Records and Library, Record Group 45. The most important of the many series of letters sent and received by the secretary of the navy, from 1798 to 1886, are now available on microfilm; they amount to slightly more than twenty-two hundred rolls of film. A few private journals and records relating to certain exploring expeditions have also been microfilmed. As far as future microfilm publication plans are concerned, we expect to film additional portions of Record Group 45 during the next several years, as our resources and other commitments permit.

In this brief review, I hope I succeeded in giving you some conception of what our naval records contain. For specific research problems, the staffs of our two military records divisions are always available.

# National Archives Records on United States Foreign Relations: Captured Foreign Records

ROBERT WOLFE

It is logical, obvious, and confirmed in use, that our captured records reproduced on microfilm are invaluable direct sources for the study of United States–German relations since 1867 and to a much lesser extent of United States–Italian relations since 1920. What is less apparent, and therefore regrettably neglected in use, is the value of these records where United States relations with third countries are involved. For example, for the study of United States–French relations between the two world wars, the American records have gradually been made accessible during the last two decades, but the French diplomatic archives for the same period are notoriously inaccessible except in selective documentary publications by the grace of the Quai d'Orsay. The German governments throughout the 1920s and 1930s were of necessity avidly interested in the state and content of Franco-American relations, and there are among the records of the German embassy in Washington and the German embassy in Paris extensive files on the subject, the most pertinent bearing the uncryptic titles "U.S. Relations with France" and "French Relations with the United States," respectively. The related German Foreign Office central files are appropriately enriched with instructions sent to and despatches received from those two embassies, augmented by written correspondence and memorandums on conversations with the United States and French embassies in Berlin, members of their staffs, as well as their consular officials stationed in Germany, to say nothing of frequent visiting official firemen and private citizens.

Between 1926 and 1933 the German Foreign Office files pertaining to the League of Nations and with international conferences gradually dwindle, its Geneva delegations, would naturally contain a fair amount of knowledgeable, if biased, observations on United States–French relations, as would the files of the German delegations to various international conferences

19

from Versailles, through the series of reparations and disarmament conferences, up to and including the London Economic Conference of 1933.
During the subsequent Nazi era, of course, German records dealing with
the League of Nations and with international conferences gradually dwindle,
as those pertaining to German-American relations eventually do, but the
records of German relations with French governments from the Third
Republic through Vichy are useful, and in some cases central, to an understanding of Franco-American relations from 1933 to 1944.

The foregoing, of course, reflects the expected content and usual arrangement of the diplomatic archives of all major powers, if not of all states. It
would be a crude belaboring of the obvious were I to point out that the
example of Franco-American relations is only an illustration, and holds
true to a lesser or greater degree for German diplomatic records on Anglo-
American, Russo-American, Mexican-American, or Japanese-American
relations.

The ultimate belaboring of the obvious, I suppose, is to point out that,
just as in the German Foreign Office Archives, the principle holds true that
there is valuable material in the archives of *any* country for the study of the
relations between two other powers with which that country has relations—
particularly where access is restricted to the pertinent records of either or
both of these other powers. I suggest that the recently opened British diplomatic archives for the period between 1922 and 1938 would be at least as
rewarding as the German for the student of Franco-American relations.
However, the open British archives are to the best of my knowledge not yet
available on microfilm, while the bulk of the German diplomatic archives
can be consulted without cost at the National Archives or purchased on
microfilm for very reasonable reproduction fees.

Nevertheless, with the encouraging exception of several theses and dissertations now in progress dealing with United States relations with several
Latin American countries between 1914 and 1945, there has been relatively
little use by diplomatic historians of our microfilm of German and Italian
records. Although the language barrier is to some extent an obstacle, the
overwhelming majority of historians trained in United States graduate
schools are required to demonstrate a reading knowledge of German, and
in our experience even a rudimentary knowledge of the language enables
the researcher, when dealing with subject matter he knows so thoroughly,
to comb through the microfilm of presumably pertinent German or Italian
files and identify documents relating to his subject. These can be quick-
copied directly from the microfilm for later accurate translation. The
National Archives provides the reference advice, the finding aids, and soon,
we hope, indexes; the historian does the research, hires his own translator,

and of course interprets the documents, writes the history, and takes all the credit or blame, as the case may be.

While the seized German records have some value for direct bilateral American relations with third states, they are likely to be of greater use when approached from the broader viewpoint of multilateral diplomacy and the broader issues of international relations directly or indirectly involving the United States, such as alliances, military aid, disarmament, rearmament, trade, tariffs, financial investment, reparations, and cultural exchanges. This broader usefulness is particularly true of the German Foreign Ministry Archives, but to some degree applies also to the records of the Reich Chancellery from 1920 to 1945 and include so-called protocols of cabinet meetings, which are actually summaries rather than verbatim minutes for the period 1919 to 1938.

Among the records of the Nazi party, its formations, affiliated associations and supervised organizations, those of its Foreign Organization (Auslands-Organisation or "AO"), the German Foreign Institute (Deutsches Auslands-Institut or "DAI"), and the League of Ethnic Germans Abroad (Volksbund für das Deutschtum im Ausland or "VDA") contain information on cultural and political propaganda in the United States. There is also some related material among the seized records of the Goebbels Propaganda Ministry and of the Armed Forces High Command Propaganda Office. Examples of range and variety of the subject matter to be found in the records of these agencies are numerous record items dealing with pro-German and pro-Nazi propaganda aimed at ethnic Germans or at native elements or dissident groups in the United States, and anti–United States propaganda aimed especially at Latin America. There is also among the records of the SS (a formation of the Nazi party) some material relating to the United States in its relations with other countries, particularly among the records of the SD-Ausland, the Foreign Intelligence Office of the Reich Security Central Office (RSHA).

The National Archives also has on microfilm extensive records of German private industry, particularly of armament manufacturers and other war-related industries. Most of these records were seized in connection with the prosecution at Nuremberg on charges of conspiracy to wage aggressive war and the use of slave labor, or for use in the postwar decartelization program. Some of these records, notably those of the I. G. Farben chemical combine, are useful sources for documenting the connections of United States industries with their German and other European counterparts.

To the extent that United States foreign relations have to do with war and peace, the high-level German military records, including naval and air records, provide considerable material. The destruction by fire during the bombing of Potsdam in April 1945 of virtually all of the Reich and Prussian military records antedating 1920 forces the researcher to resort to the still intact Bavarian and Württemberg military archives, which have never been in this country and are not available on microfilm.

The German Foreign Ministry Archives, which I have already discussed, do of course contain extensive records pertaining to Reich military affairs for the 1867 to 1920 period. Particularly valuable for the World War I period are the records created by the Foreign Ministry Liaison Staff to the Grand Headquarters of The Imperial High Command. The German naval archives survived the war, and the National Archives has accessioned nearly four thousand rolls of microfilm reproducing the larger part of those records. The German naval records obviously provide a valuable partial remedy for the missing Imperial Army and High Command records for the pre-1920 period, but they are particularly useful for a study of the naval race before World War I and between the two world wars, to say nothing of the crucial Imperial German U-boat policy during World War I. The German naval records prior to 1915 are of some use for German colonial and economic policy in areas of the Pacific of prime concern to the United States. The usually high-quality reports of German military and naval attachés, whether they pertain to the Boxer Rebellion, the Russo-Japanese War, or the various Japanese "incidents" and excursions into China after 1931, are not without interest to those concerned with United States policy in the Far East.

The high-level German armed forces and German army records for the 1920 to 1945 period are substantial in quantity and offer much on some aspects of foreign relations, particularly after Hitler assumed the position of commander in chief in 1938. By that time he had made himself the effective originator of all German policy—diplomatic, civil, or military.

But even well below this top level where diplomacy and military strategy meet, there are such useful materials as (to revert to the example of United States–French relations) the records of the Waffenstillstandskommission, the German element of the Franco-German Armistice Commission established in 1940. These records most likely would reveal just what the Nazi and Vichy governments knew or suspected about the operations of American diplomats and agents in unoccupied France and French North Africa.

What I have said about the seized German records holds true to a much lesser extent for our microfilm reproduction of seized Italian civil and military records. The Italian diplomatic and civil records on film cover a shorter time period, roughly 1922 to 1944, and are only a fraction of the German in volume. In variety of provenance and in scope of subject matter they are much narrower; in short, the filming was highly selective. We also have a small collection of Hungarian records, a scattering of other European records, and the archives of the Communist party of the Smolensk Oblast—all of which are peripheral to diplomatic history.

The National Archives holds eighty-two rolls of miscellaneous high-level Japanese civil and military materials, filmed in Japan by the Far East Command, as well as some records of former Japanese diplomatic and consular missions in Germany, Austria, and Italy ranging from the 1920s to 1945. At one time we also held thirty-five hundred cubic feet of seized Japanese military and civil records, but 163 rolls produced by selective microfilming thereof before return to Japan were deposited in the Library of Congress. In fact, with these rolls and its microfilm collection of Japanese Foreign Office records and of the military monographs and Manchurian studies prepared under American aegis by former Japanese officers, as well as thousands of accessioned seized Japanese books, the Library of Congress is today much more the chief United States depository of captured and related Japanese materials than is the National Archives.

Beyond captured or seized enemy records, I should perhaps mention the records of the International Military Tribunal for the Far East, and of IMT and lesser Nuremberg tribunals, the former already available on microfilm (T918, 61 rolls), the latter to be microfilmed over the next several years. The war crimes trial records contain only scattered or peripheral records pertaining to United States foreign relations before the end of World War II, but directly represent, of course, narrow but specific aspects of United States foreign policy in action both in postwar Europe and postwar Asia. The broader aspects of United States postwar foreign policy in these two areas, the occupation of Germany, Austria, Italy, and Japan and its dependencies, are covered in State Department records falling in the closed period. The records reflecting the execution of that occupation policy, mainly those of the United States Office of Military Government for Germany, the Supreme Commander for Allied Powers, the United States Element of the Allied Commission for Austria, and the Allied Commission Italy are in the Washington National Records Center. In each of these record groups some records are open, but many are still classified, though accessible to United States citizens under procedures established by the Department of the Army.

In summary, I wish to underscore the general proposition that there may be useful, relatively accessible material in our captured or seized foreign records for students of United States foreign relations. While I have mentioned some noteworthy general categories and specific examples, the only way to establish what material, if any, these records may contain for a specific research project is to address such inquiries to the captured records staff of the National Archives and Records Service.

# Foreign Relations Materials in Presidential Libraries

DANIEL J. REED

Central, of course, in the conduct of American foreign relations is the president. Certainly, the secretary of state and his department act for the president, especially in the conduct of the nation's routine foreign relations, but recent presidents have more and more frequently played the leading role in external affairs. Some have even been, one might say, their own secretaries of state. It follows from this that the personal papers of recent presidents, the records of their office, and the papers of their aides are indispensable to the study of our foreign relations during their administrations. Generally, these materials for the last six presidents are, or will be, in one of the presidential libraries under the administration of the National Archives. Libraries for the four earlier of these six presidents—Hoover, Roosevelt, Truman, and Eisenhower—are complete and open for use. Two others— the Kennedy and Johnson Libraries—are currently under development. While these six libraries cover all administrations from 1928 to the present, foreign relations materials in our custody extend back to 1914 by virtue of the career of Herbert Hoover. In general, each of the more recent libraries has more material relating to foreign relations than the older ones, but it is also true that more of their holdings are unavailable for various reasons—but chiefly because not enough time has elapsed since the documents were created.

Restrictions on the use of sources because of the time factor is not a great problem at the Hoover Library, which contains material on foreign affairs extending over a period of thirty years. The material begins with typescripts of records relating to the Commission for Relief in Belgium, 1914. It continues with typescripts of the more important records of the American Relief Administration which Herbert Hoover created some four years later at President Wilson's request. The original ARA records remain in the Hoover Institution at Stanford University. Hoover's relief work extended to revolutionary Russia in 1921–23. In 1919–20, as a delegate to the Supreme Economic Council of the Paris Peace Conference, Hoover collected a great deal of material relating to the decisions that affected the future of Germany and Europe for years to come. Again, he had typescripts made of the more important documents, and bound sets are now in his library at West Branch, Iowa.

When Hoover became the secretary of commerce in 1921 he revived and expanded the Bureau of Foreign and Domestic Commerce. His papers reflect this as well as his years contending with foreign debts arising from the war. Other papers relate to such varied events as his preinaugural tour of Latin America, the revolt in Mexico, the Japanese invasion of Manchuria (1931), and the question of Philippine independence. After the Second World War, former President Hoover was again in relief work and public service. In 1946 President Truman gave him responsibility for surveying the world's food needs and resources. The records of this undertaking are also in the Hoover Library.

In addition to the papers of President Hoover, the Hoover Library has those of a number of officials important in the president's career. Notable among these are the papers of Ambassador Hugh R. Wilson, Hanforth MacNider, William Hallam Tack, E. Dana Durand, and Vice-Admiral John F. Shafroth. The staff of the Hoover Library has lately concentrated its acquisition program on foreign relations materials.

It is obvious that the papers of Franklin D. Roosevelt must be consulted by everyone studying the diplomacy of the period 1933 to 1945, but what is not obvious to prospective researchers is the extent and diversity of these papers. Roosevelt has been accused of acting as his own secretary of state. Clearly, he did enjoy directing the day-by-day operations of the great departments, especially affairs of state, with other departments, especially War, Navy, and Interior. For instance, Roosevelt's desire to occupy certain miniscule but strategic Pacific islands during the 1930s is revealed in his correspondence with Secretary of the Interior Harold Ickes.

The last and least interesting category is the correspondence with heads of state. The president was polite, formal, and invariably cautious. His communicants usually reciprocated.

These categories reflect the president's interest in and impact upon foreign affairs. In addition, there is a special group that documents his role as war leader—this is the map room collection. The so-called map room of the White House served as a military information office and a communications center. Its files include communications between the White House and the following: Allied civilian and military leaders, United States diplomatic representatives in Russia, China, and Great Britain, liaison officers in war theaters, and presidential emissaries on special assignment. There is information on the Allied conferences at Cairo, Tehran, Quebec, and Yalta. (Approximately three-fourths of these diplomatic materials can now be made available to the researcher with a State Department clearance through 1945.) The bulk of the map room collection, however, concerns military operations rather than foreign relations and his papers reflect this fact.

Diplomatic materials in the Roosevelt papers can be described in four arbitrary categories, the first of which is the correspondence from representatives abroad. Roosevelt instructed his ambassadors and ministers (they were always *his* ambassadors and ministers) to write to him personally—this in addition to the reports they were expected to file with the secretary of state. Many of these men were old friends; they did not hesitate to write candidly and at length.

The second category concerns the information that came through unofficial channels. This includes communications from the public at large, comments from prominent persons outside government, and reports from citizens abroad. This "outside" intelligence provided an added and very necessary dimension to official knowledge.

The third group concerns communications between the president and the great departments. Memorandums passed almost daily between the president and the principal officers in the State Department—Cordell Hull, Sumner Welles, William Phillips, and R. Walton Moore. But there is also useful material in the files representing exchanges.

I will digress a bit and mention that Roosevelt's presidential papers were arranged as current files; this arrangement does not lend itself to research purposes. The scholar often must go through many scattered files and much extraneous material before he is certain he has seen everything on his subject. To make easier the work of the researcher, each existing presidential library has developed a finding aid program which includes indexes, cross-reference sheets, inventories, shelf lists, calendars, and bibliographies. As part of their task of making presidential papers available for research, libraries have also instituted or will institute a documentary publication program. In April 1969 the Roosevelt Library and Harvard University Press issued *Franklin D. Roosevelt and Foreign Affairs, 1933–1937*. This three-volume work contains approximately fourteen hundred of the principal documents relating to foreign affairs during the first administration. The staff will continue to publish volumes in this series in chronological order until they reach the end in 1945.

Among the adjunct collections relating to foreign affairs in the Roosevelt Library is the massive collection of Henry Morgenthau, Jr., Roosevelt's secretary of the treasury. In 1970 the Morgenthau "diaries" for the third Roosevelt administration will be opened to research. These are not diaries at all; rather, they are correspondence, memorandums, transcribed telephone conversations, stenographical accounts of conversations in Morgenthau's office, and summaries of other meetings Morgenthau attended. Here is the detail historians crave from a man who was always an important counselor; from 1939 on he worked considerable influence on foreign and defense policy.

The papers of Harry Hopkins for the period he served as assistant to the president are clearly fundamental to any study of wartime relations with our Allies. The papers of R. Walton Moore are worth attention. Moore was Cordell Hull's closest advisor, and his collection is particularly good on the evolution of United States neutrality legislation and arms and munitions control. The papers of Oscar Cox, general counsel and deputy administrator of the Foreign Economic Administration, are useful for the legislative origins and general operation of the lend-lease program. Other collections of personal papers of interest to diplomatic historians are those of Herbert Claiborne Pell, United States minister to Portugal and Hungary, Charles Taussig, head of the Anglo-American Caribbean Commission, and Sen. Elbert Thomas of Utah.

The Roosevelt Library also houses the papers of Eleanor Roosevelt, rich in materials on foreign affairs, but these are not yet open for research and not likely to be for some time.

As we come to the record of the next president, Harry S. Truman, we enter a period still encumbered with many restrictions on access to materials, especially materials on foreign relations, intelligence, and defense. In the case of this library we also come to a living president in residence who still holds many of his papers that we believe to be important, including most of the documents quoted in his memoirs. We expect these papers to come eventually to the library.

The library, however, does have custody of the bulk of the records of Truman's presidency. The White House files make up the core of the library's holdings. These contain material relating to the administration of some foreign affairs programs and quantities of public opinion mail on various foreign matters, especially those which aroused national passions, such as the recognition of Israel, the invasion of Korea, and the firing of Gen. Douglas MacArthur.

Closely related to the general files are the papers of Truman's staff. Notable are the papers of Samuel Rosenman, Clark Clifford, and Charles Murphy. Unfortunately the library does not yet have the papers of anyone who served as secretary of state under Truman; however, Dean Acheson, who was assistant secretary and undersecretary of state in the early Truman years and secretary of state through all of the president's second term, has committed his papers to the library. Over the years the library has acquired, quite naturally, the papers of a number of Truman's ambassadors and other officials.

As a result of its acquisitions the Truman Library holds material dealing with a wide variety of subjects, including the Point Four Program, the Truman Doctrine, the Marshall Plan, and foreign aid in general.

The Truman Library, in common with all other presidential libraries, has conducted a series of oral history interviews. Most of those completed thus far have had to do with the impact of the Marshall Plan in western Europe. Plans are now being made for a new campaign to extend greatly the range of recorded interviews in the field of external affairs.

The career of Dwight D. Eisenhower was noteworthy long before he became president. The Eisenhower Library, in Abilene, Kansas, near his boyhood home and grave, holds about one hundred cubic feet of his papers for the years 1942 to 1952, years when Eisenhower was prominent in military and diplomatic service abroad.

Eisenhower's presidential papers fall largely into the category familiar in later administrations as the White House Central Files. A subdivision of this, called the Official Files, has perhaps three hundred cubic feet of records relating in some way to foreign affairs. A large amount of this material is of little interest to most historians, for it constitutes routine matter relating to appointments of ambassadors and other officials or to the ordinary proclamations and official statements. Also in this mass are countless letters from the general public on foreign matters and many greetings from heads of state. Yet within all this are found here and there significant documents on such topics as the Connally amendment, disarmament, the security of Israel, and developments in Vietnam.

As happened with earlier presidents, Eisenhower withheld from the library until his death a part of his papers. These are just now on their way to Abilene from Gettysburg. We do not yet know exactly what this last addition contains, but we expect to find in it some of the most informative and sensitive records for the years of the presidency. It will most likely be some time before much of this material can be available for examination.

The Eisenhower Library has its collateral collections of papers of presidential aides such as Bryce Harlow, Gerald Morgan, and Henry R. McPhee, Jr. Probably the most important supporting groups are the papers of John Foster Dulles and Christian Herter. Dulles has given about twenty-five cubic feet of his more detailed and confidential "working papers" as secretary of state. Access to these is still highly restricted. The same is true of the smaller group of Herter papers. They are precisely the same kind of material as those of Dulles. Obviously there will be many additional bodies of personal papers added to the holdings of the Eisenhower Library before the library's development is complete.

It should be apparent that most presidential libraries hold large quantities of material relating to foreign affairs. In some instances the amount is vast, not yet well organized for research purposes, and not yet under intensive control. In these circumstances a knowledgeable staff is indispensable; we try to provide that staff. Also apparent is the fact that the more recent a president's administration, the larger is the percentage of his material under one or another kind of restriction. Thus, because library archivists are familiar with the collections and can provide information on restrictions (and for other reasons), I close with the admonition that the researcher should always consult the library for information about papers in its custody.

# National Archives Records on United States Foreign Relations: Nontextual Records

## A. PHILIP MUNTZ

I am happy to have this opportunity to discuss some of the more unorthodox forms of federal archives that might be useful in studies of United States foreign relations. I shall refer specifically to cartographic archives, which include maps, charts, and aerial survey photographs; and audiovisual archives, which comprise still pictures, motion pictures, and sound recordings.

From the viewpoint of both the custodian and the potential user, it is unfortunate that these special forms of archives have not received the attention from researchers that their importance warrants. All too often a researcher is concerned with maps and photographs only when his paper or book is ready to be published and an attractive photo or map is needed to embellish it. I am not, of course, arguing against the proper use of maps or photographs as illustrations in scholarly publications; I am emphasizing that their usefulness extends far beyond that rather limited role.

There are certain hazards, however, in the use of photographic materials as a source of historical evidence. This is particularly true of motion pictures, which tend, by their vivid recreation of past scenes, to create an aura of authenticity that may be highly misleading. But other forms of records may also be misleading. It is the responsibility of the historian to evaluate the reliability of his sources, whatever their nature, and in this effort the archivist, through his concern with the provenance of all records under his control, can make a substantial contribution.

## AUDIOVISUAL RECORDS

### Motion Pictures

Of the approximately eighty-five thousand reels of motion picture film in our Audiovisual Archives Division, a considerable number contain footage that relates directly to foreign affairs or diplomacy. Among these are some fifty-seven reels, recently copied from nitrate film in the custody of the United Nations, that deal with the activities of the League of Nations. Some of the more noteworthy footage involves the Sino-Japanese conflict, the Italian aggression in Ethiopia, the Spanish Civil War, and sessions of the League dealing with disarmament.

Other films from nongovernment sources that should be of interest to historians include the large quantity of newsreels from Paramount, Movietone News, and News of the Day and the various documentaries, including the March of Time series and the CBS Eyewitness to History series. Much of this film is probably more valuable as a source of information on the interpretation of events by our mass media than as a direct record of the events themselves.

From government sources there are many films covering a wide variety of subjects bearing on international events and foreign affairs. Important conferences, meetings, and ceremonies are generally well covered. There are, for example, films of the siging of the Treaty of Versailles and of the Cairo, Tehran, Yalta, Quebec, and San Francisco Conferences. There are also films dealing with foreign aid and assistance programs and with international scientific and cultural endeavors. Military activities in World War II and the Korean War are the subject of many films, usually made by the air force and its predecessors.

Some of our most interesting motion pictures are German films that are a part of the National Archives Collection of World War II War Crimes Records, Record Group 238. They deal with the Nazi rise to power, civilian and military activities in wartime Germany, and the Allied march into Germany. Somewhat similar coverage is included in our Collection of Foreign Records Seized, 1941–, Record Group 242, which includes Japanese and North Korean films relating to political and military matters.

I have mentioned only a few examples from our film collections. There is a great deal more that might be useful to students of foreign affairs, particularly as a source of background information. The unpublished subject catalog to these collections, which is available for use in the research room of the Audiovisual Archives Division, along with supplementary lists, should be invaluable to anyone wishing to use these records.

STILL PICTURES

The still picture holdings of the National Archives are among the largest of any depository. They contain about 3.5 million items, which are allocated to some one hundred thirty record groups, representing agencies from the Bureau of Accounts in the Treasury Department to the Bureau of Yards and Docks. Between these alphabetical extremes are a number of record groups whose contents are likely to be of interest to students of foreign relations. The records of the Department of State, the Bureau of Insular Affairs, the Bureau of Foreign and Domestic Commerce, the Panama Canal Company, the Boundary and Claims Commissions and Arbitrations, and the Office of Inter-American Affairs are a few of the more obvious examples. In addition, the records of various military and civilian wartime agencies contain thousands of photographs that could be useful in a wide range of studies.

One of our most interesting and significant groups of photographs is that of the United States Information Agency and its predecessors. In addition to photographs of diplomatic functions, and agency activities and propaganda photographs for use abroad, there are at least three hundred thousand news photographs from the Paris Bureau of the *New York Times* for the period from 1923 to 1950. This outstanding collection was purchased from the *Times* in 1950 by the Economic Cooperation Administration and was subsequently transferred to the National Archives.

Two other collections of still photographs from European sources are of particular interest. These are the von Ribbentrop albums and the Hoffman Collection of Nazi party photographs, both in our World War II Collection of Foreign Records Seized. The sixty-five von Ribbentrop albums contain many pictures of Nazi and other Axis leaders at official and private functions. The Hoffman Collection, which has been described as the official photographic collection of the Nazi party organization for the period from 1919 to 1945, contains almost sixty-five thousand items. It is, or should be, an indispensable source for anyone interested in recent German history.

SOUND RECORDINGS

Our approximately thirty-one thousand sound recordings are among our least-used resources. That fact is difficult to explain in view of the present interest in oral history and the popular enthusiasm for so-called spoken word recordings. Undoubtedly our sound recordings contain material that would be valuable in historical research. Some of the speeches on foreign relations, for example, may not be available in any other form. Examples that might be of interest are an address by Cordell Hull on the reciprocal trade program on February 6, 1938; speeches by the delegation chairman at the signing of the United Nations Charter at San Francisco; Eleanor Roosevelt's speech rebuking the Russians at the United Nations in 1948; the entire proceedings of the International Military Tribunal at Nuremberg; and the round table discussion on the Pan-American Bird Treaty before the Sixth North American Wildlife Conference from the records of the Department of the Interior. Although there is no central catalog of the sound recordings, alphabetical lists arranged by title and name of speaker are available for the use of researchers.

## CARTOGRAPHIC RECORDS

The holdings of our cartographic branch include well over 1.5 million maps and charts and about two million aerial photographs. Although a large percentage of these records may be considered to be of at least peripheral interest in the study of foreign relations, I will mention here only selected files that are directly relevant to the topic.

By far the largest body of pertinent maps is a part of the Records of Boundary and Claims Commissions and Arbitrations, Record Group 76. It comprises about twenty thousand maps and aerial photographs, forty-four hundred of which pertain to the delineation of the United States boundaries. The demarcation of international boundaries is an eminently mappable diplomatic activity; an examination of the boundary records reveals geographers, surveyors, and cartographers to have been importantly involved at practically every stage of the boundary-making process. The products of their activities include not only highly detailed maps of specific boundary segments but also a large variety of maps showing topography, settlement, land use, transportation and communication routes, and other physical and cultural phenomena in the regions traversed by the boundaries. In addition to the maps compiled by agents of the State Department and the major federal mapping agencies, there are many maps produced by foreign agencies and by private mapmakers. Besides the maps delineating United States boundaries, there are also some fifteen thousand maps and aerial photographs produced by the United States government during its role as arbiter in a number of Latin American boundary disputes.

International boundaries and political subdivisions are also treated by maps that have been produced by the State Department's Office of the Geographer. These are in General Records of the Department of State,

Record Group 59. Included are several map-illustrated serial publications, among them the *Geographic Reports,* the *International Boundary Studies,* and the *Geographic Bulletins.* State Department research in mapping and political geography is well documented by a lengthy series of reports, studies, and correspondence from the files of Geographers Lawrence Martin (1921–24) and Samuel W. Boggs (1924–54).

The General Records of the Department of State also include the records of the Foreign Service Inspection Corps. Among these are 250 foreign city plans from the period 1906–39, many of which were annotated by United States consular representatives to show the embassies and consular establishments of the United States and other nations as well as key commercial buildings and transportation and communication facilities.

One of the most significant instances in which the expertise of geographers and cartographers was employed in the conduct of United States foreign policy was the Versailles Peace Conference of 1919. The Records of the American Commission to Negotiate Peace, Record Group 256, include more than eleven hundred maps researched and compiled by a distinguished group of social scientists. Although maps of Eastern and Central Europe predominate, the commission's maps cover areas throughout the world and exhibit virtually every mappable phenomenon that was considered potentially relevant to the postwar territorial restructuring of Europe. Particular emphasis was given to ethnic, religious, and linguistic distributions and to political boundaries, existing and proposed.

A considerable amount of cartographic material relating to foreign affairs is among the records of the War and Navy Departments. The largest group of these is the War Department Map Collection, filed with the Records of the Office of the Chief of Engineers, Record Group 77. This includes approximately twenty-seven hundred maps accumulated chiefly during the period 1895–1939 by various army intelligence offices. Among these are many items forwarded, some with annotations, by United States military observers and attachés. The geographical coverage is worldwide, but the chief emphasis is on the principal areas of American economic, political, and military activity during the late nineteenth and the early twentieth century—namely, Latin America, China, and the Philippines. Smaller files including similar material on these same areas are in the Records of United States Army Overseas Operations and Commands, 1898–1942, Record Group 395; Records of the Military Government of Cuba, Record Group 140; Records of the Provisional Government of Cuba, Record Group 199; Records of the United States Marine Corps, Record Group 127; and Records of the Office of the Chief of Naval Operations, Record Group 38.

Many of the cartographic records I have mentioned are described in preliminary inventories, and there are also unpublished finding aids—catalogs, indexes, and lists—available for much of the material. And soon a guide to the entire holdings of the Cartographic Branch will also be available.

In summary, the cartographic and audiovisual records in the National Archives contain an immense amount of information that is either unique or that is not easily accessible in other documents. When used in conjunction with related textual documents, these records can provide an added dimension to research in American foreign affairs.

# Some Neglected Sources for the Study of United States Foreign Relations

## MEYER H. FISHBEIN

Scholars in the field of foreign relations often fail to recognize the research opportunities in records of federal government agencies other than those of the State and Defense Departments; nevertheless, all but a few of these other agencies maintain some foreign liaison—a fact frequently overlooked. Indeed, important foreign relations policies may originate in some of these other agencies, and foreign liaison officers have recorded important links in the chain of international decision making.

I shall deal with only a few such nondiplomatic and nonmilitary agencies that create substantial records relevant to the study of United States foreign relations. Most of these records are neglected as sources for such studies, even though the matters to which they relate are often common concerns of the foreign relations historian: international trade, monetary policy, immigration, and foreign aid, among other topics. For example, many historians have written about "dollar diplomacy" or, less pejoratively, the economic influences in foreign relations; yet few researchers examine pertinent records of the United States Tariff Commission and of the Treasury, Commerce, Labor, and Agriculture Departments.

Records relating to such international economic matters as trade, money and banking, foreign claims, and war debts appear not only in the Office of the Secretary of the Treasury, but also in several Treasury Department bureaus. Searchers, for instance, should examine the Bureau of the Mint records for sources relating to several international monetary conferences: the conference of 1892 was specifically proposed by the United States, and records show how we gained support for that conference. One letter dated May 26, 1892, from George W. Wurts in St. Petersburg reported:

On calling yesterday at that [the Foreign] Ministry to ascertain if a decision had been arrived at in regard to the invitation, I was referred to the Ministry of Finance, which is more interested in the subject than the Foreign Office. I failed, however, to find any one in authority there, though I went twice to enquire, but in the evening I received a verbal message from Mr. de Thoerner, Acting Minister, that he would see me to-day at his house, the Ministry being closed on account of this being a great holiday.[1]

Extensive global economic data appear among Bureau of Accounts records. The files relating to Argentina, 1917–41, for example, concern Argentina's gold deposits in the United States, credits to various foreign countries, securities in the United States held for the British government, wheat purchases, and international loans. The Bureau of Customs records include many reports on the enforcement of the Chinese Exclusion Laws and considerable correspondence about the effect of custom laws and regulations on international trade and our balance of payments.

International trade is also dealt with in depth by the Commerce Department. A few researchers know that reports of commercial attachés for the 1920s and 1930s are contained among the records of the Bureau of Foreign and Domestic Commerce; they are nevertheless largely unfamiliar with the correspondence and reports concerning international trade and United States investments abroad. Labor Department files contain many references to foreign economic conditions and documents concerning diplomacy, including several significant letters relating to the World Court and the League of Nations. How many of those who are interested in the lend-lease program are aware that records of the Office of Business Economics include many detailed accounts dealing with reverse lend-lease that predate the office?

Records of the Tariff Board, 1909–12, are filed with the accessioned records of the United States Tariff Commission, the board's successor. The entire record group includes investigative materials and correspondence relating to exports and imports. One professor of history examined tariff records for a study of a trade agreement between the United States and Japan. The correspondence of European agents (1919–35) and of Tariff Board Chairman F. W. Taussig, a well-known economist and historian whose letters include his comments about the Paris Peace Conference of 1919, are of unusual value for research. Other related foreign trade sources for the New Deal period may be found among the records of the Office of the Special Representative for Trade Negotiations, the Office of the Special Adviser to the President on Foreign Trade, and the National Recovery Administration.

The National Archives stores approximately one thousand cubic feet of records received from the Office of Agricultural Relations, 1901–54. They include consular reports, varied records relating to international conferences and technical assistance to underdeveloped nations, and reports and studies relating to an Italian land utilization program (1933). The consular reports are arranged by country and thereunder by subject—for example, agricultural policy, farm management, foreign trade, tariffs and trade regulations, and trade and economics.

Emergency agencies for both world wars, such as the War Trade Board, the Office of Foreign Assets Control, the Alien Property Custodian, the Office of Price Administration, the War Food Administration, and the Production Board, gathered and analyzed considerable data about foreign economic relations.

While it is no startling revelation that the Post Office Department is involved in international communications, few if any researchers examine its records for this topic. The records, however, include many documents relating to postal congresses and conventions since 1853. A few examples will illustrate the content of postal records:

Australia walked out of the International Postal Union of 1885 because each of its colonies was not granted a separate vote;

Morocco permitted the British, Spanish, and German postal services to handle its mail although the sultan refused to allow any inland delivery of parcels;

Several hundred letters written during 1892–1910 deal with proposals to increase the efficiency of Far Eastern mail in order to promote our China trade;

A list of money orders sent to Russia in 1914 may have more than curiosity value; and

Records concerning a 1911 survey of postal laws and regulations evaluate worldwide postal services.

Our voluminous records relating to immigration require at least passing attention. The records of the Treasury and Justice Departments, as well as of the Department of State, include numerous references to the effect of immigration policies on international relations. I recommend the article entitled "The United States Government and the Irish . . ." by Homer L. Calkin that appeared in the March 1954 issue of *Irish Historical Studies* for those who are interested in the variety of such records relating to a single ethnic group.

Finally, let me call attention to another obvious, though neglected, source. Congressional reports have remained one of the most important sources for information about our foreign relations, yet diplomatic historians rarely explore the unpublished records of congressional committees. A few files may illustrate the types of congressional materials available. The files of the Senate Foreign Relations Committee for the Seventy-seventh Congress include many letters and petitions concerning the Neutrality Act. One by a professor of law expresses the wish that the committee would "press relentlessly for the speedy repeal of this unfortunate legislation, so contrary to every one of our traditions and so detrimental to the enlightened self-interest of the American people."[2] Similarly, the committee's records of the Seventy-ninth Congress deal mainly with the establishment of the United Nations. For the Eightieth Congress, the records relate to a wide variety of subjects, including the Marshall Plan, the crisis in Greece, German revival, and Aid to Palestine. They have some special interest because, for example, they reflect Sen. Arthur Vandenberg's role in developing the bipartisan foreign policy characteristic of the post–World War II period, which prompted another Republican to accuse him of representing "the best Roosevelt squandermania Do-Good New Dealer."

## NOTES

1. Wurts to William Wharton, enclosed in Wharton to the Secretary of the Treasury, June 14, 1892, File 91054, Letters Received by the Bureau of the Mint, Records of the Bureau of the Mint, Record Group 104, National Archives Building, Washington, D.C. The original is among the Diplomatic Despatches, Russia, General Records of the Department of State, Record Group 59, National Archives Building.
2. Francis Deak to Sen. Tom Connally, Sept. 25, 1941, Tray 226, SEN 77A-F11, Records of the United States Senate, Record Group 46, National Archives Building.

# National Archives Records on United States Foreign Relations Discussion

## DISCUSSION

*John A. DeNovo, University of Wisconsin:* I would like Milt Gustafson to comment on the following quotation from an article by Walter Rundell in the *AHA Newsletter* [7(June 1969):42–43] on access to records:

There should be a central agency in Washington to handle researchers' inquiries concerning access to all government records. Such an agency, if located high within the executive department and invested with adequate authority, could greatly simplify and facilitate research in official documents. One would hope that it could promote uniform and liberal policies of access to those records and that it could standardize security clearances.

*Milton O. Gustafson:* When I read that sentence I wondered if Dr. Rundell had heard of the National Archives and Records Service, because I think that should be our job. But he used to work in the office where I now work, and so I know he has. I think what he has in mind is something that Prof. Ernest May talked about last Christmas. If this is indeed what he had in mind, there should be something in the Executive Office of the President— an agency or an office—that would be able to standardize security clearances and so forth. But I see in the first few rows Bill Franklin from the Department of State and Jim Hewes from the Department of the Army, and maybe they have additional comments on this question.

*James E. Hewes, Office of the Chief of Military History, Department of the Army:* I will speak as an individual rather than as a member of the Office of Military History. I have been reading in the papers lately that the Congress of the United States is interested in promoting the career of a gentleman by the name of Otepka and giving him a higher role in the problem of security clearances. Perhaps this is a job they could give Otepka. [*Laughter.*]

*William M. Franklin, Historical Office, Department of State:* We were aware years ago of difficulties in researchers' using Department of State records and then finding that the trail, of course, led to the War Department records, or vice versa. Thus for quite a number of years now we have had what we call preaccess consultation between the departments concerned in order to decide whether a researcher can be admitted to the records which he needs in both departments or, in a few cases, more than two departments. Obviously it is discouraging to him to be admitted to one and then denied access to the other. This has been worked out. I do not believe there have been any difficulties for years on this score.

As far as security checks go, those are fairly well standardized. They are not the complete security investigation that government employees undergo. They are name checks, which are made rapidly; thanks to modern improvements in mechanization, I presume, they can now be made in a matter of a few weeks.

They are designed to indicate to the granting officer that the researcher does not have a record—that his record is not in the police category. If the investigation comes up clean, and almost all do, then a researcher is supposed to be a trustworthy citizen.

On this basis access is granted in these restricted cases. There is very little delay. There seems to be a queer canard going around that different departments take months to go over the same records to find out whether you really were born in Toledo and so on. This is certainly not true. We obtain clearances within a matter of a couple of weeks, and they are accepted by the security offices on the basis of quick telephone calls.

I suppose someone will have had an experience to the contrary, but I think that a number of you who have worked in recent records, classified records under restrictions, will bear me out that neither the Potomac River nor separate security offices have been any great trial to you in your access to records of the Defense and State Departments in particular.

*Gustafson:* I have one other comment to make about the Rundell article, and that is his point that professors ought to send their graduate students to the National Archives and to other research institutions a little bit better prepared than they are currently doing. It is appalling to sit down and talk to someone who has not heard of the *Foreign Relations* series, or that State Department records are restricted, and in fact closed after 1945. This makes my job particularly difficult, and so this is another point that he made that I would support wholeheartedly.

*Richard W. Leopold, Northwestern University:* I would like to comment on two aspects of John De Novo's question that do not involve, I think, the question of security.

Some of you may remember that a few years ago the question of a research center in history was raised, and this idea of course now is being carried forward in some way. Some of you are more aware than I am of the details under the proposal of the Woodrow Wilson Center, and some of you may have received a questionnaire recently under the name of Hubert Humphrey asking your opinions on what sort of a research center it should be. And I certainly would like to encourage all of you who have not received questionnaires about this Wilson Center to find ways in which you can make your views known. Research assistance needs to be provided for you, for your graduate students, and, of course, for foreign scholars coming to this country who are even less equipped than we.

The other point that I would like to make I will put in the form of a question. Some of us have been dealing with the National Archives to our great benefit for a number of years. We have received over the years the excellent finding aids, the preliminary inventories, the reference bulletins. As I look over the pamphlet listing National Archives publications that was in our folders, I am impressed by the number of these that are out of print. For those of our students who are coming to Washington properly equipped it would be most valuable if some of these earlier reference aids could be made available.

Now presumably they are in our libraries. Presumably they are in any government depository. I am wondering—and here is this old question—what steps are now being taken to make readily available to our graduate students and to those professors teaching in new institutions this magnificent battery of finding aids. And—the inevitable question—when will the new edition of the *National Archives Guide* be available?

*Herbert E. Angel, Deputy Archivist of the United States:* I suppose I should attempt to answer that one. You can select various dates for the *Guide.* Work, however, is very definitely in progress and quite well along.

As for the other finding aids, we, of course, have copies of those here. We have not gone so far as to chain them to the pulpit yet, but we do have them. We also have quick copying machines. And National Archives publications are available in their entirety on microfilm. So we are not completely devoid of these things. And if there are shortages, let us know.

One of the reasons, of course, we have not reprinted many of these finding aids is that with the passage of years things have happened to the different rceord groups, and there is a matter of updating the publications so that they represent our current knowledge. That is the reason that we have not gone back to press just to keep the supply up. But if there are copies that definitely are needed, we will supply them.

*Wayne S. Cole, University of Maryland:* I would like to ask someone to describe the restrictions on the use of navy and army records, and I would also like to ask—if I am correct in believing that these restrictions are substantially more severe than those on the use of State Department records—what possibilities there may be in obtaining some relaxation on those restrictions.

*Angel:* The logical person to talk about restrictions on army and navy records would be Bob Krauskopf, who has responsibility for both of those groups, although he talked today only about navy records.

*Robert W. Krauskopf:* This is a troublesome area, as we all know, both on the researcher's side of the fence and ours. We would just as soon see no restrictions if that could possibly be worked out. The situation is complex, and I can only speak in generalities here. If anyone has specific problems, I think it would be well to discuss them with the Archives staff directly and individually.

There are many types of restrictions. There are restrictions on various types of records by subject, that is, personnel-type information and investigatory data, things of that sort that have no bearing on security. I think, however, that the problem that affects most people working in the diplomatic area is the security classification.

One great advance that was made in the area of security classifications within the last decade, of course, was the issuance by the Department of Defense in 1959 of a directive that had the effect of declassifying military records created before 1946, with certain exceptions. The exceptions still present many problems, but we have advanced this much. We are much better off than we were ten years ago.

That directive, however, left many areas in which the records are still security classified, and classification cannot be reduced yet. But as far as the remainder is concerned, for those areas in which classification cannot be reduced, we still have to require that the individual researcher go to the agency responsible and obtain a security clearance. That is the only way under which admittance can be granted. And that usually involves, as far as the agency is concerned, clearance of the notes and eventual clearance of the manuscript.

I am not quite certain, but I think the situation with regard to State Department records is a little more clear-cut, not as complex perhaps. I am sure that all elements of the Department of Defense are constantly working on this problem and are seeking ways and means of narrowing the areas in which security classifications still have to be maintained. If anyone from that department is here and wishes to comment further on that, I think this might be an opportune moment for him to do so.

*Hewes:* The problem in the Department of the Army is that very often the documents should have been declassified when the records were retired; someone simply forgot to do it. And in that case, generally speaking, when a researcher finds the document and cannot get access to it because it is classified, the National Archives is able to get the document declassified if the originating agency agrees. Is that not correct?

*Krauskopf:* Yes, we can always do that. When it is a simple problem, the case of an individual document, then, of course, we can always go back to the agency involved and ask them to review it and get it declassified. That is true.

*Dean C. Allard, Jr., Naval History Division, Department of the Navy:* Two of the basic problems in access to the navy records that have anything to do with the policy and strategy formulation is the existence of the Joint Chiefs of Staff material and material originated by other countries. On one of those categories I think there is some progress or at least some hope for progress in the near future. That is, the Joint Chiefs of Staff material, which is now being reviewed by a group, as I understand it, in the Joint Chiefs office. The Joint Chiefs hope to have some declassification action in the next two or three years.

As far as the foreign material that is interfiled in the Navy Departments records is concerned, I frankly cannot see much hope of immediate declassification. But at least if there is some action on the declassification of the Joint Chiefs of Staff material I do think that access to the navy records on the policy and strategic formulations will be much easier.

*David Green, Ohio State University:* This is a question for Dr. Gustafson, and since Dr. Franklin is here perhaps he might want to comment also. You mentioned in your paper the possibility of opening up some documents from 1945 to 1949. Presumably this would be adding to the restricted material that is available after 1939. As I understand it, the rules of the game so far are that documents are opened as each succeeding volume of *Foreign Relations* is published. Thus we probably cannot expect those volumes through 1949 to be available for quite some time. Is there any way that the unpublished material can be liberated for our use independently of the publications of *Foreign Relations* volumes, and would it be helpful to you to have some request of that kind made by this group? Because if a resolution would be helpful, I am sure we could get someone to propose it.

*Franklin:* What Mr. Gustafson said did not refer to access but to the transfer of the records dated from 1945 to 1949 to the National Archives. This is not the same as opening them. There should be a relationship between the transfer of records from the State Department to the Archives, but for various technical reasons the exact coincidence of transfer and access is not the same.

The National Archives at present has records of the Department of State in the restricted period to which access can be granted only through application to and approval by the Department of State. As Mr. Gustafson said in a very polite way, this is a damned nuisance to him. And we regard it so in principle. We would like to see our records transferred to the Archives at a time when those records can be opened. At present there are records in the restricted period which scholars are researching in the National Archives, and for the year 1945 in the Department of State; this situation causes both the Archives and the State Department considerable headache. We are not set up in the Department of State to service scholars. Mr. Simon, who is the head of our Records Service Division, has gone to great lengths to prepare study areas and finding aids and facilities to handle scholars researching files in the Department of State Building. It would be much better if those records had been transferred to National Archives so that the nuisance would be Mr. Gustafson's problem and not ours directly.

Ideally—ideally, I repeat—it would be better to have only an open period and a closed period, with the open period covering all those records transferred to the National Archives by State. For various reasons this has not been possible. But the most particular reason is that the records are arranged in five-year groupings. I believe for later periods the span is reduced to three years; the three-year period would be more helpful. But we cannot break up the five-year group. Besides, we are still compiling the 1949 records for *Foreign Relations.* So, begging your pardon, we would like to have those handy in the Department of State. We do not want to transfer them to Archives until we are through with them because we are the principal users.

On the question of declassification, this is a huge problem. The security agencies of all departments have been doing nothing now for about two decades but cranking out ever more severe security requirements to make sure that everyone locks his desk and puts nothing in it and the safe has triple combinations and fireproof lining. And that the classifications are maintained, that if there is anything in the file that is secret, the whole file becomes secret, along with every paper in it, and so on and so forth.

This entanglement will now have to be unraveled. I repeat, the security people for two decades have been working towards ever greater security. Now with the lapse of time the situation has reached the point that they are quite aware of this problem, but what are they going to do about it? Who is going to do anything about it? How does one declassify, or even downgrade? There are only two methods. One is to have teams of people with both knowledge of the current political consequences and the significance of the records and knowledge of the records in large enough quantities to go through and actually read them and pass a judgement. The number of such records is staggering.

Someone mentioned the fact that the Army and Navy Departments have declassification teams. They have had the manpower, I say jealously, to establish these teams, but the State Department never has had anything close to that much manpower. We rely on another method of declassification—time. Time. Lapsed time. That is all. We can also handle individual papers in small quantities, and we do under the Freedom of Information Act. We did it long before the act was thought of. We now have a desk designated by the act. One can apply at that desk, and if possible the paper will be shipped around to pertinent officers who do know its political significance at the moment. A decision will then be made as to whether it can be declassified and made available to the researcher. Very large numbers of papers have been made available, but still the number is very small in comparison to the totality of classified records.

I do not know how well I have answered your queries, but we are aware of the problems. The ideal solution would be to move records from the Department of State—and I would think from other active agencies also— to the National Archives at a time when the Archives could open them. If declassification had not been effected sooner, it could then take place at that point.

# Publication of Records on United States Foreign Relations

# National Archives Microfilm Publications as a Resource for Foreign Relations Research

## ALBERT H. LEISINGER, JR.

Nearly three decades ago the National Archives launched a microfilm publication program. Under this program microfilm copies of significant series of archival materials are prepared. The negative microfilm, equipped with introductions and such finding aids as tables of contents, lists, or indexes, is retained by the National Archives; and positive prints, which we call microfilm publications, are sold at nominal cost to scholars, libraries, or research institutions. It is National Archives policy to expand this program to the limit of our resources by making available microfilm copies of more and more primary source materials.

The major factor in beginning what was at the time a unique program and a new adventure in publication was the need to preserve our nation's most valuable records. Moreover, the historian not only desired easy access to and copies of these records, but he (as well as the archivist) desired more extensive publication of archives. At that time the outlook for any systematic or comprehensive program of publication of archival resources by conventional means was pessimistic: the records were vast, the costs were high, and the funds were not forthcoming. Microfilm copies, however, could be produced at just a fraction of the cost and with greater accuracy than letterpress; an edition was never out of print as long as the master negative existed, since copies could be produced on demand at any time.[1]

## SELECTING RECORDS FOR FILMING

Only a small part of our archival holdings is available on microfilm—probably not more than 4 percent of the total volume. At the present time, about one hundred thousand rolls of microfilm, containing approximately one hundred million pages of documentary materials, are available to researchers through our microfilm publications program. The equivalent of six hundred million documentary pages of reproductions of archival materials has now been distributed to institutions in the fifty states, Puerto Rico, Guam, and nearly sixty foreign countries.

The eighth revision of the *List of National Archives Microfilm Publications,* published in 1968, describes the film available. Since 1950 the National Archives has been publishing descriptive accompanying pamphlets for each series of records microfilmed; more than 450 of these pamphlets have now been produced. These pamphlets are available without charge to those purchasing the microfilm as well as to those interested in the content of the records reproduced.

The selection of archival series or groups of records for publication on microfilm is made from the approximately nine hundred thousand cubic feet of records in our custody. These include practically all of the permanently valuable records of the federal government from 1774 to 1950 that have survived, that are still in government custody, and that are free of restrictions on their use. Records are selected for microfilming if they have a high degree of research value for a variety of studies; if the ratio of research value to the overall volume is high; if they are in, or close to, a good state of arrangement; if they are so organized, indexed, or controlled that a researcher can easily retrieve information from the film copy; and if they are not readily available in published form. In the selection process each series of records is, in effect, competing with all other series of records in the National Archives. The values of filming a particular series of records have to be compared with the values of filming other series.[2] In this competition, records relating to foreign relations and the history of other countries have fared well. For example, it has been possible for us to film in their entirety the Papers of the Continental Congress; the records of the Russian-American Company; the diplomatic, consular, and miscellaneous correspondence of the Department of State through 1906; and practically all of those sections of the 1910–29 decimal files of the State Department that concern internal affairs of foreign states, our diplomatic relations with them, and their relations with other states.

Several facts about our filming program should be kept in mind. We are, with rare exceptions, microfilming each series of records in its entirety, and we have avoided the microcopying of selected materials from a series. This policy is based on our belief, as archivists, that the filming of selected materials will often destroy the integrity of the series, that is to say, the relation that documents in each series have to each other; that it is easier to film an entire series than to film selected items; that any canon of selection will find dissenters, if not in this generation then in the next; and that it is cheaper.

When the program was first started, most projects grew out of routine reference service on the records. It was not until 1948 that we began to plan our program systematically. As the program has developed, increased emphasis has been given to filming related series of records. We now believe (and have thought for some time) that all main series of records relating to the same broad subject or field of interest should be filmed so that the researcher can obtain good coverage. Thus we have microfilmed about half a dozen series of records that relate to the suppression of the African slave trade and Negro colonization. Similarly, literally scores of projects document relations between the United States and Mexico.

## EARLY PUBLICATION PROGRAMS FOR DIPLOMATIC ARCHIVES

The value of filming record series in their entirety is demonstrated in part by the dissatisfaction of many scholars with past publications of our diplomatic archives during the nineteenth century and the first twenty-five years of this century. We may begin with Jared Sparks's *The Diplomatic Correspondence of the American Revolution.*[3] Sparks's carelessness and obvious errors—both of omission and commission—led to the publication of a new edition edited by Francis Wharton that has superseded the Sparks edition.[4] But Wharton's edition also has its defects. A recent comparison of the originals of six of John Adams's letters by a member of the staff of the National Historical Publications Commission with the Wharton version revealed at least thirty errors both of omission and commission.

The diplomatic correspondence by itself, of course, tells just part of the story of our revolutionary war diplomacy; when using the microfilm edition of the Continental Congress papers, for example, researchers have available to them the committee reports, journals, drafts and proposals for treaties and agreements, as well as other pertinent documentation that is not included in Wharton.

Although no comparison has been made, to our knowledge, between the printed and the original diplomatic correspondence for 1783 to 1789, it would be very surprising if there are not gaps, in addition to numerous transcription errors, in these as well. The materials were prepared for publication under the direction of State Department clerk William A. Weaver, who prepared the seven volumes for publication in only two years.[5]

Andrew C. McLaughlin, in his analysis of the six volumes of *American State Papers* dealing with foreign relations for 1789 to 1828, stated that not more than one-quarter of the relevant materials in the custody of the State Department were included in this publication; that many documents "appear only in extract"; that invaluable printed enclosures were omitted; and that numerous documents dealing with political and social conditions were not published. Mentioning specifically the omission of unpublished reports of William Short, John Quincy Adams, Jonathan Russell, and Benjamin Rush, McLaughlin printed a few of these to show their significance. He affirmed that his examination of the archives showed "conclusively . . . the need of printing in ex tenso the diplomatic correspondence for . . . 1788–1828," and the need for printing those materials from 1828 to 1860 for which there was "no single printed compilation of diplomatic correspondence." Yet despite the fact that McLaughlin's recommendations received substantial support from the historical profession and the Department of State, they have never been implemented.[6]

Richard Leopold, in discussing the need for publication for this later period, states that "many documents were published by order of the Senate or House, but they are widely dispersed, capriciously selected, and badly edited. . . . we have no reliable estimate of the percentage of archival records in print for the period."[7]

My own favorite example of an omission during this period is in the despatch sent by our chargé d'affaires in Great Britain, Aaron Vail, Vail informed the secretary of state that the United States had received a windfall in the form of a bequest from James Smithson "to found at Washington, under the name of the Smithsonian Institution, an establishment for the increase and diffusion of knowledge among men." An extract of the despatch was forwarded to President Jackson, who, in turn, transmitted it to the Congress. Congress, we know, came close to rejecting the bequest because of strong anti-British sentiment. Interestingly enough, the original despatch was marked for the copyist with brackets to show the following deletion, and I quote:

The caption of the will is in language which might induce a belief that the Testator labored under some degree of mental aberration at the time it was made, tho' I understand that its allegations are not destitute of probability at least.[8]

Whether the State Department was at the time justified or unjustified in making this deletion from the despatch is beside the point. The scholar now working in this area should certainly know that it had been made.

Similar marked deletions are to be found on many nineteenth- and early twentieth-century despatches in the National Archives. They often indicate to the researcher that a document has been printed or copied only in part. An advantage in using microfilm publications of the originals is that the film copy will reproduce the brief notes made by the secretary or other high department officials indicating their reactions or the nature of the reply, stampings or other notations showing the date of receipt by different offices within the department, notations of referrals to their departments, Congress, or the White House, and memorandums of State Department officials.

John P. Harrison in his *Guide to Materials Relating to Latin America in the National Archives* assesses despatch enclosures from nineteenth-century diplomats in this manner:

The research value of the enclosures . . . has frequently been overlooked. Among the enclosures are copies of correspondence between the diplomatic officers and officials of the governments to which they were accredited, United States naval officers, other diplomatic and consular officers, and private persons who were in conflict with the local government; official gazettes and other government publications; and newspapers, broadsides and printed pamphlets. . . . Approximately 95 percent of these newspapers are the only extant copies in the United States. Many of the pamphlets, broadsides, and other imprints, especially for the years before 1830, are very rare items.[9]

Harrison's generalization about the research value of the enclosures to despatches from diplomatic representatives in South America is probably valid for consular and diplomatic despatches from other geographic areas of the world, with the exception of Western Europe.

It is not my intention to discuss the *Foreign Relations* series published since 1862 other than to state that it was not until 1921, as Richard Leopold pointed out, that *"Foreign Relations* entered the modern era" with "scholars in command" and with "a long overdue set of principles to govern its compilation."[10]

## MICROFILMING DIPLOMATIC RECORDS AT THE NATIONAL ARCHIVES

The National Archives has issued a great many microfilm publications that are of value for studies in the fields of foreign relations and the history of other countries. As early as 1942 we began to microfilm the more than twenty-two hundred bound volumes of diplomatic despatches dating from

1789 to 1906. These are arranged in series according to the name of the country and thereunder chronologically. In preparing these series for microfilming we attempted to facilitate the use of the film by researchers as much as possible. We did this, first, by reproducing on the first roll selected pages from a number of registers that when taken as a unit, comprises a calendar for each series of despatches. Second, we prepared an alphabetical index to the writers of the despatches. This reference tool supplies the writer's title, inclusive dates of his communications, and the roll numbers of the film on which his communications are reproduced. Third, we included a statement concerning the scope and major subject matter content of the microfilm publication. For example, the introduction to the despatches from China contains the following statement:

The despatches contain a wealth of information concerning not only China Proper but also Manchuria, Tibet, Formosa, Korea, the Philippine Islands, and Indochina. They relate to such subjects as the opening of treaty ports and the extraterritorial rights of American citizens, the Opium Wars, The Taiping Rebellion, the Sino-Japanese and the Russo-Japanese Wars, the Boxer Rebellion and other anti-foreign disturbances, and the need for more United States naval vessels in China waters. There are despatches and reports in which are discussed the problems of piracy, the treatment of shipwrecked American seamen, the protection of missionaries, the emigration of Chinese from the United States, claims of American citizens in China against the Chinese Government, prohibition of the opium trade, the "coolie trade," floods and famine, and epidemics of such diseases as cholera and the bubonic plague. There is also information on the growth of shipping and trade, China's natural resources and her agriculture, public health, education (by the Chinese Government, by missionaries, and by admitting Chinese students to educational institutions in the United States), and communications—roads, river transport, mail services, construction of the Trans-Siberian Railroad and other railways, and telephone and telegraph lines.[11]

In addition, the introduction to the microfilm publication contains a table of contents and data on related series of records whether microfilmed or not.

For the period to 1906 we have also microfilmed all of the series of consular despatches, more than thirty-five hundred volumes. Although these deal primarily with economic affairs and the protection of American life and property, they often contain reports on political developments and disturbances. During the first half of the nineteenth century reports on political affairs occurred more frequently, especially when there was no diplomatic representative on the scene. The consular despatches also contain a great variety of enclosures, both printed and unprinted.

Most of the letters received by the State Department before 1906 that were not filed in the diplomatic or consular despatches were filed in a series of "Miscellaneous Letters" consisting of 1,533 volumes, all of which have been microfilmed. This valuable but lengthy series contains an enormous quantity of documents relating to international affairs and events abroad. The writers include United States citizens with interests or claims abroad, foreign citizens, members of Congress, army and navy officers, officials of government departments, and presidents of the United States. For the period through 1820, for example, there are about eight hundred presidential letters, many of which are significant for studies of our foreign policy. Although a calendar and supplements covering the period through 1825 as well as a register for 1860–1906 have been filmed for this series, it may best be exploited by those interested in specific events or a particular subject covering a relatively short time span.

Another series well worth consulting for those interested in the political background and biographical data of United States diplomatic and consular representatives is the Applications and Recommendations for Office, 1797–1901, most of which has now been filmed through 1869. Each subseries contains as part of the editorial apparatus a list of applicants or persons recommended, arranged by presidential administration and thereunder by name of applicant or officeholder.

One of our most ambitious microfilming projects is that of the decimal files of the Department of State, 1910 to 1929. These records are arranged by a decimal system of subject classification in nine major subject classes. Although we were well aware of the tremendous research value of these files, it was the urgent need for preserving the records from the deterioration caused by excessive wear and tear that forced us to film them. A careful investigation revealed that the only feasible way to preserve these records was to microfilm those sections of the file that were subjected to the greatest use and then to substitute the microfilm copies for the paper records. Those sections of the file most in need of preservation were the 800 class, relating to the internal affairs of states, and the 700 class, concerning relations between states. Fortunately the file arrangement, by using subordinate numbers to represent individual countries, makes it possible to select and microfilm as units the documents relating to the internal affairs of a particular country (class 800) or the relations between the United States and a particular country (711.——) and that country's relations with other countries. With a few minor exceptions, all of these files have now been microfilmed. The pertinent parts of the purport books for each section of the file have also been microfilmed along with the records. They are, in effect, a list of the documents filmed; they serve, along with the accompanying pamphlet, to facilitate use of the records and to offer to the research scholar a great reservoir of research materials comparable in value to the microfilmed series of diplomatic and consular despatches through 1906. Recently we have begun to plan the filming of decimal files of the State Department for the period 1930 to 1939. We will continue to select the files that are filmed, for this period and the earlier period, on the basis of research value and the need to preserve the original records.

These, then, are the major microfilm publication projects from records of the Department of State. An examination of our most recent *List of National Archives Microfilm Publications* will reveal many others.

## FILMING RELATED SERIES OF RECORDS

It is not possible, of course, to describe all the records the National Archives has microfilmed that contain significant data relating to foreign affairs or to the history of particular countries. Of particular importance, however, are the major series of letters received and sent by the secretary of the navy to 1886, all of which have been microfilmed. These include letters from commanding officers of squadrons, 1841–86; from captains, 1805–61; from commanders, 1804–86; from officers below the rank of commander, 1802–86; and from the secretary of the navy to officers 1798–1868.

Also microfilmed are the "area files" of the Office of Naval Records and Library. Included in these files are unbound papers from private sources, chiefly naval officers or their heirs, and unbound papers removed from the files of the Office of the Secretary of the Navy and other offices of the Navy Department. The file, arranged by eight geographic regions and thereunder chronologically, covers roughly the period from 1775 to 1910.

The commanding officers of ships and squadrons left no small imprint on our foreign relations in the nineteenth century. Not only did their ships frequently carry our diplomatic and consular officials, as well as special agents, to and from their assignments, but naval officers on occasion served in diplomatic assignments during the absence of official representatives. At times they were even trusted with diplomatic assignments of their own. Some of the more important missions, such as those of Perry and Shufeldt, were turning points in our foreign relations. Navy squadrons ranged the seven seas, while navy ships were often rushed to areas of crisis. The reports of their commanding officers—who frequently were acute observers—are often of the highest value. In areas where the United States had special interests, as in Latin America and the Caribbean, their reports are often essential for an understanding of the United States role. During the nineteenth century, also, such naval officers such as Wilkes, Ringgold, Rodgers, Gilliss, Herndon, and Page led exploring expeditions to many areas of the world. Because of the peculiarities of their arrangement, most of the navy records are best exploited when specific incidents, dates, or names are at hand.

## MICROFILMING CAPTURED RECORDS

Of significance also are the more than twenty-five thousand rolls of microfilm now in our custody as a result of the capture of enemy records, mostly German, at the end of World War II. These records cover primarily all of the period from 1867 to 1945 and have now been restored to German depositories. The more important ones were first microfilmed, and the master negatives or copies were deposited in the National Archives. With few exceptions, all of the film has been brought under microfilm publication controls. The filming was started in Whaddon Hall, Buckinghamshire, England, as a tripartite project of the governments of Great Britain, France, and the United States; other filming at Whaddon Hall was done by various American universities, Saint Anthony's College, and the American Historical Association. Filming at the Berlin Document Center was accomplished by the American Historical Association, the Hoover Institution, and the University of Nebraska. The oldest records of all, from the Heeresarchiv Potsdam, some of which date from as early as the seventeenth century, were filmed at the National Archives. The bulk of the materials was filmed at Alexandria, Virginia, beginning in 1956. The Alexandria filming, undertaken initially by the American Historical Association but with foundation support and the cooperation of the Departments of State and Defense and the National Archives, became a National Archives project about eight years ago. Guides for most of these captured records have been published, including fifty-nine guides—with more still to be issued—to the Alexandria records alone.

As a result of these filming projects the National Archives has probably become the most important center in the world, outside Germany itself, for studies of modern German history. The National Archives was privileged to host the Conference on Captured German and Related Records in November 1968, the papers and proceedings of which will also be published by the Ohio University Press.

These, then, are three substantial groups of archival materials available for foreign relations research. There are, of course, other microfilmed records, especially those of the War and Treasury Departments, that have significant value for students of foreign relations and the histories of other countries. With few exceptions, however, microfilmed records of these departments do not contain continuous runs of material on these subjects.

## LETTERPRESS AND MICROFILM:
## AN ASSESSMENT AND COMPARISON

It is not possible to predict what the future holds for our microfilm publication program. We at the National Archives should be aware, and I hope all of us are, that as long as we continue to select for filming materials that have continuing and significant research values we can expect the program to flourish. We are fortunate that our microfilm publication program operates on a trust fund basis with a small part of the proceeds from every sale returned to the fund to be used for the production of additional master negatives. I doubt whether it will ever be possible to begin to exhaust our store of archival materials that have value sufficient to justify their filming for scholars.

This paper has stressed the values of microfilm publications as a means of bringing exact reproductions of archival materials to the scholar. Through such a program a university or a research library can expand and develop its collections. A new university, crippled by a paucity of research materials, can at a comparatively small cost obtain research materials; and graduate students can be trained to work with primary sources.

It should be emphasized that both letterpress and microfilm have a place in scholarly publication programs. Letterpress is generally more suited for the publication of materials of the highest value that are not extensive and that merit the widest possible circulation. Microfilm publication is best suited for reproducing extensive bodies of records quickly and efficiently. All too often, only one or the other method is used; actually, many combinations of both are possible. One type of combined project is illustrated by the Adams family publication project. In 1952 the trustees of the Adams Manuscript Trust decided to microfilm the Adams family papers in order to ensure their safety and to make them available to scholars everywhere. Although a comprehensive letterpress edition of these papers has been under way since 1954, it will not be possible to print every document or to cover every subject: in these cases, the microfilm may be consulted.

Another type of combination project is illustrated by the one now in process at the National Archives for the Wisconsin volumes of *The Territorial Papers of the United States*—the oldest continuing documentary publication undertaken by the United States government, with the exception of State Department's *Foreign Relations* series.[12] Dr. John Porter Bloom has been editor of the *Territorial Papers* series since 1964, following the death in 1961 of Clarence Carter, who began the publication project in 1931. In this case, the microfilm supplement was prepared first. The editor then made his selections from the film, which he had enlarged, and he then prepared his printer's copy from the enlargement. The film supplement thus contains all the records from which the selections were made, and the letterpress publication makes direct reference to materials reproduced on the film supplement by roll and frame number. An editor may print only a few documents relating to a specific incident, but in his footnotes he may refer to other documents relating to this incident that are reproduced on the film. The scholar may also view, if he so desires, exact reproductions of the documents that the editor has chosen to print.

All of us should be aware of the gaps now existing in the *Foreign Relations* series and the probability that publication may, of necessity, become more and more selective. In closing, I should like to address just one question to my good friend, Dr. William Franklin of the Department of State: Would it be feasible to issue a microfilm publication supplement to the *Foreign Relations* series?

## NOTES

1. For a history of the National Archives microfilm publication program, see Albert H. Leisinger, Jr., "Selected Aspects of Microreproduction in the United States," a report prepared for the Extraordinary Congress of the International Council on Archives held in Washington, D.C., May 9 to 14, 1966. This report has been republished in *National Archives Accessions,* no. 60 (Dec. 1967): 29–49, and in *Archivum* 16 (1966): 127–50.

2. For a more detailed listing of the criteria governing the selection of materials for microfilm publication see U.S., National Archives and Records Service, *The Preparation of Records for Publication on Microfilm,* Staff Information Paper no. 19, by Albert H. Leisinger, Jr. (Washington, D.C., 1951) as well as Leisinger, *Microphotography for Archives* (Washington, D.C.: International Council on Archives, 1968).

3. U.S., Department of State, *The Diplomatic Correspondence of the American Revolution,* ed. Jared Sparks, 12 vols. (Boston: N. Hale Gray & Bowen; New York; G. & C. & H. Carvell, 1829–30).

4. U.S., Department of State, *The Revolutionary Diplomatic Correspondence of the United States,* ed. Francis Wharton, 6 vols. (Washington, D.C.: Government Printing Office,1889).

5. Carl L. Lokke, "The Continental Congress Papers: Their History, 1789–1952," *National Archives Accessions,* no. 51 (June 1954): 8–9.

6. Andrew C. McLaughlin, *Report on the Diplomatic Archives of the Department of State, 1789–1840* (Washington, D.C.: Carnegie Institution, 1904), p. 4.

7. Richard W. Leopold, "The *Foreign Relations* Series: A Centennial Estimate," *Mississippi Valley Historical Review* 49 (1962–63): 597.

8. Aaron Vail to John Forsyth, July 28, 1835, #197, Diplomatic Despatches, Great Britain, vol. 43, General Records of the Department of State, Record Group 59, National Archives Building, Washington, D.C.

9. U.S., National Archives and Records Service, *Guide to Materials on Latin America in the National Archives,* by John P. Harrison (Washington, D.C.: Government Printing Office, 1961), p. 47. It might also be mentioned that William R. Manning, ed., *Diplomatic Correspondence of the United States concerning the Independence of the Latin-American Nations,* 3 vols. (New York: Oxford University Press, 1925), and idem, *Diplomatic Correspondence of the United States: Inter-American Affairs, 1831–1860,* 12 vols. (Washington, D.C.: Carnegie Endowment for International Peace, 1932–39), omit numerous documents and enclosures relating to economic affairs.

10. Leopold, "The *Foreign Relations* Series," pp. 599–600.

11. U.S., National Archives and Records Service, *Despatches from United States Ministers to China, 1843–1906,* Pamphlet Accompanying Microcopy no. 92 (Washington, D.C., 1958), p. 5.

12. For a description of this series, see William M. Franklin's article included in the present volume.

# The Future of the Foreign Relations *Series*

## WILLIAM M. FRANKLIN

The *Foreign Relations* series was, and still is, unique: it is the only continuous, annual, official publication in depth of diplomatic correspondence and foreign policy documents. The uniqueness of this series has been largely ignored or obscured for a hundred years. When the series started in 1861, it was obviously a novel republican venture based on the then shocking idea that the people had a right to know on a current basis how their foreign affairs were being conducted.[1] Despite its uniqueness in principle, the *Foreign Relations* series seems to have made little impact at the time of its birth or for decades thereafter. The reason, of course, was that United States policy in those years was so limited, overt, and doctrinaire that the only secret revealed by the series in those early days was that the American Republic had no secrets to reveal.

In the early twentieth century, the uniqueness of the *Foreign Relations* series was further obscured by the substantively more important documentary collections published by the great powers of Europe. This all began in 1910 when the French government released the first volume of its twenty-nine-tome collection of documents on the diplomatic origins of the war of 1870–71. The late and eminent Italian scholar, Dr. Mario Toscano, writing in 1966, characterized this French publication as "the first great collection of diplomatic documents in the modern sense."[2] The fact that he did not even mention *Foreign Relations* in this connection indicates that Dr. Toscano, as many another scholar, was so impressed by the substantive importance of the French documents that he did not consider the American publication—although much earlier in origin—to be in the same league. Before the French series could be completed and before the inevitable German counter-collection could even be started, along came World War I, followed by a huge outpouring of top-level documentation by the great powers of Europe on the origins of that conflict. *Foreign Relations,* although publishing far more recent documentation, was lost to sight in the scholarly gold rush to dig out the top-secret paydirt from the German publication *Die Grosse Politik,* the French publication *Documents Diplomatiques Français,* the British documents on the origins of the war, and many others. For the most part, European governments published through the July crisis of 1914 and then stopped; the Bolsheviki, being revolutionary, began with the war-time secret treaties and worked backward to the age of imperialism. Nobody except the United States went right on through the war period.

Now it so happened that for the brief interval of 1917 through 1919 the United States, for the first time in its history, suddenly played a major role in the main arena of world politics. Would this high-level, secret material be released in the normal course of publication, which at that time was put-ting the documents out with a lag of about eight years? I am sorry to say that even back in those courageous times—appreciably closer to the virtues of the Founding Fathers—the world war material went into supplements that were not released until about fourteen or fifteen years after the event. And the really top-secret documentation—the Paris Peace Conference documents of 1919—was put aside into another subseries, with the result that historians of the world war were "shackled" (as we have been taught to say) for twenty-seven years until the Department of State smote their chains asunder by publishing the minutes of the Council of Four in the *Foreign Relations* series. After that Paul Mantoux, Premier Clemenceau's interpreter at the Paris Peace Conference, was emboldened to publish his version of what the Big Four said.[3]

For the interwar years of 1920 to 1939 the *Foreign Relations* series again led all the rest, but no one cared very much. The volumes could do nothing but reflect the largely negative policies and often petty concerns of the United States government in this second period of aloofness from the broils and toils of world diplomacy.

With the end of World War II, the Europeans resumed, as they had after the First World War, publication of their documentation on the origins of the fracas. Most of these series begin with 1919 and continue only to the outbreak of war in 1939. Only a few venture into the period of the war. The Italians, who missed out on the previous postwar publishing spree, are working on a comprehensive series that will go up to the Italian surrender in 1943. The Hungarians are publishing six volumes in Magyar that will run through the war. (For those whose Magyar is rusty, there is a calendar of documents in German in each volume.) The German documents, unique in being edited by an international committee, will eventually go up to 1945. The Vatican, a dark horse in this documentary race, has brought out five interesting volumes on the Holy See and World War II[4]. But meanwhile

*Foreign Relations,* plodding along in its quiet, chronologic sort of way, has blazed a broad path all the way through the diplomacy of World War II. The Russians, whose interwar series was planned to go only to the 1930s,[5] were obviously stung into action by our publications on Tehran, Yalta, and Potsdam.[6] They released their own documents on these summit conferences in English translation in various issues of their *International Affairs* magazine[7] and then gathered them together for a book published in Russian in 1967.[8] Incidentally, these Soviet documents are worth looking up and comparing closely with the State Department Conference Series volumes; you will not learn much more about the conferences than you already know from our publications, but I guarantee that you will gain shocking insights into what a totalitarian system can do to historical evidence.

While the other governments are still working on the war and the prewar periods, *Foreign Relations* has again moved ahead of the entire pack into the documentation of the postwar period; but this time it will be neither ignored nor obscured. This time it is really in the spotlight, being first not only in the time of publication but also in the importance of the content. This uniqueness is a cause for pride but also for concern, because this postwar period poses a number of very special problems for the series in addition to the obvious difficulty of being painfully conspicuous.

First of all, there is the quantity. Publications for the year 1945 ran to twelve volumes, including those on Yalta and Potsdam. That, we thought, was a wartime abnormality—a hump that we would soon get over. Then, as we dug into the files from 1946 on, we soon came to the depressing realization that this time there would be no return to normalcy anywhere in the department, from the secretary's office on top to the files down below. Hostilities had ended, but the number of problems, people, and papers kept rising. We could not continue, however, to put out twelve or more volumes per year on a steady basis: it would take too long, cost too much, and break too many bookshelves. Our advisory committee, with whom we discussed this problem, agreed. So for the year 1946, for the first time in the history of the series, we drew up a plan in advance of compilation—a plan that listed the subjects and rated them as first, second, or third priority. Compilation would proceed from the top down, and subjects of lower priority would be handled in brief editorial notes (with file numbers), enabling us to stay within our goal of ten volumes. (Actually, there will be eleven volumes, including the two on China.)

But with our existing staff in the Historical Office we could not regularly compile even ten volumes in a year; and if we could not compile the documents for a year in a year, the series would continue to slip. The staff would have to learn how to compile faster and at the same time more selectively.

They have done just that; for the year 1947 there will be eight volumes, and for 1948 there will be seven. Even if it takes us a little longer to compile a smaller number of tight volumes rather than a larger number of loose ones, we will save time in the long run by having a smaller number to be selected, cleared, edited, indexed, printed, and bound before they finally drop off our long assembly line.

The postwar documentation is not only huge; it is also scattered within the State Department and among other departments and agencies. During the war, records were produced faster in the Department of State than they could be indexed and filed. Many never reached the central files but were kept in the various offices and bureaus and were later stored as "lots." Despite the perennial shrieks of the Historical Office, this system (if it can be so called) was perpetuated into the postwar world. Although our present Records Service Division has made vigorous efforts to improve this situation, the department still has more than three thousand separate lots, in addition to its huge central files and in addition to the post records. Each lot may be anything from a few boxes to a score of packing cases filled with papers of a particular office or officer, arranged in whatever way they were left by the last secretary who kept them or by the last researcher who pawed through them to find something.

Many of these lots can be ignored by the historians compiling *Foreign Relations* volumes, but many of them are highly important, particularly for policy papers. If *Foreign Relations* provided only diplomatic correspondence, as it used to do, then we would not have to bother with these annoying lot files; but scholars want to know how a policy developed and the alternatives that were considered, and this type of information may often be found only in unindexed lots. In the wartime conference series volumes some of the most important papers came from special lots. For the volumes of the postwar period we have regularly combed all pertinent lots. The cost in historian man-hours has been huge, but the volumes will be much richer for it. (Incidentally, this system of unindexed lots will increase difficulties in administering grants of access to nonofficial scholars.)

During the war period we had what the Department of State was inclined to regard as presidential "interference" with foreign policy and a sprouting of new agencies "dabbling" in foreign affairs. This, too, became normal in the postwar world, although in a more organized manner. The result has been that for many of the important documents needed for *Foreign Relations* we have had to go to other executive departments (notably Defense and Treasury), to the National Security Council, the Atomic Energy Commission, and to presidential libraries. Some of this necessitates additional clearances; all of it requires much more time and effort than was ever dreamed of in the balmy prewar days when the entire records of United States foreign policy as in the basement of "the" department. (Again I might note in passing that in this matter our problems will be shared by private scholars as they work into the files of the postwar period.)

The difficulties growing out of the size of the postwar documentation and its disorganized and scattered condition can be surmounted by the application of man-hours; but we have other problems that could not be solved even by doubling our staff, particularly the question of permission to print certain papers within a given period of time. This touchy subject may be divided into two aspects: personal and topical.

With reference to individuals, the *Foreign Relations* series has always had a reputation—good or bad—for being outspoken. As early as 1870 the series tramped on its first toes by publishing a despatch of that year from George P. Marsh, our minister in Florence, in which Marsh said that the Italian government had followed the lead of Napoleon III for so long that it was unable to formulate a policy of its own and that its future course would be characterized by "vacillation, tergiversation, and duplicity, as it has always been since 1864."[9] What made that one so salty was that it appeared in Italian translation in the leading Florentine newspaper on the very day that Mr. Marsh was invited to an official dinner with the minister of foreign affairs and several other government leaders. Was Mr. Marsh handed his passports? Did the ministry topple? Were relations broken? No, the only result, as Mr. Marsh had to admit, was that the Italians treated him better than ever. He continued happily and successfully in his Italian post until his death twelve years later.

Despite our best efforts to sell the moral of this story to higher policy officers in the department, the problem of clearing personal references has become appreciably more difficult in recent years, even though the series has slipped beyond the twenty-year line. Of course, the editors of *Foreign Relations* have always been authorized to leave out a sentence or two containing an invidious personal reference, but the dramatic increase in longevity that we have seen since World War II will make these problems more numerous and more touchy as more prominent officials here and abroad stay active in government or politics well beyond a quarter century.

The topical or substantive aspect of the clearance problem is even more serious. Basically, this problem is the result of periodicity. A war, even though it lasts but a few years, creates an abyss—a sharp discontinuity—between the eras before and after, each of which has its own distinctive set of problems and policies, its own configuration of friend and foe, its own atmosphere and language. Obviously, it is easy in a postwar period to publish the documents of a dead-and-gone prewar period, and that is exactly what the European powers have always done with their great documentary collections. We found it not too difficult to publish the record of our diplomatic and politico-military policies for the period of World War II, since most of the wartime problems were peculiar to the war and ended with it. And if we did not have many official fellow travelers on our safari through the wartime documentary jungles, we certainly did enjoy the company of a goodly crew of unofficial but authoritative autobiographers, who helped by letting a lot of top-secret cats out of the bag before we ever arrived on the scene.

But with 1946, even reliable and detailed memoirs become few and far between. And suddenly the major subjects have a contemporary ring, a characteristic that becomes much more pronounced by 1948–49. This is the beginning of the same era that we are—fortunately—still in. Here we have the start of those hardy, perennial problems of Berlin, Germany, the cold war, NATO, communism in China, Korea, United States aid, United States bases, the Arab-Israeli conflict, the India-Pakistan controversy, and many others. They have not been solved; they have not gone away; and the United States has been continuously and importantly involved. In some cases, publication of the record may be helpful to the current United States position; in other instances, where publication would be detrimental, we may have to accept a delay.

In the latter cases, we in the Historical Office have a choice: deletion or delay. We have had this painful choice before, but with the documentation of the postwar period we are going to have it, I fear, in a more acute form and more frequently.

There are compromise procedures: if the difficulty lies in only a few paragraphs or papers that we believe are not really necessary to the main line of the story, we will drop them. We will not do so, however, if we feel that a significant distortion would result. In that case we have a further compromise possibility; namely, to mention the subject in an editorial note, indicating that we are not publishing the documents but giving the file numbers so that in years to come researchers can track the subject and turn out revealing articles exposing our sins of omission. I may add that our advisory committee has supported us in feeling that compromise along these lines is justifiable if it will avoid holding up a volume of, say, fifteen hundred pages on twenty subjects because of a few pages on one subject.

We had a classic case of this sort in the long-continued dispute between the United States and Mexico over El Chamizal, that portion of El Paso, Texas, separated from Mexico by the change in course of the Rio Grande in 1864. *Foreign Relations* carried documents on the subject from time to time, beginning with the volume for 1910. In 1933 there was considerable negotiation on the subject, which did not produce a settlement but which did come up with a convention for flood control in the area. In *Foreign Relations* for 1933 we published the convention, but we did not publish the correspondence and memorandums that lay in back of it because the policy officers of the department, including our ambassador in Mexico City, were convinced that such publication would exacerbate feelings on both sides of the river and would make a real settlement all the harder to achieve. But the editor of *Foreign Relations* did receive permission to include a long, bracketed note giving the gist of the developments and concluding with the following paragraph:

Since no settlement of the territorial issues had been achieved when this volume was ready for publication, it was decided, after consultation between the two Governments, to omit at this time documentation on this phase of the negotiations for the years 1931–1933. This decision is in accordance with that section of Department of State Regulation 045.2 which permits certain omissions of documents from *Foreign Relations* to "avoid publication of matters which would tend to impede current diplomatic negotiations or other business."[10]

The story, of course, has a happy ending. *Foreign Relations* said nothing more about El Chamizal, and the dispute was finally settled in 1967 (El Chamizal means "the thicket." I can see thickets of this sort all along our path from 1947 on.)

This completes my somber list of the major problems to be overcome by the *Foreign Relations* series as it progresses into the postwar era. The department has already moved to alleviate some of these problems. I believe that all of them can be resolved with that ever-reliable team of courage and time; and if we show too little of the former and take too much of the latter, I am sure that we can expect scholarly impatience to help us over the hurdles.

## NOTES

1. For background on the *Foreign Relations* series, see E. R. Perkins, "*Foreign Relations of the United States:* Ninety-one Years of American Foreign Policy," *Department of State Bulletin* 27 (Dec. 22, 1952): 1002–7; Robert R. Wilson, "A Hundred Years of *Foreign Relations*," *American Journal of International Law* 55 (Oct. 1961): 947–50; Richard W. Leopold, "The *Foreign Relations* Series: A Centennial Estimate," *Mississippi Valley Historical Review* 49 (Mar. 1963) 595–612.

2. Mario Toscano, *The History of Treaties and International Politics* (Baltimore: Johns Hopkins Press, 1963–), 1:105.
3. Paul Mantoux, *Les délibérations du Conseil des Quatre, 24 Mars–28 Juin 1919* (Paris: Éditions du Centre National de la Recherche Scientifique, 1955).
4. For descriptions of the Italian, Hungarian, and German collections, see Toscano, *History of Treaties,* pp. 161, 251, 295. The Vatican series is published by the Libreria Editrice Vaticana under the title *Actes et documents du Saint Siège relatifs á la seconde guerre mondiale.*
5. U.S.S.R., Ministerstvo inostrannykh del SSR, *Dokumenty vneshney politiki SSSR,* vols. 1–14, 7 noyabrya 1917–31 dekabrya 1931 g. (Moscow: Izdatelstvo politicheskoy literatury, 1959–69).
6. U.S., Department of State, *Foreign Relations of the United States: The Conferences at Cairo and Tehran, 1943* (Washington, D.C.: Government Printing Office, 1961); idem, *Foreign Relations of the United States: The Conferences at Malta and Yalta, 1945* (Washington, D.C.: Government Printing Office, 1955); idem, *Foreign Relations of the United States: The Conference of Berlin* (Potsdam), 2 vols. (Washington, D.C.: Government Printing Office, 1960).
7. U.S.S.R., Soviet Society for the Popularization of Political and Scientific Knowledge (Moscow), *International Affairs,* nos. 7–8 (1961)—Tehran; nos. 6–9 (1965)—Yalta; nos. 10 and 12 (1965) and nos. 1–9 (1966)—Potsdam.
8. *Teheran, Yalta, Potsdam: Sbnorik Dokumentov* (Moscow: Izdatelstvo "Mezhdunarodnye otnosheniya," 1967).
9. U.S., Department of State, *Papers Relating to the Foreign Relations of the United States . . . 1870* (Washington, D.C.: Government Printing Office, 1870), p. 450.
10. U.S., Department of State, *Foreign Relations of the United States, Diplomatic Papers, 1933,* vol. 5, *The American Republics* (Washington, D.C.: Government Printing Office, 1952), p. 824.

## Publication of Records on United States Foreign Relations

DISCUSSION

*Bryce Wood, Social Science Research Council:* I am interested in some of Dr. Franklin's remarks, particularly those regarding the decision about what are important and what are unimportant collections or topics in any given year. The staff might decide a particular group of documents is not important enough to be printed, but five years later something might happen to generate considerable interest in that topic. Would *Foreign Relations* then publish those documents?

*William M. Franklin:* It has been done, as in the case of El Chamizal, which I mentioned to you, where several times the series picked up from previous years. This could be done again, but it is a little awkward in a series in which the whole format is chronological and annual.

Some years ago, a member of our advisory committee suggested that every fifty years we could produce a special volume containing those passages in documents that were deleted for policy purposes, not just eliminated or condensed because of lack of importance. We could sell this for enough to finance the series.

*Bradford Perkins, University of Michigan:* Do you think it is going to be possible to maintain a year-for-year schedule, not because of the lack of labor on your staff, but because of the difficulty in getting clearance for publishing from Foreign Service personnel and desk officers?

*Franklin:* I said only that with our present staff, we may be able to compile a year in a year. I did not say anything about getting the volumes out to the public in a year, and my remarks indicated that there were other difficulties. For example, I did not mention the technical editorial problems. Getting

69

clearance to publish documents that are controversial for personal or political reasons also constitutes a very, very high hurdle that we have to jump before we can give the final green light to bind and release the volumes.

*William L. Neumann, Goucher College:* Could you comment briefly on the 1947 and 1948 materials in regard to intelligence documents that seem to bear on policy decisions?

*Franklin:* Intelligence materials, as materials from other agencies, must be considered in the postwar period in order for one to get a true perspective of United States foreign policy. They are extremely high level, and they are copious. Some years ago it was decided that it would be impossible to include all such documents—they were not worth it from the point of view of foreign policy—except those for which we had some indications that the paper in question had come to high-level attention and had been particularly influential in the formation of policy. As you know, many others of a very high-level classification circulate routinely, but we are unable to find or identify their impact on policy makers. If they come up for discussion at a meeting they will be included, provided we can get permission to declassify them for this purpose, and I think we can.

# Administrative History
# of the
# Department of State

# Research on the Administrative History of the Department of State

ELMER PLISCHKE

Because of the very nature of the family of nations and its astaticism, foreign relations by definition constitute a continuum. Because the interests of world powers are inherently competitive, foreign relations are challenging and exciting; because most Americans harbor their own individual views on the subject, United States foreign relations are believed to be everybody's business; because the United States is a world leader with global interests and responsibilities, its foreign relations are a vital concern of the collective polity.

Reflecting some of these considerations is the intensified research that has been launched since World War II and the literature that has emerged respecting certain aspects of the changing American foreign relations role—especially including, insofar as administration is concerned, the presidency,[1] the secretaryship of state,[2] the Foreign Service,[3] and top-level and interdepartmental coordinating and decision-making positions.[4] On the other hand, as might be anticipated, the greatest research and literary attention has centered, not upon the management of foreign affairs, but upon matters of substantive policy and United States relations with specific countries, areas, institutions, developments, and crises.[5] While these are certainly worthy ventures, diplomacy as a method of conducting intergovernmental relations and, more specifically, the national administration of foreign affairs—with the president and the Department of State at its epicenter—appears to be less attractive to either the researcher or the publicist—or even the professional diplomatist.[6] Nevertheless, in the search for truth it is as important to know *how* foreign policy is made and implemented and to understand *how* external relations are conducted as it is to apprehend and appreciate the substance of the foreign policy itself. Therefore, greater scholarly attention—particularly planned research—might profitably be devoted to the professional institutions and processes of diplomacy and to the management of foreign affairs by the Department of State and American overseas missions.

The objective here is to define and rationalize succinctly, in the historical context, the problem of research on the conduct of United States foreign relations, focusing primarily on the principal executive institutions below the cabinet level which are charged with handling this responsibility in the United States and abroad. This survey concentrates largely on the organization, functions, operations, and procedures of the administrative mechanism and its personnel. To assist those concerned with such research, it identifies the principal elements of the subject; it suggests areas of research approach, potentiality, and need; it comments upon certain aspects of basic official and unofficial resources; and it alerts the researcher to a few of the more obvious problems that confront him.

## ASSUMPTIONS

It may be taken for granted that it is useful to understand the past in order to manage the present and prepare for the future intelligently. Where relevant, the researcher must be familiar with certain landmarks of historical development and analysis, including the principal stages in the history of Department of State organization and reorganization; the Livingston reports of the 1830s;[7] the Rogers,[8] Moses-Linthicum,[9] and Foreign Service Acts;[10] the Hoover Commission recommendations;[11] the Rowe, Wriston, and Herter Committee reports;[12] the Jackson Subcommittee studies;[13] and the American Foreign Service Association proposals of 1968[14]—together with such key unofficial assessments and proposals as those of the American Assembly[15] and the Brookings Institution.[16] These need to be supplemented by the more general background accounts of such writers as Robert E. Elder, William Y. Elliott, Malbone W. Graham, H. Field Haviland, Stephen D. Kertesz, James L. McCamy, Arthur W. Macmahon, John M. Mathews, Burton M. Sapin, Smith Simpson, Graham H. Stuart, Benjamin H. Williams, and Quincy Wright.[17]

It is also self-evident that, in order to be of value, the serious research study needs to possess a fixed focus and defined parameters. These may be chronologically or functionally delimited, and they need to be determined with care on the basis of the purposes of the study, the resources obtainable, the amount of time available, and the end product envisaged. In view of the breadth of the spectrum projectable, choices are virtually unlimited;

there clearly is room for the contributions of biographers, diplomatists, historians, journalists, legalists, institutionalists, administrationists, politicists, behavioralists, and cyberneticists, as well as polimetricians, quantifiers, and other "scientizers." Treatments may be reportorial, descriptive, normative, analytical, or empirical.

Discussing changes in diplomatic method some years ago, former Secretary of State Dean G. Acheson said: "There are fashions in everything."[18] It takes little but superficial knowledge of the field to realize that while everyone presumes to know what is meant by the concept "diplomacy"—the prime preserve of the Department of State—the concept has been subjected to an extensive series of refinements since the founding of the Republic. Thus, early concepts include "revolutionary age diplomacy," "transcontinentalism diplomacy," and "golden age diplomacy." Prior to World War I the terms "expansionist" or "manifestly destined" diplomacy, "dollar diplomacy," "gunboat diplomacy," and "open door diplomacy" crept into American practice and public consciousness.

In the twentieth century these refinements also came to reflect changes in diplomatic method. Thus, since Woodrow Wilson emphasis has been attributed to the New Diplomacy, which consists of "parliamentary diplomacy" in the international organization, "personal diplomacy," and "open diplomacy." In the more recent times, since World War II, more attention has been paid to "summit diplomacy" and "ministerial diplomacy," "nuclear diplomacy," "crisis diplomacy," and "total diplomacy." Most of these variations, particularly those of the twentieth century, have been inadequately studied in any systematic way, and the Department of State's relation to them warrants serious investigation.

Similarly, fashions have pertained in matters of research method and treatment, the most prominent in the past generation having been concerned with organization and management theory, decision making, systems analysis, gamesmanship, opinion surveys and quantification, automation of information retrieval and documents control, and cybernetics. These, too, have been inadequately involved in contemporary research and literature. In short, a review of published accounts reveals such a dearth of organized study of most aspects of the process of United States foreign relations that there is ample room for future investigation. The areas or phases subjected to the most widespread concern are the reform and strengthening of the Department of State, the Foreign Service, and the foreign policy-making process; and most recent research and analysis has concentrated on these matters largely in the context of currency or immediacy—thereby slighting administrative history.

Both substantive and methodological interests—irrespective of their intrinsic importance—as all fashions, tend to be ephemeral. Their treatment in published literature and in-house studies and reports is, often for good reasons, selective and fragmentary. Comprehensive analyses of the administration of the Department of State—to say nothing of the broader field concerned with the overall management of foreign relations—are lacking; and conversely, serious research gaps and subject biases occur. Much-needed fundamental, mundane, "bread-and-butter" studies often are regarded as too prosaic and pedestrian to be appealing or rewarding; and the time-consuming, costly work of compendious compilations is frequently shunted aside. Moreover, judgments may be rendered without adequate factual foundation, conceptualization may be ventured by the novitiate, and reformative panacea may be projected by the uninformed.

Finally, it is axiomatic that there is value to any public institution in self-evaluation as well as in outside review and assessment. Both kinds of evaluations are mutually complementary, and both may be useful. It appears that all too often the "professional" outsider, particularly the former Department of State officer, either turns apologist or, departing his office in disgruntlement, is moved to excoriate the practice of diplomacy by the United States. The journalist, on the other hand, is more concerned with producing an interesting and, if possible, a revealing story, while the academician needs to squeeze his research into an otherwise full academic schedule and, therefore, may be rash or insufficiently informed. Evaluation and criticism within the Department of State and Foreign Service should be most knowledgeable but may fail to achieve full intellectual or emotional detachment and perspective. After nearly two decades of career service, Smith Simpson, writing of the *Anatomy of the State Department,* concluded that the insider "is inclined to go off on personal or trivial tangents," that he generally lacks the courage "to raise basic issues," and that, even among those who do, "too few have the final determination to put them down in cold print."[19] Sometimes this is true even of the professional diplomatic retiree. Perhaps this helps to explain the fact that many of the published accounts are produced by academicians.[20]

From the perspective of the Department of State, in summary, it would seem both reasonable and desirable to have devised a systematic projection of the complete anatomy of the administration of United States foreign relations in which all of its main and secondary, and some of its tertiary, organs, and functions are defined and interwoven into a logically determined pattern of interrelationships. Such structuring of the subject should not be overly difficult and could even be diagrammed graphically, and this process and its results should be helpful to both in-house and outside research interests. Effort also needs to be focused on studying the entire taxonomy in some depth; if this is unfeasible, priorities may be prescribed. This undertaking, it seems, would be a compelling first step in producing meaningful developmental analysis and evaluation, as well as in determining the merits of change and the institution of improvement.

## RESEARCH COSMOGRAPHY

As with most studies of public affairs, the conduct of United States foreign relations—as a research field—may be structured in various ways. The historian generally elects to use the chronological route, hinging his study on identifiable sequential periods. Others may prefer a topical approach, organizing their dscriptions and analyses on a series of separable but parallel topics arranged in an ordered fashion. Depending on varying criteria, the latter may stratify the components of the subject on the basis of organizational factors, functions, or issues. These primary and subpatterns are not fully mutually exclusive and may be combined in such a way as to contribute to each other. The framework employed by the researcher naturally reflects his particular perception, focus, and emphasis. Or he may commence, a priori, with some contrived preconception or hypothesis, which he seeks to prove or disprove, and, consequently, the elements or phases of the subject he incorporates will be selective.

### HISTORICAL APPROACH

To be more precise: using the chronological method, one fundamental arrangement is to treat the subject on the basis of such an arbitrary formula as the administrations of either individual presidents or secretaries of state. This would appear to have limited value, except for comparative rather than developmental or analytical purposes, or for the investigator who wishes to restrict himself to a particular incumbent or era. The most obvious, chronologically related approach, however, is to organize the subject into cohesive time-oriented segments, using key developments as landmarks on which to found delineations. The diplomatic chronicler who concerns himself with the entire span of foreign relations normally structures his treatment on such relationships.[21]

On the other hand, analysts of the administration of foreign relations (as distinguished from general diplomatic history and substantive foreign policy)—who nevertheless pay some homage to historical progression—generally employ the institutional treatment. Aside from writings restricted to the presidential, secretaryship of state, and congressional roles, they fall into two main categories. The first consists of those who regard the subject primarily from the organizational and staffing point of view and therefore confine themselves largely to analysis of the Department of State and its personnel system, especially the Foreign Service. These include, for example, the works of Graham H. Stuart on the Department of State, William Barnes and John Heath Morgan on the Foreign Service, and E. Wilder Spaulding on ranking diplomats.[22]

In the second category, the historian approaches the subject from the broader perspective of the diplomatic function—or, to put it another way, from the focus of diplomacy as the primary means of rationalizing international relations—rather than concentrating simply on national governmental machinery and personnel. This research attitude, though sparingly employed in comprehensive surveys, penetrates beyond the Department of State and the Foreign Service. It introduces consideration of such additional factors as the policy-making system; functional coordination at the presidential, departmental, and mission levels; and diplomatic and consular practice—the latter embracing the appointment, reception, and credentials of diplomats and consular officers; the types and functions of overseas missions; privileges and immunities; activities and services of diplomatic and consular officers; and a variety of such foreign relations instruments and practices as participation in international conferences, treaty making, the granting of asylum, and the like.[23]

## TOPICAL OR FUNCTIONAL APPROACH

Turning from the historical approach to the potentialities of the topical treatment, we find that one of the basic perspectives, functionally oriented, is simply to distinguish between the network of elements contributing, respectively, to policy making and policy implementation. In theory this should be simple and ought to have merit, but on the basis of published results this focus does not appeal widely to researchers as a comprehensive method of treatment of the subject—especially not in the historical context—although attempts have been made to apply it to specific activities in the contemporary period. On balance, this approach is less popular with researchers dealing with the administration of foreign relations than it is with those analyzing limited areas of substantive policy or recounting the American experience in crisis handling.

Another topical perspective focuses upon the inclusive panoply of broad foreign relations functions. This might be structured, for example, as an analysis of such primary activities as intelligence and information gathering and assessment, decision making, policy and program execution, and action evaluation. Or it might be organized on the basis of the principal traditional diplomatic activities, including representing, reporting, negotiating, implementing programs, servicing private Americans and their interests abroad, and other activities contributing to the maintenance of communication among governments.

On the other hand, the research framework might combine elements from both of these basic arrangements. Whatever the treatment, to these factors might be added such matters as the management of foreign relations respecting peaceful settlement of disputes, collective security, alliances, and other forms of institutionalized international cooperation, as well as the mastering of relations in the process of nation building and in handling matters of recognition and nonrecognition. To be complete, each of these approaches, however structured, must also be overlayed or paralleled in some fashion with description and analysis of national administrative institutions and internal procedures for the control and exercise of these activities.

A third fundamental perspective employing the topical orientation is founded, essentially, on management and administration elements in the more precise sense. These embrace structural organizaiton, personnel, procedures, processes, and other supporting factors. Structural design and formalization is central to this treatment, and it encompasses five primary elements: (1) executive-legislative relations, together with the role of the judiciary; (2) presidential-level organization, including interagency coordination through the presidential inner team, the cabinet, the National Security Council, and similar facilities; (3) the Department of State mechanism; (4) other departments and agencies and their coordination among themselves and with the Department of State; and (5) diplomatic and operational missions in the field.

The personnel factor entails distinguishing such groupings as State Department versus Foreign Service officers, careerists versus noncareerists, traditional diplomats versus special agents, respresentative versus technical and other levels of service, generalists versus specialists, diplomats versus consular officers, and regular diplomats versus operational program implementers. While the problem of personnel types may be common to the field of personnel administration, some of these juxtapositional considerations are unique to the administration of foreign affairs. Consideration of the personnel factor also involves the standard elements of recruitment, training, assignment, career development, promotion, perquisites, and related matters, as well as the nature of the personnel power structure and its influence on diplomatic relations, elitism, and professional morale.

Foreign relations procedures and processes embrace, among others, some of the primary functions previously noted, including intelligence analysis and research, policy making, representation, negotiation, reporting and information gathering and processing, program implementation, service to Americans, and a variety of odds and ends. The supporting functions—some of which are often ignored completely in the area of published research—might include, for example, activities concerned with protocol, central secretariat services, contingency planning, operations center management, budgeting and financing, communications, public relations, records control, security, physical facilities, and the like. This patterning can be extrapolated substantially through various layerings of primary and secondary elements.

Most general analyses of the administration of United States foreign relations employ some variant of this third topical arrangement.[24] However, the majority of researchers, not unnaturally, concern themselves with some limited though basic aspect of the subject. Many of these, as previously noted in part, concentrate on such factors as the secretary of state and the Department of State, the personnel system, the congressional role and public opinion, the role of the military, and decision making.[25] A few are concerned with intelligence, special presidential representatives, specialized attachés, and the administration abroad of such operational programs as foreign assistance and information/propaganda.[26] It is interesting but should not be surprising that—because of its inherent nature and because of the legislative-executive conflict over the Versailles treaty, the reaction to the Yalta commitments, and the "Bricker amendment" proposals—the matter of treaty making and executive agreement making has occupied the center of substantial investigative and reportorial attention.[27]

ISSUES APPROACH

By way of comparison, the issue-oriented approach to the subject, as a systematized research technique that has gained increasing credence since the 1950s, has come to be applied primarily to the analysis of specific historic developments, to matters of substantive policy, and to crisis diplomacy. It is still relatively untried in the realm of foreign relations management, although from time to time it has been employed in reviewing a single important issue or area of concern (such as Department of State organizational structuring, international presidential commitment making, Foreign

Service personnel reform, and decision making). To some extent it also has been broached, though not made central, in broader studies; and it has become the focus of some short and restricted analyses. Since World War II, such basic issues as the changing role of the public in determining United States foreign policy and relations; presidential authority to deploy military forces abroad in time of peace; treaty-making authority; top-level machinery and procedures for foreign and defense policy coordination and implementation; the fusion of Department of State, Foreign Service, and other overseas personnel systems; civil-military relations in foreign policy decision making; and the demarcation between secret and open diplomacy—each directly relevant and material to the conduct of American diplomacy—have become the subjects of serious study and in several cases have even evoked "great debates."[28]

A list of other issues, also of general significance but less seriously researched, could include the development of the presidential inner foreign policy team; contingency foreign policy planning; the effectiveness of United States engagement in summit, ministerial, and parliamentary diplomacy; the political management of the bureaucracy; the Department of State's assumption of responsibility for operational programs abroad; the primacy overseas of diplomatic chiefs of mission; the coordination of diplomatic, consular, economic assistance, propaganda, and other functions and missions in the field (including the concept of the country team); the role of military, scientific, and other specialized attachés; professional elitism; the presidential use of special diplomatic representatives and such specialized officers as the ambassador at large and the political adviser (POLADS); other specialized diplomatic missions, including those assigned to international organizations and observership functions, and the like.[29]

Moreover, some important issues have been receiving little outside research and even less publication attention. These are represented by such topics as the application of modern organization theory to the management of foreign relations; the personal qualities essential, respectively, to effective policy making and negotiation; the treatment of diplomats by host governments and peoples; diplomatic functioning at the ministerial level, specifically within the forums of international organizations; physical headquarters facilities and the creation of diplomatic enclaves in national capitals; the modernization of documentary information retrieval; and the declassification, opening, and publication of diplomatic archives.

To conclude, the need for planned research programs is obvious. Several aspects of the subject have been grossly neglected; others have been studied in the past but warrant updating; and still others, because they reflect the concerns of the moment, prove to be of ephemeral interest and value. Many phases of the subject need to be analyzed in much greater depth than has previously been the case. The treatment of certain elements represents the newer research techniques—for example, attitude studies, quantification extrapolations, comparative analyses, and theory development—and these may produce a greater appreciation of the foreign relations process, providing methodology is perceived as the means to achieve a more profound understanding and not as an end in itself.

But when all is said and done and we consider the very nature of the situation, it is reasonable to conclude that research on the conduct of United States foreign affairs is likely to continue to be piecemeal, spasmodic, and unintegrated.

## RESEARCH DESIGN AND RESOURCES

Rewarding research requires certain obvious essentials. Most basic—in addition to motivation, need, time, and ideas—is the availability of informational resources and their fabrication into an effective research design. Study of the administration of United States foreign relations juxtaposes the active concern of primarily three communities: the government itself, the academic family, and the information media. The first two have a good many parallel and complementary interests, while those of journalism are often unique—with the story of the moment generally outranking the complete chronicle or the analysis in depth. Yet, though really not surprising in the American democratic system, more immediate attention often seems to be devoted to satisfying the informational demands of journalism rather than the more complex demands of either the government historian or the academician.

### PLANES OF RESEARCH DESIGN

As with any subject of human knowledge, the researcher concentrating upon the conduct of foreign relations may vary both his breadth and depth. Thus, on the most elementary plane, his research design may be broad but shallow, so that he might limit himself to a few readily available basic sources of information.[30] And for certain very limited and rudimentary purposes, these may suffice.

If the researcher penetrates to a more comprehensive level, however, he needs to rely on additional resources, largely of an end-product nature, such as presidential proclamations, executive orders, key presidential memorandums, statutes and congressional resolutions, administrative regulations, reorganization plans, budgets, diplomatic notes, treaties and agreements, periodic reports, public addresses, and the final acts, policy declarations, and communiqués of international meetings and conferences. These may provide a general understanding of what has transpired, or been said, or decided.[31]

A third level of research design delves deeper still, embracing resources which contribute directly to the production of such end-product documentation. Much official, officially supported, and private academic research penetrates to this level. This category is represented by the original texts of diplomatic communications, policy memorandums, staff studies, briefing papers, international conference working documents, files of the agencies of international organizations, congressional hearings and debates, in-house departmental reports and memorandums, officially oriented compilations and listings of data, and task force or review committee studies and recommendations. These may be supplemented by the preliminary drafts of various kinds of documentation, often with revealing marginal comments; for example, the draft versions of treaties, statutes, reports, diplomatic notes, policy papers, and communiqués.[32]

The final plane—even more fundamental—penetrates to the all-encompassing mass of written and other raw material: drafts; interunit preliminary documentation; and the individual views of participants, either inscribed in memorandums, commentaries, diaries, memoirs, and personal papers or, if necessary, elicited by interview.[33] Research that plumbs the recesses of these primary resource reservoirs is likely to be the most original and innovative, the most sagacious, and often the most contributory to understanding. The depth of treatment by the researcher is naturally related directly to both his research objective and the availability of resources, and, just as research design and intent to circumscribe treatment may obviate the need for the more basic resources, so the unavailability of those resources may delimit the research experience and its consequences.

RESEARCH RESOURCE AVAILABILITY

Contrary to popular belief and the repeated allegations of an insatiable press, the government of the United States pursues a remarkably liberal official publication policy for its foreign relations information and documents, a practice begun early in the nineteenth century.[34] The impressive list of regular publications of the Department of State—ranging from the

texts of treaties and agreements to diplomatic communications, policy statements, reports, and periodic lists of diplomatic and consular officers and
their biographies—are supplemented by special compilations and an extensive range of publications on individual subjects of current or historical
relevance.[35] It is not generally realized that the Department of State would
have an even more extensive publishing program if it were more adequately
funded and staffed for this purpose. Additional published materials on particular aspects of United States foreign relations are made available by
Congress, the White House, and various administrative agencies.[36] It is
questionable whether any other government currently has, or in the past has
had, a more generous disposition to propagate information and publish its
documentation.

The government of the United States also has a liberal policy regarding
the opening of its documentary archives to research and public use. Many
countries have no publicly designated open period whatsoever for their governmental archives, and approximately three-fourths of those which do have
a precise policy respecting the matter generally grant no access to documents less than fifty years old. In comparison, the Department of State's
files are in essence "open" in the National Archives after thirty years, and
every January 1 the availability of documentary resources automatically
advances another year.[37]

In addition, American researchers who meet certain qualifications—
including scholarly or professional need—may be admitted to the active
files of the Department of State for the restricted period, which comprises
the years between the open period and the last year covered by the published documentary compilation entitled *Foreign Relations of the United
States,* reputedly the most extensive and the most nearly current printed
compilation of diplomatic papers in the world.[38]

Unfortunately, more because of lack of funds and personnel than from
capricious or willful policy, the time gap between the issuance of the *Foreign
Relations* volumes and the years to which they pertain has grown to approximately twenty-three years, so that the restricted period is narrowing. Should
the *Foreign Relations* publication time gap increase to thirty years, the
restricted period will disappear altogether.[39] For more recent years,
researchers may obtain copies of specific documents which are either
already unclassified or which may be declassified, and they sometimes may
have access to pertinent in-house compilations and studies not available for
general distribution.

Although United States governmental resources are singularly open, it
is nevertheless taken for granted that there must be some dividing line to
limit the kinds of official documentary materials that are not generally and
immediately available or that may be used by the researcher only on a

restricted basis. In this connection, working papers obviously need to be distinguished from end products. Whereas many of the latter are introduced into the public domain with facility, and sometimes even before their formal consummation, often the preliminary drafts and working papers, for understandable reasons, are not.[40]

It is essential for the researcher to understand that, while the results of Department of State action and the diplomatic process are intended to be made public when perfected, it may very well be that what goes into achieving the end product is not everybody's business—at least not immediately.[41] This applies to the processes of policy making respecting important foreign relations matters, as well as to forging an end product in the field and to aligning national interagency views and relations respecting them. Negotiation, by its inherent nature, involves bargaining and normally entails concession and accommodation to be fruitful. Yet, governments that become involved in a great deal of negotiation are reluctant to reveal the original positions on which compromise is accepted, the argumentation that may have failed to gain complete acceptance, or the details of draft proposals that are adjusted—especially in those polities in which irrational factions come to view any concession as a cowardly cession, if not an abject surrender.

Furthermore, the Department of State cannot, on its own authority, publish documents that involve foreign governments or other United States governmental agencies without their consent. Sometimes, while it may be anxious to publish and may actually have material ready for the press, the Department of State must stand by awaiting acquiescence, for the securing of such clearance is both delicate and time consuming. Moreover, the more recent the documentation, the higher the security classification, the more controversial or delicate the substance, and the more distant from the end products—the more unlikely are foreign governments and other United States administrative agencies to accord such consent to publication.

Nevertheless, despite these and other impediments to the availability of certain documentary materials, if the researcher really works diligently enough, not only can he become well informed, but he may also be able to obtain a great deal more information and research resources respecting the process of foreign relations than he thought possible.


CONCLUSION

A final word should be added concerning three subjects: the need for immediate, advance, topical, or subject systematization; for the delineation of research subject area priorities; and for the creation of a facility to provide a continuous flow of at least minimal contemporary research on a planned basis.

It has been noted earlier that research will be facilitated if the entire field of the administration of United States foreign relations were deliberately projected in an integrated, structured, and logical fashion. Its organizational, personnel, functional, and problem areas should be identified, interrelated, and extrapolated in a series of tables, codes, and charts, for ready apperception by practitioner and researcher alike. These could be enriched by supporting glossaries of diplomatic terms, institutional titles, and key reference lists in order to facilitate the refinement of terminology and conceptualization.

The primary objectives of this venture would be to expose the field in a manner as succinct, comprehensible, and rational as possible; to clarify language and concepts; to specify areas of research concern; and to contribute to the development of cognition, thinking, reporting, and writing in the field of diplomatic affairs. This task might be undertaken by the Department of State itself, by a research foundation or some other outside agency, or by a single individual, and it should involve relatively little time or expense. Naturally, it would need to be updated from time to time.

Second, serious attention needs to be paid to identifying and proclaiming areas of research priorities. These may be determined on the basis either of existing topical gaps or of urgency. Priorities may vary, for example, from a review of the roles and functioning of certain agencies or processes—such as the Policy Planning Council, international conferencing, or the country team—to more specific factors, illustrated by the development of the office of ambassador at large, the scientific attaché, and the observership at international organizations; or even to the precise physical process of preparing and transmitting diplomatic credentials and the manufacturing of the official engrossed copies of treaties and agreements that, when signed, flow into the archives of signatory governments.

Even a cursory acquaintance with the field reveals a number of major priority areas on which little published research has been undertaken. Examples are the effectiveness of varying coordination methods for foreign relations functions and responsibilities among the agencies concerned both in Washington and the field; the organization and facilitation of the diplomatic community in Washington and other national capitals; the systematization of determinations on diplomatic forum selection for negotiatory endeavors; the simultaneous employment of multiple diplomatic methods and forums, especially during crisis negotiations; and the public image of the Department of State and the Foreign Service. Even more fundamental, perhaps, are such areas as personal diplomacy, practiced increasingly by the

Secretary of State at the ministerial level; the process and value of ad hoc bilateral and multilateral negotiation at the headquarters of international organizations; and the practices and problems involved in financing United States diplomacy. Such subjects may be treated historically as well as functionally.

Finally, central to coping with the exigencies of research, it would be helpful if the Department of State augmented the Historical Office by establishing a small research staff devoted to "contemporary history" or if it appointed a number of experienced, well-qualified, and highly motivated researchers as an adjunct to the Historical Office. The mission of this special staff would be to concentrate entirely on basic research matters in order to produce—in the guise of pure rather than applied research studies—a continuous flow of largely unclassified descriptive and analytical monographic surveys on specific aspects of the diplomatic process. These should be relatively succinct though refined and sophisticated accounts of organizational, functional, procedural, and related matters. While imagination and innovativeness respecting subject selection, focus, and research method should be encouraged, in-house reform would not be among their primary objectives, and they should not presume either on the preserves of the policy-making, intelligence, public relations, documents management, and archival functions or on the traditional responsibilities of the Historical Office for publishing documentary compilations, white papers, and other studies. By maintaining close contact with the leaders of the academic community, this special research contingent could encourage and guide outside investigative ventures in support of its own research program.

Unless some such steps are taken to systematize research on the conduct of United States foreign relations, that research is likely to remain fragmentary, desultory, uncoordinated, and unsatisfying.

## NOTES

1. Some forty books—not including autobiographies, biographies, chronicles on particular administrations or presidencies, and analyses of presidential handling of particular foreign relations issues—have been published since World War II specifically on the presidency of the United States. In the 1960s these averaged nearly three per year.

   Most of these volumes deal with the office and its general powers, including foreign relations; a few are more limited in scope; and some focus on presidential leadership. But surprisingly few restrict themselves entirely to the matter of external affairs. Among the contributors to this growing literature are Thomas A. Bailey, Wilfred E. Binkley, Louis Brownlow, James MacGregor Burns, Edward S. Corwin, Herman Finer, Sidney Hyman, Louis W. Koenig, Richard E. Neustadt, Clinton Rossiter, Merriman Smith, and Rexford Guy Tugwell. Article literature on the presidency has been equally prolific.

2. Although the literature on the secretary of state is less plentiful than that on the presidency, it is more substantial than it was before World War II, when the standard resource was Samuel Flagg Bemis, ed., *The American Secretaries of State and Their Diplomacy,* 10 vols. (New York: Alfred A. Knopf, 1927–29). This series is being brought up to date under the editorship of Robert H. Ferrell (New York: Cooper Square, 1963–) as follows: Kellogg and Stimson by Ferrell; Cordell Hull by Julius Pratt; Stettinius and Byrnes by Richard L. Walker and George Curry; George Marshall by Ferrell; Dean Acheson by Gaddis Smith; John Foster Dulles by Louis L. Gerson; and Christian A. Herter by George Bernard Noble.

Also illustrative of books and monographs on the subject during the 1960s are Alexander DeConde, *The American Secretary of State: An Interpretation* (New York: Frederick A. Praeger, 1962); Norman A. Graebner, ed., *An Uncertain Tradition: American Secretaries of State in the Twentieth Century* (New York: Frederick A. Praeger, 1961); Deane and David Heller, *Paths of Diplomacy: America's Secretaries of State* (Philadelphia: J. P. Lippincott, 1967); Norman L. Hill, *Mr. Secretary of State* (New York: Random House, 1963); Henry M. Jackson, ed., *The Secretary of State and the Ambassador* (New York: Frederick A. Praeger, 1964); Don K. Price, ed., *The Secretary of State* (Englewood Cliffs, N.J.: Prentice-Hall, 1960).

To these may be added such official publications as U.S., Department of State, *The Secretaries of State: Portraits and Biographical Sketches* (1956); U.S., Congress, Senate, Committee on Government Operations, *Administration of National Security: The Secretary of State* (1964); idem, *The Secretary of State and the Problem of Coordination* (1966). All were published in Washington, D.C., by the Government Printing Office.

3. Studies on the Foreign Service since World War II embrace the following:
(a) Official and quasi-official surveys: William Barnes and John Heath Morgan, *The Foreign Service of the United States: Origins, Development, and Functions* (Washington, D.C.: Government Printing Office, 1961); James Rives Childs, *American Foreign Service* (New York: H. Holt, 1948); "Forty Years of the Foreign Service, 1924–1964," *Department of State News Letter,* no. 39 (July 1964). See also 14 below.
(b) Official executive department reports: James H. Rowe, Jr., et al., "An Improved Personnel System for the Conduct of Foreign Affairs: A Report to the Secretary of State by the Secretary's Advisory Committee on Personnel"—Rowe Report—processed (Washington, D.C.: Department of State, 1950); U.S., Department of State, *Toward a Stronger Foreign Service: Report of the Secretary of State's Public Committee on Personnel*—Wriston Committee Report (Washington, D.C.: Government Printing Office, 1954); idem, *Personnel for the New Diplomacy: Report of the Committee on Foreign Affairs Personnel*—Herter Committee Report (Washington, D.C.: Carnegie Endowment, 1962).

(c) Congressional reports: House, Committee on Foreign Affairs, *Reorganization of the Foreign Service,* 79th Cong., 2d sess., 1946, H. Rept. 2508; idem, *An Analysis of the Personnel Improvement Plan of the Department of State,* 82d Cong., 1st sess., 1951; idem, *Foreign Service Act Amendments of 1965,* 89th Cong., 1st sess., 1965; Senate, Committee on Foreign Relations, *Recruitment and Training for the Foreign Service of the United States,* 85th Cong., 2d sess., 1958; idem, *Establishment of a Single Foreign Affairs Personnel System and Nominations of USIA Officers as Foreign Service Officers,* 89th Cong., 2d sess., 1966.

(d) Unofficial books and monographs: Juvenal L. Angel, *Careers in the Diplomatic Service,* 4th ed. (New York: World Trade Academy, 1961); Nathaniel P. Davis, *Few Dull Moments: A Foreign Service Career* (Philadelphia: Dunlap, 1967); Robert F. Delaney, *Your Future in the Foreign Service* (New York: Richard Rosen, 1961); John E. Harr, *The Anatomy of the Foreign Service—A Statistical Profile* (New York: Carnegie Endowment, 1965); idem, *The Professional Diplomat* (Princeton: Princeton University Press, 1969); idem, *The Development of Careers in the Foreign Service* (New York: Carnegie Endowment, 1965); Arthur G. Jones, *The Evolution of Personnel Systems for U.S. Foreign Affairs: A History of Reform Efforts* (New York: Carnegie Endowment, 1965); David Lavine, *Outposts of Adventure: The Story of the Foreign Service* (Garden City, N.Y.: Doubleday, 1966); Harry E. Neal, *Your Career in Foreign Service* (New York: Julian Messner, 1965); Charles E. Saltzman, *The Reorganization of the American Foreign Service* (Washington, D.C.: Government Printing Office, 1954); Achilles N. Sapell, *Careers in the Foreign Service* (New York: Walck, 1962); Zara S. Steiner, *Present Problems of the Foreign Service* (Princeton: Center of International Studies, Princeton University, 1961); idem, *The State Department and the Foreign Service: The Wriston Report—Four Years Later* (Princeton: Princeton University Center of International Studies, 1958); Regis Walther, *Orientations and Behavioral Styles of Foreign Service Officers* (New York: Carnegie Endowment, 1965).

The Foreign Service also receives prominent attention in the extensive periodical literature on American diplomacy and in the general literature on the Department of State and the diplomatic process.

4. Representative of the burgeoning monographic literature on decision making are Marcus Alexis and Charles Z. Wilson, *Organizational Decision-Making* (Englewood Cliffs, N.J.: Prentice-Hall, 1967); David Braybrooke and Charles E. Lindblom, *A Strategy of Decisions: Policy Evaluation as a Social Process* (New York: Free Press, 1963); Irwin Bross, *Design for Decision* (New York: Macmillan Co., 1953); C. West Churchman, *Prediction and Optimal Decision: Philosophical Issues of a Science of Values* (Englewood Cliffs, N.J.: Prentice-Hall, 1961); C. H. Coombs and D. G. Pruitt, *A Study of Decision-Making under Risk* (Ann Arbor: University of Michigan Willow Run Laboratory, 1960); Joseph D. Cooper, *The Art of Decision-Making* (Garden City, N.Y.: Doubleday, 1961); Donald Davidson et al., *Decision-Making: An Experimental Approach* (Stanford: Stanford University Press, 1957); Joseph Frankel, *The Making of Foreign Policy: An Analysis of Decision-Making* (New York: Oxford University Press, 1963); Joseph

de Rivera, *The Psychological Dimension of Foreign Policy* (Columbus, Ohio: Charles Merrill, 1968); William J. Gore and J. W. Dyson, eds., *The Making of Decisions: A Reader in Administrative Behavior* (New York: Free Press, 1964); Roger Hilsman, *Strategic Intelligence and National Decisions* (Glencoe, Ill.: Free Press, 1956); Bartholomeus Landheer et al., *Ethical Values in International Decision-Making* (The Hague: Nijhoff, 1960); Harold D. Lasswell, *The Decision Process: Seven Categories of Functional Analysis* (College Park, Md.: University of Maryland, 1956); Wayne A. R. Leys, *Ethics for Policy Decisions* (Englewood Cliffs, N.J.: Prentice-Hall, 1955); Sidney Siegel et al., *Choice, Strategy, and Utility* (New York: McGraw-Hill, 1964); Richard C. Snyder, H. W. Bruck, and Burton Sapin, *Decision-Making as an Approach to the Study of International Politics* (Princeton: Princeton University Press, 1954); idem, eds., *Foreign Policy Decision-Making: An Approach to the Study of International Politics* (New York: Free Press, 1962); Theodore C. Sorensen, *Decision-Making in the White House: The Olive Branch or the Arrows* (New York: Columbia University Press, 1963); R. M. Thrall et al., *Decision Processes* (New York: John Wiley, 1954).

Illustrative of the expansive article literature on decision making, the following apply specifically to foreign affairs: Jacques de Bourbon-Busset, "Decision-Making in Foreign Policy," in *Diplomacy in a Changing World,* ed. Stephen D. Kartesz and M. A. Fitzsimons (Notre Dame, Ind.: Notre Dame University Press, 1958), pp. 77–100; idem, "How Decisions Are Made in Foreign Policy: Psychology in International Relations," *Review of Politics* 20 (Oct. 1959): 591–614; Joseph Frankel, "Rational Decision-Making in Foreign Policy," *Yearbook of World Affairs* 14 (1960): 40–66; idem, "Towards a Decision-Making Model in Foreign Policy," *Political Studies* 7 (1959): 1–11; James A. Robinson and Richard C. Snyder, "Decision-Making in International Politics," in *International Behavior: A Social Psychological Analysis,* ed. Herbert Kelman (New York: Holt, Rinehart, & Winston, 1965), pp. 435–63; Richard Rosecrance and J. E. Mueller, "Decision-Making and the Quantitative Analysis of International Relations," *Yearbook of World Affairs* 21 (1967): 1–19.

Bibliographical guidance can be found in William J. Gore and F. S. Silander, "A Bibliographical Essay on Decision-Making," *Administrative Science Quarterly* 4 (1959): 97–121; and Paul Wasserman and F. S. Silander, *Decision-Making: An Annotated Bibliography* (Ithaca: Cornell University Press, 1958), with supplement for 1958–63 (1964).

5. For a series of seventeen essays on various aspects of the resources and needs of American diplomacy, see Smith Simpson, ed., "Resources and Needs of American Diplomacy," *The Annals of the American Academy of Political and Social Science,* vol. 380 (Nov. 1968). Also see U.S., Department of State, "Relationship of the Government and Private Research Communities in the Field of Foreign Relations," External Research Report, ER-68, (July 1, 1963); U.S., Department of State, Office of External Research, *Government Resources Available for Foreign Affairs Research* (1965), both published in Washington, D.C., by the Government Printing Office.

6. Taking cognizance of the general posture of the United States in world affairs

and of its complex governmental mechanism for conducting diplomacy, the subject of this survey is deliberately interpreted broadly as encompassing the development of the management of American foreign relations, in which the Department of State is the principal and central subcabinet-level executive agency. Perspective and treatment, therefore, exceed the more restricted interpretation that might be applied to the conceptualization of both "the administrative history" and the "Department of State."

7. Resulting in enactments in 1855 and 1856; see U.S., *Statutes at Large,* vols. 10 and 11, 33d and 34th Cong., pp. 619–26, 52–65.
8. Ibid., vol. 43, pt. 1, 68th Cong., Public Law 135, pp. 140–46.
9. Ibid., vol. 46, 71st Cong., Public Law 715, pp. 1207–17.
10. Ibid., vol. 60, pt. 1, 79th Cong., pp. 999–1040, Public Law 724, as amended, as given in U.S., Congress, Senate Committee on Foreign Relations and House Committee on Foreign Affairs, *Legislation on Foreign Relations: With Explanatory Notes,* revised and published annually.
11. U.S., Commission on Organization of the Executive Branch of the Government (Hoover Commission), *Foreign Affairs* (1949); idem, *Task Force Report on Foreign Affairs* (1949), Appendix H; and idem, *Task Force Report on Overseas Economic Operations* (1955), all published in Washington, D.C., by the Government Printing Office.
12. See note 3(b) and Steiner, *The Wriston Report,* cited in note 3(d).
13. U.S., Congress, Senate, Committee on Government Operations (Jackson Subcommittee), Reports and Hearings, 1959–, including, for example, *Administration of National Security: The American Ambassador,* 88th Cong., 2d sess., 1964; *Administration of National Security: The Secretary of State,* 88th Cong., 2d sess., 1964; *Administration of National Security: Selected Papers,* 87th Cong., 2d sess., 1962; *The Ambassador and the Problem of Coordination,* 88th Cong., 1st sess., 1963, Sen. Doc. 36; *Organizational History of the National Security Council,* 86th Cong., 2d sess., 1960; *Organizing for National Security,* 3 vols. (1961).
14. American Foreign Service Association, *Toward a Modern Diplomacy: A Report to the American Foreign Service Association* (Washington, D.C.: Foreign Service Association, 1968); also "Toward a Modern Diplomacy: A Report to the American Foreign Service Association," *Foreign Service Journal* 45 (Nov. 1968); Lannon Walker, "Our Foreign Affairs Machinery: Time for an Overhaul," *Foreign Affairs* 47 (1969): 309–20.
15. American Assembly, *The Representation of the United States Abroad* (New York: Columbia University Press, 1956); Don K. Price, ed., *The Secretary of State* (Englewood Cliffs, N.J.: Prentice-Hall, 1960).
16. Brookings Institution, *Governmental Mechanism for the Conduct of United States Foreign Relations* (Washington, D.C.: Brookings Institution, 1949); idem, *The Administration of Foreign Affairs and Overseas Operations* (Washington, D.C.: Government Printing Office, 1951); H. Field Haviland, Jr., *The Formulation and Administration of United States Foreign Policy,* (Washington, D.C.: Brookings Institution, 1960); Burton M. Sapin, *The Making of United States Foreign Policy* (Washington, D.C.: Brookings Institution, and New York: Frederick A. Praeger, 1966); Also U.S., Congress, Senate, Committee on Foreign Relations, *United States Foreign Policy: The*

*Formulation and Administration of United States Foreign Policy*, 86th Cong., 2d sess., 1960, prepared by the Brookings Institution (Washington, D.C.: Government Printing Office).

17. Robert E. Elder, *The Policy Machine: The Department of State and American Foreign Policy* (Syracuse: Syracuse University Press, 1960); William Yandall Elliott et al., *United States Foreign Policy: Its Organization and Control* (New York: Columbia University Press, 1952); Malbone W. Graham, *American Diplomacy in the International Community* (Baltimore: Johns Hopkins Press, 1948); H. Field Haviland, Jr., *The Formulation and Administration of United States Foreign Policy* (Washington, D.C.: Brookings Institution, 1960); Stephen D. Kertesz, ed., *American Diplomacy in a New Era* (Notre Dame, Ind.: Notre Dame University Press, 1961); James L. McCamy, *The Administration of American Foreign Affairs* (New York: Alfred A. Knopf, 1950); idem, *Conduct of the New Diplomacy* (New York: Harper & Row, 1964); Arthur W. Macmahon, *Administration and Foreign Policy* (Urbana: University of Illinois Institute of Government and Public Affairs, 1957); idem, *Administration in Foreign Affairs* (University: University of Alabama Press, 1953); John M. Mathews, *American Foreign Relations: Conduct and Policies,* rev. ed. (New York: Appleton-Century-Crofts, 1938); Burton M. Sapin, *The Making of United States Foreign Policy* (Washington, D.C.; Brookings Institution and New York: Frederick A. Praeger, 1966); Smith Simpson, *Anatomy of the State Department* (Boston: Houghton Mifflin Co., 1967); Graham H. Stuart, *American Diplomatic and Consular Practice,* 2d ed. (New York: Appleton-Century-Crofts, 1952); idem, *The Department of State: A History of Its Organization, Procedure, and Personnel* (New York: Macmillan Co., 1949); Benjamin H. Williams, *American Diplomacy: Policies and Practice* (New York: McGraw-Hill, 1936); Quincy Wright, *The Control of American Foreign Relations* (New York: Macmillan Co., 1922).

18. Dean Acheson, "Meetings at the Summit: A Study in Diplomatic Method" (Lecture delivered at the University of New Hampshire, Durham, N.H., May 8, 1958), mimeographed.

19. Simpson, *Anatomy of the State Department,* p. ix, cited in note 17.

20. It is interesting to note that of the nearly thirty major, unofficially published books and monographs on the administration of foreign relations, the secretary of state, the Department of State, and the Foreign Service produced since World War II, two-thirds were written or edited by academicians. However, although many of the major contributions on the Foreign Service were the products of government officials, most of the general volumes on foreign relations (such as those in note 17) and on the secretary of state have been prepared by academicians. The same generalizations apply to authorship of earlier books on these subjects, except that in the 1930s and 1940s a few were written by journalists.

21. One of the broadest treatments has been employed by the eminent diplomatic historian Samuel Flagg Bemis, who identifies three sweeping periods: the time when the foundations of United States policy were laid, the era of expansionism, and the twentieth century; see *A Diplomatic History of the United States,* 5th ed. (New York: Henry Holt & Co., 1965). Another gen-

eralized structuring, but emphasizing topical rather than chronologically oriented primary distinctions, was applied by Richard W. Van Alstyne, who developed his historical treatment within three broad captions: national security, territorial expansionism, and neutrality and isolation; see *American Diplomacy in Action,* 2d ed. (New York: Henry Holt & Co., 1947). To be somewhat more definitive, however, the colonial, revolutionary, postrevolutionary, continental expansion, Spanish-American War, World War I, interwar, World War II, and contemporary periods may be identified. Most diplomatic historians avoid the formal use of these delineations and, in recent comprehensive surveys, generally fragment the subject into some forty to fifty-five separate chapters—or a lesser number if the treatment is less exhaustive and sophisticated—and with this process, as history continues to unfold, additional chapters may conveniently be added.

22. Stuart, *The Department of State,* cited in note 17; Barnes and Morgan, *Foreign Service of the United States,* cited in note 3(a); E. Wilder Spaulding, *Ambassadors Ordinary and Extraordinary* (Washington, D.C.: Public Affairs Press, 1961).

23. The principal broad treatments of this nature are Stuart, *American Diplomatic and Consular Practice,* cited in note 17; Elmer Plischke, *Conduct of' American Diplomacy,* 3d ed. (Princeton, N.J.: Van Nostrand, 1967).

24. Much of the published unofficial literature representative of this approach has previously been mentioned in notes 2, 3, 14–16, and especially 17 and 23. The broader treatments are to be found in such works as those of the Brookings Institution, William Y. Elliott, H. Field Haviland, James L. McCamy, Arthur W. Macmahon, Elmer Plischke, Burton M. Sapin, and Graham H. Stuart. Additional materials of value in this respect, though more limited in scope, include Cecil V. Crabb, Jr., *American Foreign Policy in the Nuclear Age,* 2d ed. (New York: Harper & Row, 1965); John Gange, *American Foreign Relations: Permanent Problems and Changing Policies* (New York: Ronald, 1959); Harry Howe Ransom, *An American Foreign Policy Reader* (New York: Thomas Y. Crowell, 1965).

25. Aside from the publications cited previously, the following represent the extensive monographic literature on—

(a) Congress and foreign relations: Holbert N. Carroll, *The House of Representatives and Foreign Affairs,* 2d ed. (Boston: Little, Brown & Co., 1966); Daniel S. Cheever and H. Field Haviland, Jr., *American Foreign Policy and the Separation of Powers* (Cambridge: Harvard University Press, 1952); Robert A. Dahl, *Congress and Foreign Policy,* 2 ed. (New York: W. W. Norton, 1964); Eleanor E. Dennison, *The Senate Foreign Relations Committee* (Stanford: Stanford University Press, 1942); David N. Farnsworth, *The Senate Committee on Foreign Relations* (Urbana: University of Illinois Press, 1961); George Grassmuck, *Sectional Biases in Congress on Foreign Policy* (Baltimore: Johns Hopkins Press, 1951); Joseph P. Harris, *The Advice and Consent of the Senate: A Study of the Confirmation of Appointments by the United States Senate* (Berkeley and Los Angeles: University of California Press, 1953); Malcolm E. Jewell, *Senatorial Politics and Foreign Policy* (Lexington: University of Kentucky Press, 1962); James A. Robinson, *Congress and Foreign Policy-Making: A Study in Legislative*

*Influence and Initiative* (Homewood, Ill.: Dorsey, 1962); Albert C. F. Westphal, *The House Committee on Foreign Affairs* (New York: Columbia University Press, 1942).

(b) Public opinion: Gabriel A. Almond, *The American People and Foreign Policy* (New York: Frederick A. Praeger, 1960); Thomas A. Bailey, *The Man in the Street: The Impact of American Public Opinion on Foreign Policy* (New York: Macmillan Co., 1948); Max Beloff, *Foreign Policy and the Democratic Process* (Baltimore: Johns Hopkins Press, 1955); Andrew Berding, *Foreign Affairs and You: How American Foreign Policy Is Made and What It Means to You* (Garden City, N.Y.: Doubleday, 1962); William Buchanan and Hadley Cantril, *How Nations See Each Other: A Study in Public Opinion* (Urbana: University of Illinois Press, 1953); Bernard C. Cohen, *The Press and Foreign Policy* (Princeton: Princeton University Press, 1963); Leonard S. Cottrell, Jr., and Sylvia Eberhard, *American Opinion on World Affairs in the Atomic Age* (Princeton: Princeton University Press, 1948); Walter Lippmann, *Public Opinion and Foreign Policy in the United States* (London: Allen & Unwin, 1952); Lester Markel et al., *Public Opinion and Foreign Policy* (New York: Harper, 1949); Arthur Ponsonby, *Democracy and Diplomacy: A Plea for Popular Control of Foreign Policy* (London: Methuen, 1915); William L. Rivers, *The Opinion Makers* (Boston: Beacon Press, 1965); James N. Rosenau, *National Leadership and Foreign Policy: A Case Study in the Mobilization of Public Support* (Princeton: Princeton University Press, 1963); Henry M. Wriston, *Diplomacy in a Democracy* (New York: Harper, 1956).

(c) Military role: Harry L. Coles, ed., *Total War and Cold War: Problems in Civilian Control of the Military* (Columbus: Ohio State University Press, 1962); Michael Howard, *Soldiers and Government* (New York: Frederick A. Praeger, 1959); Samuel P. Huntington, *The Soldier and the State: The Theory and Politics of Civil-Military Relations* (Cambridge: Harvard University Press, 1957); Jerome G. Kerwin, ed., *Civil-Military Relationships in American Life* (Chicago: University of Chicago Press, 1948); Milton Offutt, *The Protection of Citizens Abroad by the Armed Forces of the United States* (Baltimore: Johns Hopkins Press, 1928); Burton M. Sapin and Richard C. Snyder, *The Role of the Military in American Foreign Policy* (Garden City, N.Y.: Doubleday, 1954); Burton M. Sapin, Richard C. Snyder, and H. W. Bruck, "An Appropriate Role for the Military in American Foreign Policy-Making: A Research Note," mimeographed (1954); Louis Smith, *American Democracy and Military Power: A Study of Civil Control of the Military Power in the United States* (Chicago: University of Chicago Press, 1951); Alfred Vagts, *Defense and Diplomacy: The Soldier and the Conduct of Foreign Relations* (New York: King's Crown, 1956).

26. The following are representative of monographic literature on these subjects:

(a) Intelligence: Allen W. Dulles, *The Craft of Intelligence* (New York: Harper & Row, 1963); Roger Hilsman, Jr., *Strategic Intelligence and National Decisions* (Glencoe, Ill.: Free Press, 1956); Sherman Kent, *Strategic Intelligence for American World Policy* (Princeton: Princeton University Press, 1949); Washington Platt, *Strategic Intelligence Production: Basic Principles* (New York: Frederick A. Praeger, 1957); Harry Howe Ransom,

*Central Intelligence and National Security* (Cambridge: Harvard University Press, 1958); Andrew Tully, *CIA, the Inside Story* (New York: Morrow, 1962).

(b) Presidential special representatives: Charles O. Paullin, *Diplomatic Negotiations of American Naval Officers, 1778–1883* (Baltimore: Johns Hopkins Press, 1912); Maurice Waters, *The Ad Hoc Diplomat* (The Hague: Nijhoff, 1963); Henry M. Wriston, *Executive Agents in American Foreign Relations* (Baltimore: Johns Hopkins Press, 1929). More recent analyses are embodied in such articles or essays as: Elmer Plischke, "Presidential Personal Diplomatic Representatives," chap. 4 of *Summit Diplomacy: Personal Diplomacy of the President of the United States* (College Park: University of Maryland, 1958); Maurice Waters, "Special Diplomatic Agents of the President," *Annals* 307 (Sept. 1956): 124–33; Henry M. Wriston, "The Special Envoy," *Foreign Affairs* 38 (Jan. 1960): 219–37.

(c) Specialized attachés: Howard L. Nostrand, *The Cultural Attaché,* Hazen Pamphlet no. 17 (n.d.); Alfred Vagts, *The Military Attaché* (Princeton: Princeton University Press, 1967).

(d) Foreign assistance: David A. Baldwin, *Foreign Aid and American Foreign Policy: A Documentary Analysis* (New York: Frederick A. Praeger, 1966); George Liska, *The New Statecraft: Foreign Aid in American Foreign Policy* (Chicago: University of Chicago Press, 1960); Wallace J. Parks, *United States Administration of Its International Economic Affairs* (Baltimore: Johns Hopkins Press, 1951).

(e) Information and propaganda: Edward W. Barrett, *Truth Is Our Weapon* (New York: Funk and Wagnalls, 1953); Wilson P. Dizard, *The Strategy of Truth: The Story of the U.S. Information Service* (Washington, D.C.: Public Affairs Press, 1961); Murray Dyer, *The Weapon on the Wall: Rethinking Psychological Warfare* (Baltimore: Johns Hopkins Press, 1959); Robert T. Holt and Robert W. van de Velde, *Strategical Psychological Operations and American Foreign Policy* (Chicago: University of Chicago Press, 1960); Oren Stephens, *Facts to a Candid World: America's Overseas Information Program* (Stanford: Stanford University Press, 1955); Charles A. H. Thomson, *Overseas Information Service of the United States Government* (Washington, D.C.: Brookings Institution, 1948).

27. The following are merely illustrative of the extensive monographic and book-length literature on treaty making since World War II: Florence E. Allen, *The Treaty as an Instrument of Legislation* (New York: Macmillan Co., 1952); Hans Blix, *Treaty-Making Powers* (New York: Frederick A. Praeger, 1960); Elbert M. Byrd, Jr., *Treaties and Executive Agreements in the United States: Their Separate Roles and Limitations* (The Hague: Nijhoff, 1960); José S. Camara, *The Ratification of International Treaties* (Toronto: Ontario Publishing Co., 1949); James McCleod Hendry, *Treaties and Federal Constitutions* (Washington, D.C.: Public Affairs Press, 1955); John M. Jones, *Full Powers and Ratification: A Study in the Development of Treaty-Making Procedure* (Cambridge: At the University Press, 1946); Roger L. MacBride, *Treaties versus the Constitution* (Caldwell, Idaho: Caxton Printers, 1955); Mario Toscano, *The History of Treaties and International*

*Politics—Part I: The Documentary and Memoir Sources* (Baltimore: Johns Hopkins Press, 1966).

Aside from the frequently cited Samuel B. Crandall, *Treaties, Their Making and Enforcement* (New York: Columbia University Studies, 1904; 2d ed. 1916) and Wallace M. McClure, *International Executive Agreements: Democratic Procedure under the Constitution of the United States* (New York: Columbia University Press, 1941), the earlier literature also was extensive, represented by the following: Royden J. Dangerfield, *In Defense of the Senate: A Study in Treaty-Making* (Norman: University of Oklahoma Press, 1933); John W. Davis, *The Treaty-Making Power in the United States* (London: Oxford University Press, 1920); Robert T. Devlin, *The Treaty Power under the Constitution of the United States* (San Francisco: Bancroft-Whitney, 1908); Denna F. Fleming, *The Treaty Veto of the American Senate* (New York: Putnam, 1930); W. Stull Holt, *Treaties Defeated by the Senate* (Baltimore: Johns Hopkins Press, 1933); Henry Cabot Lodge, *The Senate and the League of Nations* (New York: Charles Scribner's, 1925); Francis O. Wilcox, *The Ratification of International Conventions* (London: Allen & Unwin, 1935).

28. In the field of the administration of American foreign relations, the post–World War II great debates have centered on the president's authority to deploy military forces abroad in time of "peace" and the Bricker amendment proposal to modify the president's treaty-making authority. Late in the 1960s, a similar debate was launched respecting the war-making authority of the president.

29. Published official and unofficial literature on these and similar issues, in general, has been sporadic and meager, and certain of these issues have received little or no serious scholarly research attention.

30. Such as the annually published *United States Government Organization Manual,* the weekly *Department of State Bulletin,* personnel directories, organizational charts, a few official descriptive materials (including the *Department of State, 1963: A Report to the Citizen,* published in 1963 by the Department of State), and perhaps a number of key secondary accounts cited in earlier notes. For some elementary purposes, the Department of State telephone directory may be useful.

31. A handy periodic compilation of selected materials of this nature, not including addresses, is afforded by the annual publication, *Legislation on Foreign Relations,* cited in note 10. Fundamental also are the Department of State's collections of basic documents: *American Foreign Policy: Current Documents* (annual from 1956), and its predecessor *American Foreign Policy, 1950–1955: Basic Documents* 2 vols. (1957); these were preceded by *A Decade of American Foreign Policy: Basic Documents, 1941–49,* prepared by the Department of State and published as Senate Doc. 123, 81st Cong., 1st sess., 1950, and U.S., Department of State, *Peace and War: United States Foreign Policy, 1931–1941* (1943). Also of comparable value are the international conference reports of the Department of State. All are published in Washington, D.C., by the Government Printing Office.

Central to this category are the compilations of diplomatic documents entitled *Foreign Relations of the United States* (see note 38) and a variety of materials concerning treaties and agreements, including U.S., Department of State, *Treaties and Other International Acts Series (TIAS)* and its predecessors, *United States Treaties and Other International Agreements (UST)*, *Treaties in Force,* and the like.

Also of value for certain aspects of the subject are the *Digests of International Law,* compiled by John Bassett Moore, Green H. Hackworth, and Marjorie M. Whiteman and published by the Department of State.

32. The bulk of these resources are available only in their documentary form in the files and archives of the government. Certain in-house reports may be available for distribution on a limited basis, but awareness of their existence requires direct contact with responsible government offices. Examples of recent in-house studies, prepared by the Historical Studies Division of the Department of State, include: "Assaults on United States Diplomatic, Consular, and Information Installations Abroad, 1900–1965" (Sept. 1965), "Armed Actions Taken by the United States Without a Declaration of War, 1798–1967" (Aug. 1967), "Lists of Visits of the President of the United States to Foreign Countries," and "Lists of Visits of Foreign Chiefs of State and Heads of Government to the United States," the last two being undated and republished on an occasional basis. Usually such reports are produced in processed form. Most Department of State in-house studies are classified, and some, though unclassified, are limited to internal governmental use. Occasionally they are not made publicly available because they are processed in preliminary form. Since 1946 the Historical Studies Division has undertaken some 616 research projects, and since 1950 it also has prepared more than 700 research memorandums. The projects generally are more fundamental and substantial than the memorandums. Additional in-house studies and reports are prepared by other agencies of the Department of State. Altogether, they constitute a rich research resource.

33. The total quantity of Department of State official resources amounts to 357,459 cubic feet of documentation. Of this massive reservoir, 167,000 cubic feet of records are to be found in the Department of State (including the central files of the Records Services Division, the Secretariat, and the various bureaus and offices), together with the overseas diplomatic and consular missions and posts. These are not fully processed for archival purposes and, because many are working files, some duplication occurs. The National Archives has in its custody 54,198 cubic feet of Department of State records, which have been refined for archival reposal. The National Archives also has 136,261 cubic feet of Department of State documents on deposit in federal records centers and these, not having been fully processed for archival deposit, will eventually be reduced in volume. This third of a million cubic feet of records represents only the documentation of the Department of State; quantifying considerations also must take into account the records of the other administrative departments and agencies which have foreign relations functions and interests.

34. The following are illustrative of these regularly published materials—in addition to those referred to previously in notes 30 and 31: Department of State press releases, background notes, geographic bulletins, *The Biographic Register, Foreign Service List, Diplomatic List, Foreign Consular Officers in the*

*United States,* printed and processed conference reports, annual reports such as *U.S. Participation in the UN,* and the like.

35. In considering the matter of "research resources" and their "availability," one needs to identify and understand a variety of concepts and terms. Some of these are fairly obvious, others are more subtle, and still others tend to be somewhat imprecise and confusing.

The terms "records," "papers," and "documents" often are used interchangeably, although the concept of records is broader in scope than the other two expressions and, together with "materials," is used as the most generic term by the Department of State and the National Archives. Papers and documents are distinguished in that they generally are written (or, in some cases, pictorial) as differentiated from oral documentation. Although a document, in its broadest sense, may be any written instrument that conveys information or proof, often the term is applied to the final version of an official paper. "Archives," on the other hand, are all those records which are deliberately set aside for long-range preservation.

The titles of certain types of diplomatic records and documents, by way of comparison with several of the concepts already described, are fairly precise, such as the various types of diplomatic instruments, including "aide mémoire," "circular note," "communiqué," "declaration," "final act," "note-verbale," "procès-verbal," "protocol," and "ultimatum," as well as such documentation forms as "letter," "despatch," "memorandum," "note," and "telegram." This also is the case with diplomatic credentials, such as the "exequatur," "full power," and "letter of credence."

The concepts of "drafts" (including the distinction between "initial" or "original" or "preliminary" draft and the "final" draft) as compared with "final copies" of papers or documents, and of "working papers" involved in producing "end products," also are readily comprehensible. However, it is more difficult to distinguish precisely the meaning of "publication" and "publishing" as applied to government documents and records. "To publish," in essence, means "to make public" or "to divulge" and, while this is normally assumed to apply to the issuance of printed or processed materials, in reality it also denotes revealing information in oral as well as in written form. The term "publication" pertains to the act of publishing, but traditionally it is reserved for the issuance to the public of material in written form. The dissemination of information in an oral fashion is characterized rather by the words "announcement" and "revelation," whereas the terms "dissemination," "issuance," and "release" may refer to both oral and written information and documentation. When disseminated, such information and such documents are "in the public domain." Written publications as distinct from oral information may be "printed" or "processed" (i.e., mimeographed, photocopied, or otherwise reproduced). Basic or "original" documents usually are handwritten, typewritten, teletyped, or in the form of telegrams.

A final distinction that needs to be noted is that documents and information may be "publicly available" although they are neither published nor overtly issued publicly in some other form. Such documents and information may be said to be "available," but the initiative to acquire or extract them is up to the researcher. The delineation between published, disseminated, and available documents and information, therefore, may occasion some confusion, but the distinctions among "open," "restricted," and "closed" documentation, and between "classified" and "unclassified" materials are fairly precise, at least so far as general categories are concerned. Both published and unpublished records, as well as both documents and information, may be either classified or unclassified. (See notes 37 and 41 for further discussion of these terms.)

An appreciation of the distinctiveness of these concepts and terms is essential to the study of diplomacy and the use of Department of State and National Archives records. The researcher must be cognizant of the fact that a great deal more information and documentation is publicly available than has been published by the Department of State and that far more has been published, disseminated in some other fashion, or produced in a refined form primarily for internal use than is reproduced in printed version by the Government Printing Office. On the other hand, a great deal of documentation and information is obtainable by the researcher in some organized or collated form, even though unpublished, to supplement the basic raw records of the Department of State.

36. These are represented by executive documents contained in *Public Papers of the Presidents of the United States* (published weekly and annually), the *Federal Register,* and White House press releases; congressional standing and ad hoc committee hearings, studies, reports, and compilations; *Documents of Disarmament,* issued annually by the United States Arms Control and Disarmament Agency; and a variety of reports and documents on foreign aid and assistance.

37. A report of the Department of State indicates that of the 115 countries surveyed, the diplomatic records of half are inaccessible. Of these, 38 specifically prohibit public access or make no provision for access to the records. On the other hand, 18 governments have no established or acknowledged policy regarding the matter, a fact that means the documents are not public; presumably, however, under the right circumstances bona fide researchers might have access for limited purposes under specified restrictions. An additional 14 governments have no fixed policy on the matter other than to specify that the foreign ministry, the national archives, or some other agency may authorize specific individuals to use particular documents.

The largest single category consists of those forty governments that fix particular dates for the opening of their records. Two forms of this arrangement are employed; namely, the procedure by which documents are opened automatically at the end of a specified number of years, and the procedure which fixes a specific date as the dividing point (e.g., Portugal uses the year 1851 and the Vatican 1878). About thirty governments use the fifty-year period for the opening of their diplomatic archives; the United States and a few other powers (including the United Kingdom) use the thirty-year restriction. A small number of governments use some other arrangement (the records of Germany and Japan are closed after 1945). See U.S., Department of State, "Public Availability of Diplomatic Archives," mimeographed (May 1968); also see summary report on publication policy in *Far Horizons* 2 (Jan. 1969): 6.

Analysis of governmental practices reveals that important distinctions are made between classified and unclassified documents and whether the researcher is a foreigner or native, and whether bona fide research or simply general availability to the public is involved; distinctions are also made among open, restricted, and closed periods. Availability normally is freer when the documents repose in a national archives than when they are in a foreign ministry.

38. U.S., Department of State, *Foreign Relations of the United States: Diplomatic Papers,* compiled and published on an annual basis, embraces nearly 250 volumes. From 1870 to 1932 this series bore the title *Papers Relating to the Foreign Relations of the United States,* and for the years 1861–68 these were issued under the title *Papers Relating to Foreign Affairs* and bore the cover title *Diplomatic Correspondence.* No issue was published for the year 1869. In the early decades of the series, 1 or 2 volumes sufficed for all countries and problems. Beginning with 1932, 5 or more volumes have been needed for each year.

These volumes contain the texts of diplomatic communications, exchanges of notes, reports, and other official papers relating to the foreign relations and diplomacy of the United States. Occasionally the texts of treaties and agreements are included. Materials generally are arranged by country. Each volume is indexed separately. The regular series is occasionally supplemented by special volumes dealing with particular countries, territories, or events, such as the nine volumes on World War I, thirteen volumes on the Paris Peace Conference of 1919, and the major conference series on World War II.

These series were preceded by U.S., Department of State, *American State Papers: Documents, Legislative and Executive, of the Congress of the United States,* 38 vols. (1832–61), especially *Class I. Foreign Relations,* 6 vols. (1789–1828); and Adelaide R. Hasse, comp., *Index to United States Documents Relating to Foreign Affairs, 1828–1861,* 3 vols. (Washington, D.C.: Carnegie Institution, 1914–21), which constitutes an index to published records, documents, papers, correspondence, legislation, and judicial decisions on international and diplomatic questions. The latter is concerned with the period not covered by the *American State Papers* and *Foreign Relations.*

For additional description, see U.S., Department of State, *Major Publications of the Department of State: An Annotated Bibliography* (Washington, D.C.: Government Printing Office), published periodically; and Elmer Plischke, *American Foreign Relations: A Bibliography of Official Sources* (College Park: University of Maryland, Bureau of Governmental Research, 1955), pp. 5–6, 17–19. Also see William M. Franklin, "The Future of the *Foreign Relations* Series," in the present volume, also printed in *Department of State Bulletin* 61 (Sept. 15, 1969):247–51.

39. The increasing time lag between the date of publication of *Foreign Relations* and the years to which they pertain is of considerable concern to the researcher. For many years after its inception, the *Foreign Relations* series was kept nearly current. Only a few years elapsed between the events recorded and the date of publication of the documents. However, in the course of time the lag gradually increased; following the end of World War I,

a fifteen-year lag became traditional. With the intensification of diplomatic documentation, beginning with World War II, the Historical Office was unable to maintain this schedule, and by 1960 the lag was approximately twenty years. In 1962 the secretary of state officially set the time lapse at twenty years (except for special volumes in the series), which was regarded as adequate for purposes of national security. Nevertheless, even this policy proved to be unmanageable, so that by the end of the 1960s the time lag was approaching a quarter century.

The primary reasons for this increase in the time lag are the growth of diplomatic documentation, lack of personnel and financial resources to handle the task, and the classification and clearance of documents. In so far as the magnitude of the task is concerned, it is interesting to note the following comparison: for the year 1934–35 (worked on in 1947), the department's records increased from the preceding year by 672 cubic feet, telegraphic traffic amounted to 4.8 million words, and documentation for a year could be covered in four volumes of 4,000 pages; whereas, for the year 1946–47 (worked on in 1967), the department's records increased by 1,238 cubic feet, telegraphic traffic amounted to 96 million words, and documentation for the year could be covered in nine volumes or 10,000 pages. In the meantime, the professional personnel available for the task declined from sixteen to thirteen.

For an analysis of the problem of compiling and publishing the *Foreign Relations* series, see report of the secretary of state's Advisory Committee, "Foreign Relations of the United States" in the American Political Science Association journal, *P.S.* 3, no. 1 (Winter 1970): 39–43; and in *American Journal of International Law* 64 (July 1970): 615–22.

40. Even President Woodrow Wilson who, in the very first of his historic Fourteen Points, counseled "open covenants . . . openly arrived at," discovered that when he engaged personally in diplomacy at the Paris Peace Conference in 1919, he could not negotiate effectively in the open. He concluded, therefore, that he really meant "not that there should be no private discussions of delicate matters, but that no secret agreements should be entered upon, and relations, when fixed, should be open, aboveboard, and explicit."

41. "Confidential" documentation and information need to be distinguished from that which is "in confidence." The designation "confidential" denotes security classification, of which there are three primary categories, in descending order designated "top secret," "secret," and "confidential." Some years ago the lowest ranking category—"restricted"—was eliminated, but the appellation "limited official use" came to take its place. The characterization "eyes only" limits distribution of documents, regardless of classification, to a restricted number of officials. Priority classifications—for the purposes of decision and action—also are employed. In ascending order of urgency, they are "routine," "priority," "immediate," and "flash." "In confidence," on the other hand, need not involve security restriction, but simply evidences that a particular matter is not to be publicized at the moment, or that, while the information is not intended to be withheld, its source is not to be revealed.

For analysis of the matter of secrecy and openness, see Francis E. Rourke, *Secrecy and Publicity: Dilemmas of Democracy* (Baltimore: Johns Hopkins

Press, 1961); George Seldes, *The People Don't Know: The American Press and the Cold War* (New York: Gaer, 1949); Edward A. Shils, *The Torment of Secrecy: The Background and Consequences of American Security Policies* (Glencoe, Ill.: Free Press, 1956); James W. Thompson and Saul K. Padover, *Secret Diplomacy: Espionage and Cryptography, 1500–1815* (New York: Unger, 1963); James R. Wiggins, *Freedom or Secrecy* (New York: Oxford University Press, 1964). An earlier account is that of Paul S. Reinsch, *Secret Diplomacy* (New York: Harcourt, Brace, & World, 1922). Shorter discussion is to be found in A. Maurice Low, "The Vice of Secret Diplomacy," *North American Review* 207 (Feb. 1918): 209–20; L. B. Namier, "Diplomacy, Secret and Open," *Nineteenth Century* 123 (Jan. 1938): 36–45; Elmer Plischke, "A More Open Diplomacy vs. Greater Secrecy," *Foreign Service Journal* 34 (Apr. 1957): 31–34; P. W. Wilson, "Open Methods in Modern Diplomacy," *Current History* 35 (Oct. 1931): 85–90. Also relevant are the hearings, studies, and reports of the Special Subcommittee on Government Information (chaired by Congressman John E. Moss) of the House Committee on Government Operations. For the State Department statement of its practice see, by the same subcommittee, "Replies from Federal Agencies to Questionnaire. . .," committee print, 84th Cong., 1st sess., 1955, pp. 458–80.

# Domestic Influences on United States Foreign Policy

# Domestic Influences on United States Foreign Policy: The Nineteenth Century

ALEXANDER DeCONDE

Among scholars and other men concerned with ideas, American diplomatic history has long had the reputation of having been written and having been taught in a vacuum. Taking the domestic context in the making of policy for granted, many diplomatic historians have usually concentrated on the formal, international aspects of America's foreign relations. They have, critics say, focused on the records, activities, and ideas of a narrow governing elite. Too often the result of such special concern has been history restricted to what ambassadors, foreign secretaries, and heads of governments have announced or have said to each other.

Such scholarship, even though often the product of deep and extensive archival research, is narrow, unnecessarily artificial, and unrepresentative of the deeper currents of society. It ignores too much within the nation's boundaries, or what Henry A. Kissinger calls the domestic structure, that helped shape fundamental foreign policies. It appears oblivious to cultural traits, historical traditions, social ideas, and economic complexities.

These criticisms, I think, are sound, but out of date. Much of what passed for diplomatic history before the Second World War is open to such criticism. But since that time the writing and the teaching of American diplomatic history has changed. Few professional scholars working in the history of American foreign policy today fail to take into account the domestic sources of that policy. While the better historians have always been aware of the interaction between domestic and foreign affairs, scholars are now more self-conscious than they have ever been about exploring and explaining the relationship. Not too many years ago diplomatic histories that synthesized domestic and foreign affairs were unique; now, while not common, they are no longer uncommon.

The change has been good. It has made the study of American diplomatic history deeper, richer, and more meaningful than it has ever been. But there is room for more improvement, especially in technique, theory, and attitude. I think we can learn more about ourselves and our diplomatic history by considering, examining, and testing, for example, the theory advanced by Charles A. Beard and now often by the New Left that the domestic structure determines the nature of foreign policies. I do not suggest that the historian study the domestic structure in isolation. It, too, is part of a larger environment—that of the world—but a nation's or a people's response to that international environment grows out of the special conditions of the domestic society. Since peoples often have some unique cultural traits, differing social systems, and their own historical traditions, the study of the domestic structure must take into account cross-cultural influences as well as internal American problems.

Even though the domestic system has been important in shaping foreign policies in any period, the American experience in the nineteenth century can illustrate how the principle worked under circumstances that were particularly fortunate for a young, growing people. That century witnessed the growth of the United States from a small, agrarian nation, largely isolated from the mainstream of world politics and diplomacy, to an industrial giant capable of taking—even if not ready to do so—a leading role in world affairs. During most of that century the great powers of the world were all European, sharing a basic Western cultural heritage, and acknowledging the United States as being within the mainstream of that heritage. Within each country that heritage developed variations, but in the domestic structures of all could be found a belief in the supremacy of the white race and of Western institutions. Americans held these beliefs, and more. Within the Western historical tradition they believed in the supremacy of the Anglo-Saxon, of Protestantism, and of their own special way of life.

The American nation's history, from the opening of the century to its close, seemed to confirm the rightness of those convictions. It was a history of expansion, exploitation, and triumphs over lesser peoples. It was a history distinguished by an unmatched sense of security, one that the domestic society took virtually for granted. What most Americans did not realize was that few peoples at any time had enjoyed the luxury of such security, such freedom from external threat that the domestic structure could evolve virtually on its own terms, as though it were especially ordained by Providence to prosper.

As historians have pointed out repeatedly, the American nation enjoyed this internal security because of the geographic circumstances that gave it weak neighbors, because of the international structure that accepted its predominance in the Western Hemisphere, and for other reasons less obvious.

What the American people did not often realize was that their security came at the expense of insecurity for their neighbors. For much of the century the frustrations of Latin Americans stemmed from their inability to provide for their own security, from their impotence in the face of American power. For them a sense of subservience was as much a part of life as was a sense of superiority for their strong northern neighbor. Mexicans, especially, understood the plight of the insecure. "Poor Mexico," one of their most quoted aphorisms goes, "so far from God and so near the United States."

This internal security, this sense of superiority within the domestic structure, produced self-righteous policy makers, mostly lawyers and businessmen of pragmatic outlook who were convinced that American government and institutions were better than anything else anywhere else. So good was the American domestic structure, as demonstrated in a practical way by its triumphant history, they believed, that it could be planted anywhere and people would benefit from it. This self-righteous attitude prevented them from understanding—or even tolerating—the domestic structures of other peoples and from appreciating the finer qualities in other cultures. It critically affected the way they viewed, assessed, and reacted to the actions or policies of other states.

Most presidents and most other men responsible for making decisions on foreign policy in the nineteenth century fitted this pattern of leadership. They were all, or virtually all, white, Anglo-Saxon, Protestants, men shaped by their own milieu, a domestic structure they had been chosen to represent, defend, and at times enlarge, in the international environment. So convinced were they of the superiority of their way of life, of their institutions, of their ideals, that they measured other societies, or other nations, other peoples, by these norms of their own society. Naturally, in such a self-righteous means of measurement, they found other societies wanting, less idealistic, less democratic, less virile, than their own.

We can see from episodes in the very beginning of our national history how such attitudes, in various guises, have helped shape the ideas of policy makers. Alexander Hamilton and Thomas Jefferson, for example, both had mental images about the kind of nation they wanted to see evolve on the American continent, basically the kind of domestic structure that would produce the nation of their visions. In simple terms, Hamilton preferred a trading, industrialized society; Jefferson liked the idea of an agrarian society built on the widespread ownership of land. Hamilton saw England as a model; Jefferson more often looked to France for inspiration. They and their friends exerted pressure on the president and on the Congress in hopes of committing the government to the kinds of foreign policies that would promote the domestic structure they desired.

This concern for what the domestic structure should be and the influence of the existing domestic structure on foreign policy at this time can be seen in the furor over the Jay Treaty of 1794. Domestic pressures, as much as anything else, forced George Washington's administration to seek the negotiations with England leading to the treaty. When the English agreed to negotiate, domestic political considerations—essentially the views of Hamilton and other Federalist politicians—determined the nature of John Jay's mission. Finally, when the treaty was concluded, domestic considerations more than international ones stimulated the people's reaction to it. This reaction, for and against the treaty, became so violent that President Washington hesitated to ratify it. When he did ratify, he did so under pressure from Federalists who believed that the treaty and peace with England would preserve the kind of domestic structure they desired. Many Republicans considered his decision a domestic defeat for them and the kind of society they preferred.

A few years later, when the Jay Treaty contributed to the coming of the Quasi-War with France, Federalists and Republicans again took positions on foreign policy, or toward war, in keeping with their view of what would be best for the kind of domestic structure they wanted. In this instance Federalist politicians acted on the basis of an old principle: they attempted to use foreign policy for internal political advantage, mainly to bring about domestic cohesion under their leadership. For a good while President John Adams responded to such pressure from within his own party, adopting a bellicose foreign policy. As many presidents have done since his time, he reacted to internal pressures on the basis of their domestic effect rather than on the basis of carrying out or formulating a justifiable foreign policy. When he switched his policy, bringing peace with France, he also acted in large part out of domestic considerations.

The next president also made important foreign policy decisions on an ad hoc basis as reactions to domestic pressures. When Thomas Jefferson took the first steps toward the purchase of Louisiana he did not act solely because he immediately sought to add that province to the American empire. He acted when he did because internal political pressures had become so intense that he had to do something. Later, Federalists who had demanded action against the French in Louisiana opposed the purchase, nominally on constitutional grounds but really on the basis of political impulse. Domestically, the acquisition brought them no immediate gain, even some loss, so they reversed themselves and fought it.

In this respect Americans have acted no differently than have politicians and men of influence in other cultures. In China of the late nineteenth century the provincial gentry, particularly in the important central province of

Hunan, opposed railway concessions made by the imperial government to foreigners. Using various forms of pressure and working with other opposition groups, such as those headed by students, the gentry in at least one instance forced the central government to give up its policy of rail concessions to Westerners. Whether or not the policy of the central government was wise, it had to take into account the influence of the domestic structure. Old, experienced, imperial China could no more escape the influence of the domestic structure in the making of policy than could young, experimental, Federalist America.

Historians realize that their tools for measuring the influence of the domestic structure on foreign policy are crude, that often even a long-term influence, such as religion, varies and fluctuates. Nonetheless, we have enough evidence to know, as a general principle, that the nature of domestic constituencies affects decisions in foreign policy.

This principle can be seen, with some clarity, at work in a number of instances in the nineteenth century, a time of simple constituencies in comparison to our century. Negroes represented a minority that could be maltreated with impunity; they had no powerful state or international organization to protest their plight or to take up their cause. Conversely, when dealing with black peoples in other lands, or even black states such as Haiti, American policy makers were able to do almost as they pleased. Blacks within the United States did not constitute an effective constituency; for most of the century they were able to do little that could effect decisions in foreign policy. Unlike blacks of the twentieth century, they did not organize themselves into militant pressure groups that could force policy makers to take their views into account when dealing with African and other black states.

How the nature of the domestic structure and attitudes of the dominant constituency within the structure affect policy issues such as war or peace can be seen in the era of manifest destiny. In the two major controversies of that era, one with Great Britain over the Oregon country and the other with Mexico over Texas and California, American policy makers were tough and bellicose. Yet in one case they did all they could to gain what they could through compromise, and they avoided war. In the other dispute they were not only unyielding, but seemed to welcome a test of arms, as though military violence could settle the issue on its merits.

While not ignoring the discrepancy in the power of Britain and Mexico and the influence that discrepancy had on American policy makers, I suggest that the attitudes of the domestic constituency toward Englishmen and Mexicans had a great deal to do with the policies pursued by the American government. Americans respected Englishmen, shared their cultural, institutional, and religious heritage, and were reluctant to fight them, even to gain all of Oregon, a land manifestly destined to belong to Americans. In dealing with the Mexicans, Americans heard destiny speak with a clearer voice. They held Mexicans in contempt as a people, despised their institutions, and hated their religion. Americans coveted land belonging to both Englishmen and Mexicans, but it was easier for them to use violence against a people they considered inferior than against one they admired and looked upon as kin.

We could, without much effort, cull other examples from the nineteenth century, such as the issue of slavery in the fifties, to illustrate how the nature of the domestic structure has shaped foreign policies. But rather than do that, I wish before closing to suggest that the men who have written our diplomatic histories have often themselves assumed the attitudes of the dominant domestic constituencies. They are the men who have depicted American foreign policies of the nineteenth century as a series of triumphs. They have, in their books, perpetuated the self-righteous nationalism as espoused by the pragmatic policy makers of that century. They have accepted the assumption of American superiority, the assumption that foreign policy involved mainly the solution of immediate problems for the advantage of Americans, regardless of cost to others, and the assumption that the attitudes of the American domestic constituency had almost a universal applicability.

To the diplomatic historian these attitudes seem to have come easily, probably because almost by definition the study of a nation's foreign relations is an exercise in nationalism. But it makes no sense for a scholar to be defensive about his own domestic structure, to be fundamentally uncritical of it, and to be condescending and less than analytical about other cultures, the sources of adversary policies. Diplomatic historians should, it seems to me, be more concerned about intercultural history than they have been.

Only by studying foreign cultures and their unique or general attributes can we understand war and conflict. Even if those who made policy did so mainly within the context of their own domestic structure, the diplomatic historian should not write or teach history that way. He should be capable of explaining the pressures within each structure that helped shape conflicting policies. He not only should mine archives but he should also bridge the gap between cultures that the self-righteous policy makers of the nineteenth century could not.

# Domestic Influences on United States Foreign Relations in the Twentieth Century

WAYNE S. COLE

America's role in world affairs becomes meaningful partly in terms of efforts to guard national peace and security in relations with other countries, that is, in terms of coping with external influences. In addition, however, American foreign policies and actions partly grow out of internal influences. Domestic affairs and foreign affairs are intimately related to each other and influence each other. Many of the policies and actions of every state in international affairs grow out of the needs, desires, and ambitions of the dominant individuals and groups within the country. The specific objectives and actions of the United States in foreign affairs might be quite different if other individuals and groups with different values, interests, needs, and ambitions were in power at a particular time. All of this has been said before and has been widely accepted as almost axiomatic. Scholars have accomplished much research, interpretation, and publication regarding these relationships between domestic and foreign affairs.

Nevertheless, the research has little more than scratched the surface and provided a good start so far as foreign affairs in the twentieth century are concerned. And certain conditions and problems inhibit and slow the progress. One of these obstacles inhibiting research on domestic influences has been the tradition and relative ease of researching and writing old-fashioned, conventional, diplomatic history. It is perfectly logical to begin one's research in the official correspondence between diplomats, foreign offices, and heads of governments. But the tradition, the prestigious status, and the relative ease of that kind of research often discourage scholars from adventuring into the less conventional and less familiar, the more subtle waters of domestic influences.

A second and related reason for the limited progress in studying domestic influences has been the diplomatic historian's attachment to the older, conventional research methods—methods not essentially different from those von Ranke and others used more than a century ago. While physical scientists have spectacularly advanced their research methods and while social scientists have experimented with quantitative and behavioral methods, most historians of American foreign relations have made little progress in revising methods used for decades. One should not minimize the difficulties of developing and applying new research tools for the historian's craft; the methods of the physical and social scientist cannot be transposed unchanged into the context of historical research. And one should properly be skeptical of the excessive enthusiasms, narrow vision, and intellectual parochialism of some of the behavioral scientists. Nonetheless, if knowledge and understanding of domestic influences on foreign affairs are to be increased substantially, historians need to retool and explore imaginatively the possible contributions and limitations of new research methods, including quantitative and behavioral methods and the insights provided by other disciplines.

Third, the quality of research and interpretations on domestic influences has been limited by the tendency of some to grind axes and, in effect, to embrace the devil theory or great man theory of history. But headhunting is not endemic to studies of domestic influences: one need not necessarily use the good-guy, bad-guy, devil theories of history in the study of domestic influences on foreign affairs. One can and should ask "what" and "why" about domestic influences, without assuming that different influences would have created utopian peace and security in world affairs and without assuming that all imperfection was due to evil men and corrupt institutions.

Fourth and finally, research and publication on domestic influences on foreign affairs in the twentieth century have been handicapped by source material problems. In some cases the problem has been the old one of inadequate access and limited freedom in the use of essential source materials in the United States and elsewhere: private individuals and organizations (including business organizations) that have not preserved or opened their records to researchers; government departments and agencies (including military departments) that have manufactured roadblocks not really necessary for the protection of American national security and interests.

A different source problem encountered in the twentieth century has been the very bulk and abundance of source materials. The tons of records and millions of manuscripts make the total research task on some subjects quite beyond the energies and years of individual scholars; they may increase the difficulty of locating relevant needles in the awesomely huge haystacks. And the quantity and variety of sources relevant to the study of domestic influences on foreign affairs are substantially greater than those for conventional diplomatic history. I have been working for nearly twenty years on the subject of Franklin D. Roosevelt and the isolationists. Though I have carefully researched more than ninety different manuscript collections—some of them huge collections—the end is not yet in sight for my project if I expect to do it properly. In addition, the telephone, the airplane, and the conversations over lunch or cocktails have discouraged the creation of key documents and evidence at just those points when matters begin to get interesting. And, while the problem is not unique in the twentieth century, there have always been such public and private figures as Franklin D. Roosevelt who have consciously discouraged the recording of confidential conversations that might have been tremendously helpful to the historian.

Despite these and other variables slowing and inhibiting the research and publication on domestic influences on American foreign relations in the twentieth century, much work has been accomplished, and much more will be.

For purposes of analysis one may divide the study of domestic influences into three related aspects: first, domestic interests and attitudes; second, the reasons for these attitudes; and third, the influence (if any) of these domestic interests and attitudes on the shaping and conduct of American foreign relations. Each of these three deserves elaboration.

While defining each of these aspects has its special problems, probably the easiest for the scholar to determine is the first, that is, the domestic interests, attitudes, and ideas relating to foreign affairs. From the 1930s onward, both policy makers and scholars have had the advantage of public opinion polls for determining popular and group attitudes. President Roosevelt was skeptical of the validity of polls, and the *Literary Digest*'s fiasco on the election of 1936 justified his skepticism. Despite that fact, his advisers did channel poll results to him, and he kept informed on those findings.[1] The failure of the pollsters to predict correctly the outcome of the 1948 election further built distrust, and a certain degree of skepticism is justified. Nevertheless, the polls can provide both the policy makers and the scholars with some indications (however imperfect) of popular and group attitudes on foreign policy issues.

Another indicator of interests and attitudes that has been available to both policy makers and scholars has been constituent correspondence. But neither public figures nor scholars have been very certain just what use (if any) to make of the mail. Some obviously inspired mail, characterized by mimeographed form letters or by identical phrasing, is easily discounted or minimized. Chronic letter writers and crackpots can often be identified. Some people will sign almost any petition circulated in a group. Most major public officials do not personally read much of their constituent mail; their clerical staff routinely replies to the majority of it that is answered. Legislators do not always "vote their mail," and policy makers often act at variance with it. Nevertheless, even making proper allowances, constituent correspondence should not be wholly discounted either by politicians or historians.

The very act of taking time and energy to write such letters may indicate an intensity of feeling that public opinion polls may not reveal adequately. The letter crudely scrawled with a pencil on lined tablet paper and characterized by misspelled words and atrocious grammar may be as revealing and far more moving than the dictated letter professionally typed on impressive letterhead stationery. Before Pearl Harbor the White House staff tabulated pro and con mail coming to the president on foreign policy matters, and those tabulations were made available to Roosevelt.[2] Government departments, senators, congressmen, and foreign policy pressure groups have, on occasion, made similar mail counts. Among the legislative records in the National Archives are countless petitions and resolutions on foreign policy issues that may or may not have affected voting in Congress, but that will surely aid the scholar in determining group opinion on foreign affairs. After the Democratic party reversals in the congressional elections of 1938, James A. Farley, as chairman of the Democratic National Committee, systematically solicited analyses from many hundreds of local and state Democratic leaders all over the country. Flattered by Farley's personal inquiry, most of those politicians responded at length in evaluating and explaining the election results in their areas. The whole file of those responses is in the Franklin D. Roosevelt Library and is extremely illuminating on attitudes toward public issues at that time.[3] The America First Committee records at the Hoover Library at Stanford contain some twenty thousand cards and letters from persons who cared enough to contribute financially to that national foreign policy pressure group. Those cards and letters are a storehoues of raw materials for the study of noninterventionist interests and attitudes.[4] I share the widespread scholarly uncertainty about how to handle meaningfully the constituent correspondence in studying domestic interests and attitudes, but I am convinced that those letters, if properly studied, including the use of sophisticated quantitative methods and content analysis, could add to knowledge of American interests and attitudes of public issues.

In addition to polls and constituent correspondence, newspapers and periodicals may help the researcher. No one needs to be reminded that press opinion and public opinion are not necessarily the same; but press opinion, if properly used along with other indicators, can be of assistance. Many scholars depend too exclusively on the *New York Times* and a few other metropolitan dailies and neglect the smaller newspapers across the country. Some diplomats, generals, and scholars may never have learned that neither the Hudson River nor the Appalachian Mountains is the western boundary of the United States—but President Roosevelt never operated under such a misconception.[5] Admittedly, many local papers consist mostly of announcements of births, deaths, and social events along with the mass-produced fillers provided by urban commercial firms. But local editors have often been in closer touch with opinion and attitudes than most people in their communities. Many were bright, imaginative, and even bold editorial writers. Those who think isolationism was not very strong in the 1920s or 1930s, or that there was no relationship between agrarian discontent and foreign policy attitudes, would be well advised to work through the spirited editorials in a few of the small-town newspapers scattered across the Great Plains state of North Dakota. The scrapbooks and clipping files included in most manuscript and archival collections make available newspaper items that one might not otherwise see. In addition, those clipping files sometimes provide hints at what items from the press and periodicals the particular public official may have read and responded to.

In addition to polls, constituent correspondence, and the press, the resolutions and minutes of meetings of special interest groups can be helpful, including conventions of business, labor, religious, and ethnic groups. Admittedly, only a handful of people normally draft convention resolutions and dominate proceedings. At the very least, however, those few often defer to the dominant attitudes of their members; not infrequently they share and earnestly try to serve those interests and attitudes. Such resolutions are among the more obvious and clear-cut indicators of the direct relationship between group self-interest, on the one hand, and foreign policy views on the other. If one does not have access to the records of the various organizations, one can locate copies of the resolutions in the files of the public figures and the offices to which they are sent, in special interest periodicals, and in newspapers.

Similarly, literature, petitions, and letters from foreign policy pressure groups provide indications. Pressure groups may magnify the strength of particular foreign policy views, but the very diversity of those groups so helps to magnify other different views that the final composite may not be so distorted as that provided by a single pressure group. And the analysis of the leadership and membership of such pressure groups can provide clues about those who feel most strongly on particular issues.

In doing research in government archives on domestic interests and attitudes, the scholar should not limit himself to Department of State records. Increasingly in the twentieth century, most departments and many government agencies actively treat aspects of foreign affairs. Departments and agencies vary widely in their policies on the use of their records, and most are less generous than the Department of State. Nevertheless, domestic interests in some special aspects of foreign affairs channel all or part of their efforts through departments or agencies other than the State Department. In this same connection, the Senate Foreign Relations Committee and the House Foreign Affairs Committee are by no means the only relevant congressional committees in the study of domestic influences on foreign affairs. And one may locate key items in the files labeled Papers Supporting Senate and House Bills and Resolutions, organized among legislative records in the National Archives by Congress, session, and number of the bill or resolution.

One should not, of course, overlook the private correspondence, the speeches, and the published writings of the leadership elite—the public officials, businessmen, clergymen, military officers, educators, and scholars. Personally, I do not attach so much weight to leadership elites and do not minimize the attitudes of the so-called common man as much as many scholars do. Nevertheless, interests and attitudes are not limited to the "grass roots" or the "man-in-the-street"; elites are an important part of the interest-attitude-influence configuration—though not the only part.

And finally, an often overlooked type of source for information about domestic interests and attitudes may be the observations by foreigners in America. Foreign travelers, businessmen, journalists, scholars, diplomats, and consular officials conceivably may have perspectives in observing and reporting on the American scene that reveal dimensions other sources may miss. Of major importance in this regard has been the adoption of the thirty-year rule in the use of Foreign Office records in Great Britain. In any event, polls, constituent correspondence, the press, resolutions of special interest meetings, pressure group literature, records of government departments and agencies other than the State Department, expressions by opinion-maker elites, and the observations by foreigners in America are all relevant starting points for the scholar who seeks to determine American domestic interests and attitudes related to foreign affairs.

In addition to determining domestic interests and attitudes, the research process on the subject also involves the much more difficult task of determining reasons and motivation for domestic influences. Sometimes one can identify with reasonable certainty a direct causal relationship between self-interest and foreign policy views. When the independent iron and steel producers in the United States from 1937 onward urged the licensing and control of exports of scrap iron and steel from the United States, they were explicitly concerned with the supply and cost of a raw material needed in their domestic industry rather than with imposing economic sanctions against Japanese aggression.[6] It is easy to demonstrate parallels between the efforts of local areas and businesses to win defense contracts and their enthusiasm for military preparedness.[7] It is not difficult to demonstrate a relationship between shipping interests, on the one hand, and their opposition to shipping and trade restrictions in the neutrality legislation of the 1930s.[8] Though Samuel Lubell probably overemphasized the ethnic bases for isolationism, the tendency of Irish-Americans, German-Americans, and some Italian-Americans to be noninterventionists before World War II was not wholly independent of their ethnic sympathies.[9] Those and other relationships are easily demonstrated or illustrated by letters and petitions in the files of the Department of State, the Senate Foreign Relations Committee, and individual congressmen and public officials. The exact strength of such relationships, however, is much more difficult to determine.

Often it is not possible to establish that clear and direct causal relationship between interests and ideas; and sometimes the obvious explanation may not be the real one. Unmeasurable subjective and personal intangibles that are difficult to identify and weigh may operate. Despite the occasional inconoclast, most people like to win the approval of their peers. Most are reluctant to invite disapproval from their peers by taking sharp issue with the consensus within their own particular group (though they may take pride in dissenting from a different or larger consensus with which their own group does not identify). Even iconoclasts, rebels, hippies, and the New Left generally conform to the patterns that win acceptance in their particular group. Most feel a conscious or subconscious desire to win approval from the in-group or subgroup with which the individual identifies, whether the group be composed of military officers, farmers, members of the chamber of commerce, history professors, or hippies. That general tendency may be as powerful as any direct-interest idea of causal relationship. Even if that is true, however, one still needs to ask why any group (whatever the personal and status relationships within it) tends to identify with particular points of view on public issues. Broader economic, sectional, rural-urban, ethnic, religious, and psychological patterns help account for the inclinations of the various groups.

In addition, feelings of identity, empathy, or alienation may be involved. Agrarian radicals on the Great Plains in the 1920s and 1930s felt alienated from the increasingly dominant urban groups that seemed to be running the economy, the government, and foreign relations. Consumers relative to businessmen, workers relative to employers, debtors relative to lenders, elected officials relative to professional career diplomats, civilians relative to the military, women relative to men, students relative to teachers, blacks relative to whites, the young relative to the middle-aged—all forms of alienation by any out-group relative to the in-group can reduce the sense of responsibility for patterns and policies believed to be controlled by and for the dominant or in-group. Conversely, feelings of identity or empathy may build a sense of responsibility and pride of belonging. To go still further, how often does an individual's physiological and glandular makeup have as much to do with reactions to foreign policy alternatives as the pocketbook or religion? And how does the scholar go about demonstrating or disproving it?

Most historians were properly trained in so-called scientific research methods and the precise use of primary evidence, and they were cautioned about generalizing on the basis of that evidence. That is as it should be. One runs grave intellectual risks if one strays very far beyond what one can document directly in the sources. But one may also fall far short of the truth about motivation and causation if one refuses to pursue intuitively derived theories emerging indirectly from one's reading of the sources. The historian should not be excused from doing his research in depth, but he may distort the past as much by excessive caution in generalization as by daringly imaginative adventures in generalization. And new methods and sources conceivably could reduce the dependence upon intuitive bases for fresh interpretations.

In any event, sociologists, social psychologists, and others have already explored some of those avenues. Historians could benefit, more than most of us have, from studying both the contributions and the limitations of their methods and theories, modifying what they may have to offer to meet the special research and intellectual requirements of history.

In addition to identifying domestic interests and attitudes toward foreign affairs and in addition to wrestling with the problems of motivation, the scholar concerned with the relation of domestic and foreign affairs must also cope with the equally difficult task of determining what influence (if any) those domestic interests and attitudes exerted on the actual conduct of American foreign relations. Occasionally one can identify sharply and precisely the one-on-one causal relationship between domestic interests, attitudes, and agitation leading directly to a particular foreign policy. Superficially, one might identify that relationship in the case of Sen. Arthur H. Vandenberg and the ending of America's commercial treaty with Japan in 1939–40[10] or in the efforts of the American Committee for Non-Participation in Japanese Aggression that led to the licensing of exports to Japan in 1940–41.[11] But even in those and other comparable instances the obvious, direct domestic influences probably could not have prevailed had not the decision makers (for whatever reasons) been receptive to the particular influences. In other words, both the influencer and the influenced are relevant, as are the total domestic and international milieu in which both live and act.

Often key influences may be intangible and indirect. Sometimes the influences may inadvertently have effects quite different from those intended. Sen. Gerald P. Nye, in his moralistic, antibusiness, and antiwar agitation, opposed the shipment of arms to any potentially warring state; but his efforts unintentionally made it easier for the anti-Japanese, collective security, and interventionist spokesmen to win effective support for their coercive economic sanctions against Japan in 1940–41.[12] The scholar should seek to identify the one-on-one influence when it existed, but he should not overlook the nebulous and hard-to-define atmosphere, group environment, and milieu. One must turn first to careful, in-depth research in a wide variety of original sources and must not lightly go beyond those sources. But the intuitive insights arising as one studies the documents may be closer to the truth than a narrow, rigid adherence to only that part of the truth explicitly revealed by the diplomatic documents. Moreover, more daring experimentation with research methods and sources may provide insights into truth that may not be available through reliance only on old-fashioned, conventional historical research methods and sources.

In conclusion, scholars clearly should not limit their explorations only to domestic influences; conventional diplomatic historical research is essential to the whole. And one should not minimize the value of the many fine books, articles, and dissertations already available on domestic influences. But much more needs to be done, and imaginative use of sources and methods may contribute meaningfully. Older scholars need to retool their methods, and some of the younger scholars need to be trained in the use of the quantitative and multidiscipline tools that could help them expand the frontiers of our knowledge and our understanding of the limitations, the peculiarities, and the magnitude of domestic influences on American foreign relations in the twentieth century.

## NOTES

1. Robert E. Sherwood, *Roosevelt and Hopkins: An Intimate History* (New York: Harper & Bros., 1948), p. 105; Franklin D. Roosevelt to George Gallup, Sept. 23, 1942, President's Personal File 4721, 8101, and 1820, and President's Secretary's File, Public Opinion Poll 1941, 1944 Folder, Franklin D. Roosevelt Papers, Franklin D. Roosevelt Library, Hyde Park, New York. The Roosevelt Library is hereafter cited as FDRL.
2. Official File 4193, Box 8, Roosevelt Papers, FDRL.

3. Official File 300, 1938 Analyses, Roosevelt Papers, FDRL.

4. General Files: General Contributor Correspondence, Boxes 12–26, America First Committee Papers, Hoover Library, Stanford, California. The Hoover Library is hereafter cited as HL.

5. For example, see Franklin D. Roosevelt to James P. Warburg, May 23, 1934, President's Personal File 540, Roosevelt Papers, FDRL.

6. Roger I. Wensley to Eugene J. Keogh, May 8, 1937, House Foreign Affairs Committee Records, 75th Congress, Records of the United States House of Representatives, Record Group 233, National Archives Building, Washington, D.C. The National Archives Building is hereafter cited as NA.

7. For examples see telegram F. H. La Guardia to Roosevelt, Feb. 11, 1937, Fiorello H. La Guardia Papers, Municipal Archives and Records Center, New York, New York; Clyde Pharr to R. Douglas Stuart, Jr., May 21, 1941, and A. J. Dunning, Jr., to America First Committee Headquarters, July 28 and Sept. 22, 1941, America First Committee Papers, HL.

8. For examples see Leland M. Ford to Edwin Watson, Oct. 10, 1939, Official File 1561, Roosevelt Papers, FDRL; Frank S. Davis to Theodore F. Green, Oct. 18, 1939, Theodore F. Green Papers, Library of Congress, Washington, D.C.

9. Samuel Lubell, *The Future of American Politics,* 2d ed. rev. (New York: Doubleday Anchor Books, 1956), chap. 7. For a few of many possible examples, see Theodore H. Hoffman to Gerald P. Nye, Aug. 28, 1941, Gerald P. Nye Papers, Chevy Chase, Maryland; Frank Knox to William Allen White, Dec. 3, 1940, Frank Knox Papers, Library of Congress; John P. Marinaro to Edward J. Flynn, Sept. 24, 1940, President's Personal File 1820, Roosevelt Papers, FDRL.

10. Cordell Hull to Key Pittman, July 21, 1939, and attached print of Senate Resolution 166; A. H. Vandenberg to Hull, Aug. 7, 1939; memorandum of telephone conversation between Hull and Stanley K. Hornbeck, Aug. 19, 1939; Sumner Welles to Vandenberg, Aug. 22, 1939; Vandenberg to Welles, Aug. 24, 1939; memorandum of M.M.H. on "American Policy in the Far East: Lippmann-Vandenberg Controversy," Feb. 9, 1940—File nos. 711.942/174, 232, 271, 573, General Records of the Department of State, Record Group 59, NA.

11. Donald J. Friedman, *The Road from Isolation: The Campaign of the American Committee for Non-Participation in Japanese Aggression, 1938–1941* (Cambridge: East Asian Research Center, Harvard University; distributed by Harvard University Press, 1968), pp. 31–34; Harry B. Price to Key Pittman, Dec. 3, 1938, Apr. 12, 1939, Aug. 14, 1939, Oct. 30, 1939, Nov. 1, 1939, Nov. 1, 1939, Nov. 7, 1939, and June 18, 1940, Senate Foreign Relations Committee Records, Records of the United States Senate, Record Group 46, NA; Price to Pittman, Mar. 28, 1939, Cordell Hull Papers, Library of Congress.

12. U.S., Congress, Senate, *Congressional Record,* 75th Cong., 1st sess., 1937, pp. 8585–86.

# Domestic Influences on United States Foreign Policy

DISCUSSION

*Geoffrey Smith, Macalester College:* I think that diplomatic historians have finally moved into the realm where they realize that they are influenced to a great extent by domestic issues. I look at the past fifteen years or so, especially the past five years, at the diplomatic strife we have had in our nation, and I wonder what impact this might have on the writing or rewriting of American diplomatic history.

*Wayne S. Cole:* These are just random thoughts. One of the influences that comes to mind is economic. We are all, whether we are businessmen or not, in an economy that touches us directly or indirectly: an industrial, financial, capital, surplus economy affected by world markets, defense expenditures, and so on. I suspect this is a domestic influence that affects and will affect writing, either positively or negatively. Also, there are frustrations that undoubtedly all or most of us feel in the limited-war kind of involvement, earlier in Korea and now in Vietnam, and these frustrations provide part of the domestic influence explanations for attitudes and interpretations that are becoming increasingly popular. Another domestic influence in this same environment—and again, one that I imagine most of us feel—is the anonymity of a mass society, an urbanized mass society. Whether that mass society affects us in the form of big business, in personal consumer-businessman relationships, in education, or in scholarly research and endeavor, the effort of each of us as an individual to find some unique personal identity and the rebelling against this kind of mass anonymity may be part of what will affect the writing of younger people and ourselves. In this same connection, while "old fogies" like Wayne Cole are certainly affected by the post-World War II environment, nonetheless, we were also affected by the depression years and the war years in a way in which perhaps some younger scholars may not have been, at least not to the same degree. The depression and the war may have made some of us who are a bit older develop patterns of thought that may be a bit different from the ways of thinking of those who did not experience them.

*Alexander DeConde:* I do not see how any historian working in diplomatic history today can avoid being affected by what has gone on in the past and what is going on at this very moment, and I am disturbed by the reaction of diplomatic historians to certain things. In reading diplomatic history— American diplomatic history—one gets the view that the world was Anglo-American. I think that is why so many historians go into Anglo-American relations or Canadian-American relations. It is utterly ridiculous to have a twenty-volume history on Canada and the United States and not have one volume of history—one that is really first rate—on German-American relations. I do not see how anyone can look at the world without realizing that we do not understand the cultural traits of China and Japan. At this very moment we are dealing with a people who are virtually defeating the greatest power on earth. Fifteen-year-olds who cannot even read their own language are fighting and dying and having a tremendous impact upon our culture, yet we know nothing about them or their culture. At the same time, in our graduate schools, we are reducing the number of languages that people have to have to obtain a Ph.D. degree; we are going to become diplomatic historians by restricting our knowledge to maybe the English language. (Although it is true that many things have been translated.)

We also have a trend today within our domestic structure—or outside the establishment, call it what you will—whereby we are increasingly concerned with the various ethnic groups that have contributed to our culture. But one never finds such an interest in the studies of our diplomatic history or in the texts that we had ten to fifteen years ago, or even five or six years ago. So, how can one understand the various ethnic groups that have made our society unless one gets beyond the narrow confines of the histories written in the past. Assuming we care to strengthen these influences, I think we are doing the right thing in teaching and writing history for the twentieth century.

*James E. Hewes, Jr., Office of the Chief of Military History, Department of the Army:* I would like to suggest a subject for investigation: why did big business provide financial support for the major peace societies in the early twentieth century? I suspect that businessmen were carrying over their attitude in domestic affairs, identified by Gabriel Kolko, that competition was bad for business; they simply transferred this attitude to believe that competition among nations was bad.

*Paul S. Holbo, University of Oregon:* I listened to Professor DeConde's discussion of the connection between racial attitudes or images in various areas of the nineteenth century with some interest. I was not convinced in every case, I suppose. In his discussion of the 1790s he focused on politics, while he talked about racial attitudes earlier. I wonder if he might elaborate for just a moment on any racial attitudes that he sees as affecting Hamilton or Jefferson.

*Alexander DeConde:* I had several themes. I do not think I referred to the racial theme in the 1790s, and, at least in my study of the Federalist era, I do not detect the use of the term *race* in its proper denotation at that time (although there are people who still speak of ethnic groups as races—we speak of the "French race" and things of that kind). I think there was a nationalist aspect in all of this, and I am convinced, at least by the sources that I have seen, that one cannot erase the feeling of kinship between the men making policy in our government and those in England—even among the Republicans. One of the things that confuses me is that in 1812 we went to war on this basis. I feel that was a very important thing. This attitude is expressed in the writings of various French authors; for example, Talleyrand wrote that Americans could never be true allies of the French because they were of a different culture. He used the term *race* if I remember correctly, but I would not use the term *race* for the 1790s.

But I think, on the other hand, that the matter is distinct and clear in the disputes between the United States and Mexico and those between England and France. This is very apparent, I think, in the writings of Frederick Merk, one of the foremost historians of this period. Merk is condescending about it; in other words, we were dealing with a lesser race when we dealt with the Mexicans and with a superior race when we dealt with the English, and this is my point.

*David F. Trask, State University of New York at Stony Brook:* Professor Cole, as well as Professor DeConde, has assumed a previous tradition of diplomatic history which, for the sake of shorthand, can be called Rankean. I would like very briefly to suggest that there is an alternative tradition from which we flow, a tradition in which there is very little Rankean history and in which most of the work is a study of domestic influences on foreign policy. I would further suggest the possibility that perhaps this tradition still continues.

*Cole:* I am not quite persuaded by your line of reasoning. Probably my view is affected by the first book I ever read on diplomatic history—perhaps also the first that many of you ever read, Bemis's *Diplomatic History of the United States*. At least as I read his textbook, Bemis places very little—almost no—emphasis on domestic influences. Many of the monographs that I have read, in any event, are based on research very largely limited to State Department diplomatic correspondence, perhaps unlike von Ranke's; diplomatic archives of other countries are not even used. Yet not only are scholars negligent in using the archives of other countries, but they are still writing conventional diplomatic history. Such domestic influences that have intruded very often have been limited to the political realm and, for a few, to some aspects of the economic realm—and superficially at that. I am not persuaded by your position in any way.

*Hewes:* As one of Professor Bemis's students, I cannot resist a comment that his diplomatic textbook was the first one ever written—the other things were potboilers—and that shows how very young this whole school of diplomatic history is. In the beginning historians had to start with these State Department archives, and the debate just demonstrates another generation is branching out from the same tree.

*DeConde:* I was going to make somewhat the same comment, and I think you are absolutely right. The fact that we could get this large a group interested in this discipline in so short a time is amazing to me. I think we have gone a long way in a very short time. I feel that this criticism is no disparagement—but I guess it is in a sense—of what men have done in the past. They were men of their time, but that does not mean that we cannot criticize what they have done and try to do things a little better and to be broader and more understanding. After all, I think that John Higham in his little book on history does not identify diplomatic history—that is, American diplomatic history—as a discipline earlier than 1914. I think he is wrong in that; I think we can trace it back farther. Nonetheless, I think he has put it in a certain context.

But I want to get back to Dave Trask's question for a minute if I can. I do not know whether American historians have ever been in the Rankean tradition, if I understand it correctly. I do not know of anything before 1914 that in any broad sense could be conceived of as American diplomatic history in an intercultural context. There may be a few things. I think of Albert Weinberg's effort on manifest destiny, but I find it such a hodgepodge; I like it as a source rather than a coherent synthesis, but it is sort of a pioneering work. I do not know whether scholars went beyond the narrow confines of the traditional exchanges between diplomats until the postwar era. I think it is very difficult to pinpoint such work. Maybe others know of some.

*Manakkal S. Venkataramani, Indian School of International Studies, New Delhi, and Visiting Professor at the University of North Carolina:* I wonder whether some of the domestic influences Professor DeConde mentioned were still operative in the twentieth century. There may be issues about which there will not be much domestic pressure. What happens in those instances? For example, in dealing with the approach of the United States to the question of my own country's independence—Indian independence— there was not much domestic pressure in this country. There were a few religious groups and pacifists and a few socialists and other groups that were active in asking for independence for India and several other countries, but there was no constituency, as you put it, in this country. The question then arises whether other factors may have come into operation: factors like the feeling of kinship that Professor DeConde discussed—kinship with Britain and perhaps to a lesser extent with other people, like the French, the Dutch, and so on—which was very significant and which had fateful consequences for our peoples. And should this be viewed within the framework of the concept of white supremacy in this country?

The other factor that Professor DeConde mentioned was a lack of knowledge about the culture, background, and religions of those people, and even the widespread feeling that they were probably "lesser folk"—a phrase that he used. In the absence of domestic pressures, where did the responsibility for making the decisions lie? Should we then ascribe to the leaders of this country prime responsibility for the decisions that were made? Should we find in them certain devilish qualities for the decisions made in this period? Take, for example, a development that occurred in India during the war: with famine facing the country and fatalities running to some three million, the American people did not know about it at all. There were no constituencies in this country urging American action to relieve the distress and to save the people from this calamity. Adequate and exhaustive information was available only to this elite group, and certain decisions were made not to render assistance. In this kind of case there was no pressure at all; yet decisions were made, and only certain individuals or persons could be regarded as having had the information, the background, and the knowledge on the basis of which certain decisions could be made to act or not to act.

Another factor that Professor DeConde mentioned was the absence of an organized militant black group in this country. This is also important in dealing with the nonpolicy of the United States towards some of these countries, forgotten countries like India and the African countries during this period. Now, during the period of the 1930s and 1940s, which were critical years for Indian independence and for the emerging African nationalism, there was the absence of a militant black group in this country that could have been an effective help to those peoples. I find in my studies of the situation in this country in regard to Indian independence that just about the only organized group that took a firm stand in behalf of Indian independence and the emancipation of the African people from colonial rule were the black people organized as they were in those days in the National Association for the Advancement of Colored People. This organization, however, was not strong enough, not militant enough, not forceful enough, and there were no other pressures; thus the leaders made the kind of decisions they did during those years.

*Cole:* I think all of your comments are appropriate and thoughtful. I have two points to make. When a policy maker is confronted with an issue and there is not widespread interest, knowledge, or concern in organized groups or public opinion in the United States, you are, in my judgment, quite correct that the policy makers are free to arrive at decisions without regard to organized group influence within the United States; however, I am not quite persuaded that even in that kind of situation one could wholly discount domestic influences. That is, I would contend that each of the policy makers is in one way or another the product of a set of experiences through his life, a set of values that he has accumulated through a period of living and being educated, and that the kind of decision he makes in a particular situation is, in a sense, a product of the kind of environmental influences that have been exerted on him through his years as a child and an adult. Perhaps that is defining domestic influences improperly, but I think these life experiences do constitute a kind of domestic influence.

The second thought that came to my mind as you were speaking was that—mind you, I have not done research in the specific topics you asked about—there were domestic attitudes, domestic ideas, that influenced (how effectively I do not know) the question of Indian independence. One can get maudlin about it, but the idea of self-determination was a sentimental idea, an idea widely felt among the American people. I remember in college before World War II that this concept helped foster sympathy for efforts in India. Now, one can debate whether this sympathy had any effect on policy, but I think the feeling was very real and widely held, and I think it can be identified as a domestic influence.

*Hewes:* I was writing a term paper on what attitude the United States should adopt towards Indian independence at the time of the Bengal famines in World War II; consequently, I knew about these famines. *Time* magazine, the source for my information, was very strongly in favor of Indian independence. So was the army General Staff, because it was anti-British in the sense of being anti-imperialist. If one looks at the records that have been made available on the role of the General Staff in formulating wartime global foreign policy, one will find a very strong anti-British strain in all of their thinking when they went to conferences with the British. Because the General Staff was anti-British, it was, by extension, pro-Indian.

*Mitchell William Kerr, Towson State College:* One of the problems is getting adequate information about the lower level of the diplomatic corps. How soon would personnel records for promotions be available for research, not for slanderous purposes?

*William M. Franklin, Historical Office, Department of State:* Every government in the world restricts access to personnel records as a matter of public decency. If you took the king's shilling, you would feel the same way. This is the basis for a restriction of some fifty years on access to personnel records. However, it is not my impression that information useful to the evaluation of an individual's career and his biases is limited to those restricted personnel files. I am not sure just what you have in mind, but I think most of that information can be obtained readily from files that are open or that are from other open sources, or it becomes quite evident from memorandums that the man writes. I think you will find his background and prejudices very apparent if you look just a little bit between the lines. I do not think you have to probe into a man's personnel record files to find all that. I may be wrong in some cases, but the reason for limitation on access there is obvious, and it is universal.

*DeConde:* Just very briefly, I completely agree with Dr. Franklin's comments. It is much easier to get this information from memorandums of various kinds, diaries, comments from colleagues, and so forth. I think, however, that it is probably easier to get it in the early national period than it is in the later period because people were more open about their evaluations and put everything down. In the twentieth century I think our public figures are much more guarded, although I do think we get our nickies and so forth every now and then—at least this has been my experience.

# The Diplomacy of War
and Peace

# The Dimensions of American Participation in
# War and Peacemaking, 1917–1919

LAWRENCE E. GELFAND

Scholarly interest in the First World War is now riding a crest of popularity on both sides of the Atlantic that has had no parallel in the past half century. Young historians are being drawn by a combination of powerful attractions. For many the appeal is to be found in the realization that the serious international difficulties which have beset our contemporary world had their origin in, and were activated by, the military and political conflagration of 1914–18 and by the ensuing peace settlement of 1919. Supposedly, a great chain links the First World War to all the important international aberrations of twentieth-century society: the Great Depression of the 1930s, the rise of Italian fascism, Japanese militarism, and the violent drive of Germany's quest for world dominion. The Second World War and the cold war that followed in its wake also fall within the legacy. According to this perspective, Versailles was anything but a "lost peace." Its provisions were sufficiently viable to bring untold distress upon at least two succeeding generations. For today's historians, intrigued by the ring of relevancy and immediacy in order to justify their research and to give it meaning and significance, the First World War seems to meet the test.

The First World War was a time of rapid and dynamic change. The military struggle between the Allied-American coalition and the Central Powers clearly occupied the center stage, but off in the wings the revolutionary agitation in such scattered locations as Russia, Ireland, Korea, Egypt, and Hungary was hardly of less significance. For many of the world's people, the sacrifice of human life would be justified only if the war resulted in some socialist utopia or in some national self-determination. No serious study of the First World War and the peace conference can afford to ignore the revolutionary and idealistic dimensions of the struggle.

President Wilson's importance as a statesman and moral leader derives

131

from his persistent advocacy of a program that promised to reform the machinery of international relations. If the Old Diplomacy and the rival imperialisms had been the responsible agents that brought on the military confrontation in 1914, then society must overhaul this system so that the periodic bloodletting could at least be averted. The new machinery would include some system of collective security that would function through an association of nations. The rule of law, operating through a world court, would replace anarchy in the relations of states. A permanent mandates commission, which would supervise the transition of certain colonial peoples along the road to political independence, was still another reform. An international labor organization calculated to improve standards of life for millions of industrial workers was another cog in this new machinery. The element of change, the idealism implicit in the reforms, the desire to create a world order that promised mankind liberation from the scourge of war—all hold an appeal to today's often cynical, ideal-hungry generation tired of the old clichés and excuses for wars and human sacrifices.

The First World War introduced many military innovations with which twentieth-century mankind must still contend. Among these, the tank, aircraft, mustard gas, the submarine, explosive mines, and bombs capable of destroying huge concentrations of people might seem most important. All these weapons have a capacity to bring devastation to cities and farms as well as to armies and navies, to civilians as well as to soldiers. Practices like the blacklist and the violation of neutral rights on the high seas enabled belligerents to involve neutral states in hostile acts. The introduction of total warfare was still something of a novelty during the period from 1914 to 1918.

If today's young historians are drawn to innovation and rapid change in international affairs, the experience of the United States during the First World War offers a marvelous illustration of the process of escalation. Before 1917 America's defensive commitments were limited almost exclusively to the Western Hemisphere and secondarily to the Pacific. Although the greatest volume of commerce flowed to Europe, there had never been any appreciable American involvement in European international predicaments until 1914. Except for the fringes, Africa and Asia were both pretty dark continents insofar as American statesmen were concerned. Indeed, the low priority which President Wilson himself assigned to foreign affairs in 1913–14 was reflected in his selection of William Jennings Bryan as secretary of state. In addition, Wilson's ambassadorial appointments to London, Paris, Berlin, Rome, Saint Petersburg, and Constantinople all went to Democratic worthies and rank amateurs.

The First World War did not suddenly make foreign affairs important for the United States. Nor did the United States suddenly find itself a powerful nation having worldwide interests. The importance of the war lies in the fact that for the first time in its national history the United States attained a position of leadership in world affairs, a position it would not again assume until the Second World War. To be sure, the prerequisites of leadership are power and broad national interests, but these qualities America possessed in generous measure before 1917. Wartime dynamics provided the catalytic agents for American ascendancy; but in the absence of a chief executive who was willing to assume, or, was indeed insistent upon that role, American leadership would not have been attained automatically or through some magical historical or environmental determinism.

The Wilsonian notion of leadership in world affairs had two, not always closely connected, parts. In his many public speeches, Wilson the orator laid the foundations for moral suasion. His intense concern by 1917 was not limited to arranging a peace settlement for the war alone; rather, Wilson's seemingly more important concern was in establishing a peace settlement that would contain within its provisions the necessary machinery through which international sources of crisis and tension could be resolved without a military confrontation. Such a settlement would incorporate fundamental principles of justice. The Fourteen Points encompassed the basic ingredients of this Wilsonian program.

Moral leadership in and of itself, however, would not suffice if American influence was to prevail in the ultimate peace settlement. The second component of leadership called for an American parity with England and France in wartime councils. Wilson was persuaded that the military defeat of the Central Powers was essential to any desirable peace settlement, and to this end the American Expeditionary Force had to serve in France. By 1918, not only were American soldiers fighting in the trenches in western Europe, but American troops were also stationed in such remote outposts as eastern Siberia and northern Russia. An American fleet was operating in the eastern Mediterranean, and American convoys were protecting the shipping lanes of the North Atlantic. American forces were thus actively influencing the world's balance of power and supporting American interests outside the Western Hemisphere. By the time of the armistice, some 4.5 million men had been mobilized into the American army, and the American dead numbered more than thirty-five thousand.

The rapid ascent to the summit of leadership during wartime required a heavy expansion of the administrative apparatus as the scope of American foreign relations grew apace with the military escalation. Bryan's successor, Robert Lansing, discovered that the State Department was not able to cope with additional burdens arising from the war. An American Committee of

Public Information under George Creel's direction disseminated what turned out to be millions of pieces of American propaganda throughout the continent of Europe. An American Military Intelligence Corps commanded by Gen. Marlborough Churchill proved to be a necessary channel through which both covert and overt means were employed to obtain information from enemy, allied, and neutral countries. Herbert Hoover's relief program arranged to deliver foodstuffs and other necessities of life to the needy victims of the war's devastation. Edwin F. Gay's Central Bureau of Statistics gathered and coordinated information about production of raw materials—agricultural and industrial data which it received from all over the world. Wartime leadership required that scores of regular agencies of government get into the foreign affairs act for the first time: the Treasury, Justice, Agriculture, and Commerce Departments, and of course the War and Navy Departments.

During the war, the United States was granted a permanent seat on the Supreme War Council. Although American leadership did not always exploit the council to its maximum usefulness, it was important for the United States government's leadership to be so recognized. Wilson believed that while the American government must assist the Allied governments in seeking the common goal—victory—American diplomacy must never become subservient to the Allies. Therefore, throughout the months of American belligerency, until the armistice and beyond to the peace conference, Wilson insisted on both the separateness of the American commitment, with its separate military force and special intelligence service, and on an individual American preparatory program for peace. Colonel House's Inquiry, quite independent of the State Department and the preparatory apparatus of the Allied governments, was charged with drawing up the American government's blueprints for the eventual peace settlement. In a small way, the Inquiry provided a forecast of the exceedingly broad dimensions of the future peace conference. Every part of the globe was surveyed in an attempt to identify problems that might conceivably require international action. Moreover, the Inquiry's experience underscored the nation's urgent need for trained, expert personnel in the many fields of international affairs should America plan to shoulder responsibilities of leadership after the war.

Never before in American history had the United States become so deeply involved in foreign affairs as during the years of its participation in the war and the subsequent year of the peace conference. Given this newly acquired leadership, President Wilson had no realistic alternative but to attend the conference in person as director of the American Commission to Negotiate Peace. Had Wilson remained in Washington and delegated responsibilities to others, his program for peace would conceivably have been endangered. And the uncertainty of cable communication was such that from a practical standpoint, a determined Wilson, anxious to see his program for peace implemented, could not manipulate the strings of American plenipotentiaries from Washington.

. The peace negotiations at Paris were so broad and varied as to sometimes stagger today's historian who reads through its vast documentation. The United States was represented on the overwhelming majority of the sixty-three committees which served the conference. Wilson served on the Supreme Council until he departed for the United States in late June, at which time Robert Lansing took his place. In July, Frank Polk went to Paris to take charge of the American Commission and to serve as the United States representative on the Supreme Council until the American Commission was formally disbanded on December 9, 1919. In total personnel, the American Commission to Negotiate Peace numbered some 1,250 individuals, ranging from clerks and chauffeurs to plenipotentiaries.

I need not summarize here the work of the conference. Suffice it to say, the American Commission participated in the formulation of all 440 articles of the Treaty of Versailles and in all of its subsidiary protocols. Since the conference's agenda liberally addressed itself to the wide-ranging problems of Europe, Africa, and Asia, the American Commission was deeply involved in the resolution of problems that existed almost entirely outside the bounds of the Western Hemisphere. The extent of American participation in peacemaking was in no sense less important than that of the British and the French. The Americans always labored under the handicap of uncertainty, never knowing what commitments, if any, the United States was likely to accept in the final reckoning.

From this perspective of American diplomacy during 1917–19, certain other pieces fit together in the jigsaw puzzle of American foreign relations in this century. Isolationism during the 1920s and 1930s can be interpreted as a withdrawal of American leadership from world affairs and the abdication from national commitments to maintain the new machinery of the international community. Although the Versailles treaty failed to receive American ratification as such, much of the arduous labor performed at Paris in 1919 was not in vain, for it later became a part of the supreme law of the United States. In 1921 war between Germany and the United States was formally terminated by provisions of the Treaty of Berlin, which included almost half the text of the Versailles treaty.

Now, after fifty years, historians are turning their attention to the escalation of American involvement in world affairs during the First World War and American descent from the summit of leadership. The Wilsonian strategy itself is worth some close analysis. The president spoke of the need for antinational minorities; the international/aeronautical convention; the tions bills in 1916 and 1918. At times Wilson seemed to oppose any restoration of balance of power politics after the war, but at the time of the armistice, he suggested the need to maintain a semblance of strength in Germany so that the Allies would not be able to dominate a postwar Europe. What were the American priorities at the peace conference and how were these implemented? We are in need of bilateral studies concerning Japanese-American relations, Austrian-American, Italian-American, and even Franco-American relations during these years. An entire range of problems of a nonpolitical nature that were treated at the Paris Peace Conference merit investigation: the provisions providing guarantees of good treatment for antinational minorities; the international/aeronautical convention; the work of the commission concerned with the regulation of international ports, waterways, and railways in Europe. In fact, there is virtually no treatment in existing literature of the work of the Supreme Economic Council.

The reputations of both Herbert Hoover and Woodrow Wilson underwent considerable alteration as a result of their activities at the peace conference. Hoover supposedly emerged from Paris with a favorable image; Wilson, whose popularity rating was soaring at the outset of the conference, suffered a heavy loss of public confidence in both Europe and America when he returned to the United States six months later.

The historian must try to explain this metamorphosis. Perhaps part of the explanation lies with the press. We certainly need a study of the operations of the American Press Bureau, over which Ray Stannard Baker presided, and of the numerous reporters and how they "covered" the peace conference. The treatment of the conference in the American press has importance because the press was the only mass medium which informed the public of the progress of the peace negotiations. There is a need also for studies of the changing administration of foreign affairs and the modifications needed to meet requirements of American leadership. We need to explore the entire process of decision making. As I have tried to suggest, foreign affairs ceased to be the very exclusive preserve of the Department of State. Historians must begin to beat paths to the doors of other sections of the National Archives in search of the great wealth of documentation that concerns decision making in foreign policy.

During the years of war and peacemaking, 1914–19, American foreign policy became more involved in the world than had been the case previously. It therefore becomes an essential part of the historian's preparation in this field to acquire a technical competence in the geography, politics, institutional history, comparative economics, ethnography, and international law that dealt with a very considerable part of the world. To make much sense of the peace settlement in the Balkans and Turkey, the American diplomatic historian has to know something about the internal dynamics of these areas. He must know the genesis of the Bela Kun regime in Hungary just as clearly as he understands the facts behind the English Coupon Election of 1918. For the historian, the price he must pay in order to understand American leadership in world affairs is to combine an understanding of the world with an appreciation of America's own interests and policies. The expansion of American responsibilities in world affairs is clearly reflected in the broadening of the documentation which today's historians must examine.

The historian of the First World War era must learn patience. For whatever research topic that he may choose, however minute, the documentation is likely to be enormous, varied, and scattered. If the research topic is restricted and narrow, the vastness of the sources will probably not be a serious problem; the historian should take stock of the situation and plan the time to see his project through to its completion. But for broad subjects, the historian must recognize that the research is indeed open-ended; that at some point he must call a halt. My personal view is that the close of research comes when the historian finds that he is no longer learning more from his sources or modifying his hypotheses.

By and large, the principal happy hunting grounds for historians of 1914–19 are in Washington, D.C., at the National Archives and at the Library of Congress. Records of the American Commission to Negotiate Peace, Record Group 256, alone measure 262 cubic feet and became accessible to historians in 1949, though portions were still restricted until 1967. Record Group 59, pertaining to State Department records for the war years, 1914–18, measures 210 cubic feet. Concerning the extent of military records, I shall only quote from the "Essay on Sources" in Edward M. Coffman's *The War to End All Wars* (New York: Oxford University Press, 1968): "There are tons of World War I records in the National Archives, so obviously I had to be very selective in my use of them." Coffman's statement concerning his appraisal of sources can well serve as a model of how the historian should cite archival sources in his bibliography. The diplomatic historian should range widely throughout the archives before he feels satisfied that he has completed his research. For instance, papers of the United States Geological Survey bear on the peace conference because Joseph B. Umpleby and his associates in the Foreign Minerals Division attended the conference to advise on territorial boundaries.

At the Library of Congress, the scholar must start his labors with the huge collection of Wilson papers which are divided into several, often over-lapping, series. Other collections of importance are the papers of Henry White, Tasker Bliss, Robert Lansing, Josephus Daniels, Newton D. Baker, Adm. William Benson, David Hunter Miller, Gen. John Pershing, Oscar Crosby, Chandler P. Anderson, and Ray Stannard Baker. Yale University's Historical Manuscripts Division houses the huge collection of Edward M. House Papers, which includes a thirteen-volume typescript diary. Subsidiary collections include those of Charles Seymour, William Bullitt, John W. Davis, and Frank L. Polk. Stanford's Hoover Institution is valuable mainly for its excellent collection of printed sources and propaganda. The researcher will also find there one of the few extant sets of the various minutes of the committees that functioned at the peace conference. Harvard's Houghton Library has collections of more easily manageable proportions: the Walter Hines Page, Joseph Grew, William Phillips, and Ellis Dresel manuscripts. At Harvard's Baker Library, the historian should spend time on the Thomas Lamont Papers, and at the Harvard Archives there is a small collection of Archibald Cary Coolidge manuscripts; but I am sorry to report that the Samuel Eliot Morison Papers are closed until the year 2000. At the Johns Hopkins Library, the Isaiah Bowman Papers are also closed, but only until 1975. Columbia University's Special Collections Division has the George Louis Beer diary, the William L. Westermann diary, and the James Shotwell Papers. The Wellington Koo Papers, which are presently on deposit there, may be accessible to scholars as soon as Mr. Koo has completed his processing of them. Several oral interviews on file at the Columbia Library are also worthy of the historian's attention. Princeton has the Bernard Baruch Papers, some valuable portions of the Ray Stannard Baker collection, and some Wilson papers. Other small collections are located at depositories across the country, like the Albert Lybyer Papers at the University of Illinois Archives and the Robert J. Kerner Papers at the University of California Archives.

This brief survey suggests that American archival and manuscript sources are abundant to the extreme. However, today's historian of American foreign relations in the First World War period should also seriously consider making use of foreign documentation in his research. Within the past five years, the Public Record Office in London has processed and made accessible the complete British archival records on the war and the peace conference. This material is magnificently organized and, as might be expected, extremely voluminous. Also in London, there are several private collections worthy of much more than a passing interest: the Balfour and Robert Cecil Papers at the British Museum; the David Lloyd George and the Andrew Bonar Law manuscripts at the Beaverbrook Library. At the Bodleian

Library, Oxford, the Alfred Milner and James Bryce Papers await the scholar, as do the John M. Keynes Papers at the Marshall Library, Cambridge. These British documents often allow the scholar to criticize his American sources. He can, for instance, check Balfour's version of conversations with Colonel House against House's version. Also, British comments on American diplomatic negotiations and policies can often be illuminating. The Historical Registry located on Chancery Lane in London is preparing a thorough listing of manuscript sources located in the United Kingdom, and American scholars should avail themselves of this resource.

Today's historian who measures his evidence by the ton or by scores of cubic feet must bring to his research some fairly definite hypotheses. He must have a clear idea of what he is searching for in the sources. He will not be likely to retrace his steps. Despite the volume involved, the scholar must strive to handle his materials critically, noticing errors and inconsistent statements. Sampling of materials can be extremely hazardous for the historian. A competent archivist or manuscripts librarian can be of great assistance to the scholar in conserving his time and energy.

The archivist who is involved in preparing huge collections of manuscripts for scholars' research must at all times be sensitive to the problems imposed by sheer volume. Finding aids and registers should be prepared in greater detail so that the researcher will be able to locate the desired sources without having to spend an excessive amount of time. Vast collections of documents which are microfilmed (as, for example, the American records of the First World War which were recently put on some 540 reels of film by the National Archives) should be accompanied by separately bound pamphlets which describe the documentary contents of each reel by subject, title, author, and date of each item. I would also suggest that research libraries consider the advantages to the scholarly community that would come from the reproduction of registers to manuscript collections, thus making such registers available to university and public libraries throughout the country.

This generation of historians studying the period of the First World War is especially well endowed with materials, and the opportunities for significant contributions to scholarship have never been better. Today's scholars hold yet another advantage over their predecessors. Unlike the historians who wrote in the 1920s, 1930s, and 1940s—such as the Americans Ray Stannard Baker, David Hunter Miller, Frederic Paxson, and Charles Seymour, who had themselves been active participants during the war and the peace conference—today's is the first generation which does not feel personally engaged in the factionalism and animosities; it does not feel a special need to defend a particular leader or cause. Without a compulsion to serve any given interpretation, today's historians can begin to exploit the riches afforded by documentation, to treat the many dimensions of American leadership in world affairs.

# Rewriting the History of American Diplomacy during the Second World War

## GADDIS SMITH

Rather than concentrate exclusively on the nature of sources, I want to express a deep concern over the state of recent writing in American diplomatic history and to relate that concern to some new approaches for writing about the Second World War.

For a quarter of a century, from the Second World War until the early 1960s, most American political leaders and many diplomatic historians subscribed to what might be called the Great Cycle theory of American foreign relations in the twentieth century. The theory goes something like this:

The emergence of several great new or potentially great powers—Germany, Japan, and the United States—at the end of the nineteenth century upset the balance of power that had been so well and beneficently maintained under British leadership for almost a century. At first the United States had great difficulty developing a role suitable for the new conditions in the world. President Theodore Roosevelt tentatively attempted to lead the United States into participation with Britain in the maintenance of the balance of power, but his work was not sustained by Presidents Taft or Wilson initially.

Then the First World War broke out and threatened world stability. Belatedly, President Wilson realized that the very existence of American power required American participation in the war in order to bring the fighting to an end and to create stable world conditions in which the political values of the American nation could flourish. Thus from 1914 to 1917 the United States passed through one turn in this Great Cycle, from hesitation and uncertainty to resolute world leadership, proud, responsible, magnanimous, moral, for the benefit of all mankind. So goes the theory.

Yet no sooner had leadership been assumed than the next turn in the cycle began. Old attitudes were too strong, and Wilson's domestic political

141

leadership was too weak. In 1919–20 the nation repudiated the Wilsonian vision and turned not to isolation but to irresponsible selfishness. For two decades the nation was reluctant to assume international political burdens. World War II resulted in part because of American irresponsibility. The United States held rigid in a posture of noninvolvement into the late thirties, and then only after the war began did the United States under the leadership of Franklin Roosevelt again take up the mantle of world leadership, entering the war against the Axis powers. The achievement of military victory, however, was accompanied by such destruction in Europe and Asia that a power vacuum was created and with it the potential for a new totalitarian threat from the Soviet Union. This third challenge of the twentieth century, the third in the cycle, was explicitly compared by American leaders at the time with the recently surmounted challenge from Germany and Japan.

Now the question in 1945 was which way would the United States turn, back into irresponsibility, thus taking another disastrous turn in the Great Cycle, or would the United States break the cycle, redeem the vision of Woodrow Wilson, and accept the second chance to set the world aright?

With very little dissent we embarked on accepting the second chance, through our participation in the founding of the United Nations. But, still according to the theory, the United Nations, without effective power to contain totalitarian aggression from the Soviet Union, was not enough. The United States had to deploy its vast economic power and military potential directly in order to save the world. In the late 1940s and early 1950s political leaders, encouraged by most academic historians, succeeded in precisely that deployment of economic and military power, first through the Truman Doctrine and the Marshall Plan, and then, in order to provide the military security behind which European economic recovery could take place, through the North Atlantic Alliance and the military assistance programs for Europe.

But just at that point, 1950, when it appeared that this first effort had succeeded in breaking the cycle of recurring wars, just when it appeared to those making policy in Washington that the Soviet Union had been contained and that Soviet leaders had decided not to use war as an instrument, the Korean War erupted. President Truman and his advisors responded to that war in terms of the cycle theory. If the United States stood by idle as in 1914 and in the 1930s, they believed there would be a third world war. They had to take active preventive measures, and take them fast. The lessons of history seemed unequivocal. Thus was rationalized the limited and successful military intervention in Korea. For a decade the Korean War was celebrated by diplomatic historians and by the general public and by political leaders, and is still celebrated today, as an epic of American courage and sacrifice in the interests of world security.

Then in the 1960s political leaders, without distinction of political party, took up the rhetoric of the Great Cycle theory and applied it, as they are applying it today, to Vietnam. In the early stages of American participation in Vietnam the public generally seemed to accept the validity of the cycle theory to Vietnam. The Free World it seemed was faced with another challenge, the fourth in the series. Fast preventive action could contain that challenge and prevent global war. It would be prevented at very little cost, perhaps much less cost than Korea, or so it was believed.

But the predictions were not fulfilled. Month by month in the late 1960s more and more Americans refused to accept the theory as applied to Vietnam. At first there were few who challenged the theory itself. They simply raised questions as to its applicability to a particular situation. Many of the advisors of one president in the late 1960s joined in the questioning, and that president himself chose not to seek reelection.

But the new president, leader of the opposite political party, soon reaffirmed the theory and criticized the critics as if they were isolationists of 1941.

Now what does this have to do with the task of the American diplomatic historian, and more specifically with the issue of research and writing on American foreign relations during the Second World War? Let me try to make the connection.

I think that a result of the continued invoking of the Great Cycle theory by American leaders has been a revulsion among many students of diplomatic history, a revulsion against the theory and indeed against almost all of twentieth-century American foreign policy, including the policy of the Second World War. In place of the Great Cycle theory we are witnessing a hypercritical and therefore uncritical condemnation of almost all American foreign policy in the twentieth century. Just as some political leaders have superficially applied analogies of the world wars and Korea to Vietnam, some critics have moved in the other direction, applying analogies from Vietnam backwards to the earlier situations. The very foundations upon which most of our texts in diplomatic history and most of our monographs are based are being washed away, and we are in danger of losing all understanding of our past. I could illustrate this situation with a fairly simple table dividing those taking attitudes toward the past into three groups.

First there is Group A, which represents the official line, President Nixon among others. Group A looks on our intervention in the Second World War as good. Intervention in Vietnam is considered as essentially the same, in its basic purposes and assumptions, as intervention in the Second World War, and therefore intervention in Vietnam is basically right.

Group B represents what I might call establishment critics, people like Sen. J. William Fulbright, historians like Arthur Schlesinger, diplomatic historians like George F. Kennan. Group B believes that in its essential aspects our interventions in the Second World War and in Korea were right, but that the Vietnam situation is different, and therefore our policy in Vietnam is bad.

Finally there is Group C, the New Left revisionists who believe that our intervention in the Second World War was essentially bad and that our intervention in Vietnam is the same, based on similar motives, and therefore is equally bad.

Now the broad conclusion to be drawn from Group C is that American policy in the twentieth century has always been selfish, quite frequently brutal, reactionary, repressive, and almost always inimical to the interests of the peoples on whom that foreign policy impinged.

Group A and Group C share one assumption, namely that there is no essential difference between our foreign policy today and our foreign policy in other situations in this century, including the Second World War. This places a great burden on those who like myself still fall in Group B. So far historians have not done enough in their research to disprove either the favorable views of the Second World War held by Group A or the dark strictures of Group C. Groups A and C are squeezing out Group B in the middle.

What is the solution? The solution, as others have said, is more and better history. We must begin first in our research by remembering that a historical individual or institution often influences what historians write about it more by the incidental way in which it organizes and preserves its records than by its behavior. In other words, the preservation of records can lead to distortion. To put it another way, a man or a group which leaves no written record can fall into near oblivion even though its actual importance at the time was very significant.

Now all who have worked in the period of the First World War and who have plunged into the papers of Colonel House, mentioned by Professor Gelfand, know how large that self-important figure looms through his own diary and letters. How large he would be if he had not been a compulsive diarist and letter writer or if by some mischance all of his papers had been burned in 1919 it is hard to say.

To a lesser extent Henry L. Stimson and Henry Morgenthau have through the collection and preservation of letters and diaries in their lifetimes doubtless enhanced their historical stature. By the same token, the admirable institutions of the presidential libraries, with their excellent staffs, facilities, and financial support, are contributing to the presidential synthesis of foreign policy, and in diplomatic history generally to an emphasis on presidential summit diplomacy.

This word of caution should also apply to the users of the records of the Department of State. We must not be too dependent on the well-organized, accessible, and well-staffed collections—whether the diary of a House, a Stimson, or a Morgenthau, the collections at Hyde Park, Independence, or Cambridge, or the decimal file and purport books of the Department of State.

Other men and institutions, most notably temporary wartime agencies, did not preserve records quite so well or in such usable form. Fortunately, historians of both world wars are beginning to realize the importance of other agencies (as does the staff of the National Archives), but there is much more to be done. As historians we should put in a special word on behalf of the defunct agency without tradition or ongoing momentum to stimulate the preservation of its records.

Until recently most historians of American diplomacy during the Second World War have relied to an overwhelming extent on published material, on top-level State Department records, and on the cream of presidential material. Diplomatic history as written so far is largely an account of summit conferences, with a bit of filler material to get from one conference to another and a little bit more material on planning for the peaks. Much of this is good diplomatic history in a very conventional sense, but it is diplomatic history with a single focus, and with one dimension. It sets forth what the prime minister said to the president and what the foreign minister said to the foreign minister, but it proceeds on such a high, rarified level that the reader gains little sense of actual conditions in those areas of the world influenced by American foreign policy.

International politics and the archival policies of other countries make it difficult to get much beyond the printed sources on the attitudes of other countries toward the United States, but even so there is much more that can be done. Instead of confining ourselves to the summit, we must investigate more closely the local response of other people during the war to the American presence and influence.

This does not mean neglecting the State Department records, but it means using them more extensively, using them not only for material which was fed directly into summit diplomacy but also for reports by junior officials on local situations. It means exploring the records of other agencies, as historians are now beginning to do. It means more extensive use of foreign materials, newspapers, magazines, memoirs, as well as archives where available. Above all, it means expanding the limits of diplomatic history in order to go far beyond what diplomats said to each other, in order to reconstruct how people's lives were actually changed by American policies. We need to include within our universe far more than we have formerly done. We need the lend-lease official in the field, the UNRRA administrators dispensing relief, the Office of War Information staff members trying to regulate information, the officials negotiating over fuel, raw materials, shipping space, dollar reserves. And we need men in uniform liberating allegedly friendly territory and occupying enemy territory.

A start has been made in many of these directions, but we need more specific information. We need case studies of particular countries, regions, even towns. When we know what the impact of American policy was in local situations we will know for the first time more than diplomacy at the summit. What happened to local politicians when Americans appeared on the scene? What happened to the economy, to education, to the images of the United States held by the people in that country? When we know this we will know enough for the first time about American diplomacy during the Second World War either to affirm the official view of American beneficence or the revisionist view of American reaction or, most probable of all, to describe the real complexity of our impact, and having done that we will be in a better position to compare our policies during the Second World War with our policies at subsequent times.

Teachers will be able to use this new material in their courses and thereby go beyond the big generalizations and the chronicle of high-level diplomatic exchange. Students would then see more clearly than they do now that wartime diplomacy was not the exclusive province of the president or even of the Department of State, that is was not monolithic, but that in its depth and variety and contradiction it was an extension of American society in all its complexity. It will then be apparent that Americans in their wartime diplomacy were seeking to create not one rigid world on a single model, either idealistic or reactionary, but many.

I would hope that such a detailed examination of how Americans were actually changing the world during the Second World War would help us escape from the rigidity both of the Great Cycle theory, still so popular in the White House, and at the same time from the equally rigid and unlearned theories of American foreign policy as unalloyed reaction.

# The Diplomacy of War and Peace

DISCUSSION

*Mitchell William Kerr, Towson State College:* My question earlier at this conference was badly misunderstood. I think most of us here would agree that personnel records certainly should not be open for general use, but I would like to make two points. First, a comment on the first page of the program we received states that we are here to give guidance and counsel and to make a few suggestions to the Archives staff about how they can help us in the teaching of and research in diplomatic history; secondly— a point that has already been made very well—archival material relating to diplomatic history is so vast by tons and multiples of tons that it is very difficult for us to use all of it. As Larry Gelfand said, it takes two lifetimes, and we give our students a semester.

Returning to the biographical issue, my question is this: there are many people in the diplomatic scene or involved in it that we, and particularly our students, know very little about. I wonder whether or not it would be useful for our students if a diplomatic biographical directory were published— one that is very extensive, that reaches down to the attaché level and to the Department of State desk level. I think, at least for me, it would be very useful. We have many, many students who do not know the difference between Harry Hopkins and Colonel House. In my reading I have heard that there is a difference.

*Lawrence E. Gelfand:* I agree that there is an urgent need for a biographical register. The closest thing to my knowledge that we have are the annual volumes of the *Biographical Register* of the Department of State, and I think what is suggested or implied by the question is that for much of the twentieth century this register is not adequate since foreign affairs were within the province of a much larger administrative organization. The problem is much greater, I think, than the questioner is suggesting. We who are working in American foreign relations really have little in the way of biographical data on a great many of the world's diplomats in the nineteenth and twentieth centuries. The only tool I know of that is quite helpful in biographical data on, for example, nineteenth-century and early twentieth-century international diplomats is the fifth volume of the *Dictionaire Diplomatique*. There is a copy at the Yale Library, and there are a few copies at research libraries across the country, but most of our university libraries do not have the fifth volume, the biographical volume, of this set. Some libraries, such as ours at the University of Iowa, have only four volumes; some libraries, I have noticed, have only two volumes of the *Dictionaire*. We need biographical registers, I think, in all areas of history, and we need more than just the skeletal data that is the kind of who's who information we find in most of the volumes of the State Department biographical registers. Perhaps some foundation, if not the federal government, would be interested in financing this. I do not see how we are going to get such a biographical compilation without massive financial support.

*Gaddis Smith:* Just to put in a negative word: I, for one, would not advocate the profession's making a large pitch for the hundreds of thousands-of dollars of financial support necessary for such an enterprise. I think there are many other priorities that are much higher. I also think we might find ourselves supervising an enormous staff of researchers, building up this biographical material, only to find that for nineteen out of twenty attachés the material was not particularly useful; this would be a great piece of leaf-raking historical research. Many people may disagree with me but that is my opinion.

*James E. Hewes, Jr., Office of the Chief of Military History, Department of the Army:* If you are referring to military service attachés, I think you ought to investigate the process by which these attachés are chosen and sent out to their various posts. If you examined current military attachés and those we have had in the past twenty-five years, you would eventually realize that most of them are a cipher as far as their influence on policy is concerned.

*William M. Franklin, Historical Office, Department of State:* If a researcher has exhausted the biographic registers the State Department has published through the years and also the *Dictionary of American Biography* and *Who's Who,* which we ourselves use all the time, there is one other way he can find out about that particular second secretary in the American service: he can write to the Historical Office at the Department of State, and we will find out who the person was for him. It has been done many times for many decades.

*Brian L. Villa, United States Military Academy:* I have a short question for Professor Smith. I believe that towards the end of your paper you suggested a willingness to concede that during the Second World War American diplomacy tended in some sense to reflect a desire to extend American society, the principles of American society, overseas, but that the views diplomats held were not monolithic. The parts of American political and economic life different people wished to extend do not coincide in fact as easily as the revisionists or the New Left tends to think. My question, then, is whether or not in some sense what is happening in World War II diplomatic studies is that we are rushing ahead before we have good, solid histories of domestic politics, with the result that a very casual view of American society in the 1940s easily adopted by the revisionist is then used to interpret American foreign policy. Perhaps the diplomacy of World War II has to wait for some better history of American society in the 1940s.

*Smith:* I will respond to your question very simply by essentially agreeing with you that the domestic history has been seriously neglected. There is a good deal of work in progress now. There have been several recent studies on the domestic background of American foreign policy during the Second World War, and some others in progress are of very high quality. I do agree with you on that point.

*Robert Beisner, American University:* I also have a question for Mr. Smith. I am sometimes skeptical about how completely major policy makers who often enunciate what you call the Great Cycle theory really believe it themselves and how much their Munich analogies and so forth are not expressed perhaps because that is what they expect the public to believe. I wondered if your own work on Mr. Acheson might have revealed some insight into the extent to which Acheson believed his own rhetoric in this connection.

*Smith:* I think that you raise a good point, that often I think policy makers and leaders use an analogy or a rhetorical device because they think it will be persuasive with the public. But then it very often happens that the most vulnerable and susceptible audience to that rhetorical device is the person who has used it. One conclusion that I am reaching in the study of Dean Acheson involves precisely Vietnam, or Indochina. The American attitude in 1949, which was a carry-over from earlier attitudes, was that French behavior in Indochina was not an undiluted good thing, that it was not in fact one of the battles against the world communism, but that it had a good deal to do with colonialism. Initially the United States criticized the French very gently, but then, partly as a payoff to get the French to agree to a more rapid rate of German economic revival and, ultimately, German rearmament, the United States began publicly to support the French. At first it used the argument—not entirely sincerely, I think—that the French were fighting just another battle in the worldwide war against communism. This argument was first propagated publicly, and then soon it appeared in the private discussions; the public line precedes the secret line.

*John A. DeNovo, University of Wisconsin:* My question bears on something Larry Gelfand said about when to terminate one's research, but I really direct it to Gaddis Smith, too, since we are both working in the 1940s. I wonder if he has found any possible solution to the problem of the mass of material. I could not agree with him more on the need to go into Office of War Information, lend-lease, and various other administrative records, but how does one do it? Even if one is engaged in only an area study on the war years, which is my current task, I see no way to avoid overlooking tons of material.

*Gelfand:* I think Gaddis's problem in the Second World War is quite different from the problem in the First World War. I might say, though, in connection with First World War research that there are collections that are still closed or collections that are being declassified—I am thinking particularly of the General Staff records for 1918 and 1919, which are just in the process of being declassified under the terms of the 1967 Freedom of Information Act. I do not know exactly what the solution is. I made a suggestion in my paper about when I think the historian must terminate his study if he is ever going to publish at all. I think it is a real problem when one has enormous quantities of sources and when one, as a historian, cannot sample the sources as a political scientist might sample his data, say for public opinion. I think those of us who are working with enormous quantities of sources must realize the problem. I sense that this problem is going to become even greater as we obtain access to documentation in the 1940s, 1950s, and 1960s; that is to say, the last three decades. I am sure that the total accumulation of sources will eventually be vastly greater than the accumulation of sources for the First World War period. Our students taking graduate degrees today will be working with this material, and we have to devise methods for dealing with this vast accumulation. I suggested that the point at which one should terminate research is when one no longer finds anything that is novel, fresh, or adds to one's knowledge of the subject or when one's hypotheses are not undergoing any change from further research. I think all of us have to face the realities of the situation. We ourselves have been trained to end research only when every bit of source material that is available has been looked at. I do not think this is any longer possible when we are dealing with twentieth-century sources or broad subjects involving these sources in this century.

*Smith:* I might just add to that that we are a resolute group of individualists. We do not take to team history, at least in the academic settings, to the degree to which Europeans or Russians do, but we may come to it. We may have to emulate, say, our colleagues in the natural sciences. In that area a professor often has a major project, and six or seven Ph.D's are connected with that project doing component parts. I personally do not look forward to that day. I am an individualist also and do not like other people doing the research I want to do myself, but this may be one of the only solutions. I really do not see any other.

*DeNovo:* I intended to make a modest proposal tomorrow afternoon, but since there is a larger audience here, I will suggest it now. I feel that those of us working in the 1940s and later need to have some kind of structured conference at which we deal in some depth with problems of this sort. I do not know yet how this should be set up; I hope other minds will be brought to bear this. It has occurred to me that maybe the Society for Historians of American Foreign Relations might do such a pilot study if it could get a foundation grant. Regardless of whether we go to team research, or to directors of graduate study—I am not sure which direction we should take—by getting together perhaps the society can lend a little guidance, and certainly society members can compare their experiences and those of their students. If the society should be successful in devising means of attacking the problem of mass for the period of the 1940s, then such a reappraisal of needs might be pushed back into previous periods.

*Hewes:* I wish only to suggest that people make use of a source that I have found very few historians have bothered to consult, and that is congressional documents, including the *Congressional Record*.

*Paolo Coletta, United States Naval Academy:* I do not mean to be snippy, but I think the answer here lies in energy, and perhaps longevity. To which I might add: how long an editor will continue to accept parts of manuscript. I had this problem sometime ago. The manuscript had been set in type, and

I asked the editor how long I could keep sending material before the printer says this is the end of it. Her answer I pass along to you: manuscripts are never completed; they are abandoned.

*David Green, Ohio State University:* I wish to address a question to Professor Smith. In your remarks categorizing historians into your Groups A, B, and C, I had the feeling that to some degree you were sort of caricaturing Group C, in that you were putting an emphasis on the reactionary approach, an undifferentiated approach. I think that in some sense it is more helpful to look at what I suppose we call New Left revisionism as concentrating not so much on the ideological thrust as on the national impact of American policy. I prefer the question of whether or not American intervention in World War II ultimately tends to promote self-determination—quite apart from considerations of whether the internal regimes are reactionary, progressive, or whatever—to the question of whether it is our purpose to promote certain types of changes. Have I made myself clear on that point?

*Smith:* Not entirely.

*Green:* Then let me amplify a bit. It seems to me that a lot of the New Left criticism concentrates not so much on the fact that the United States wanted to promote, for example, reactionary regimes, as on the fact that the United States tended, whether by design or inadvertently, simply to transcend the limits of noninterference in other people's affairs. It may have promoted reactionary policies, or it may have sometimes promoted progressive policies as well, which were nonetheless violative of the principle of self-determination. The question of self-determination for other nations might be a more important question than the question of whether when we violate the principle of self-determination we are doing it for progressive—that is, good—purposes, as opposed to reactionary—that is, bad—purposes. From my point of view we can intervene to promote a so-called progressive regime, but the fact that the regime is progressive is not necessarily going to make us less culpable in terms of the way the object nation sees us. They see us as interfering whether we are backing the so-called liberals or the so-called conservatives.

Now, in that context I want to ask you a question about the use of the diplomatic records. I had some problem last year using the decimal file for Latin America in the Second World War period, 1944. You recall we had problems dealing with the Perón regime in Argentina during the war, and it was precisely this kind of problem. Perón was seen as a neo-Fascist, so to speak, and the question arose as to whether or not we were justified in violating Argentina's self-determination in some sense, because we were, in fact, interfering so to speak on the side of the progressive forces. I came across some despatches from Ambassador Armour to the secretary of state in which Armour related certain conversations he had had with representatives of the Perón regime. After the State Department had reviewed my notes I received a little message from the department saying to delete the sections on those conversations. Now, I do not mean to embarrass the department, but I think it is a serious question that we face.

Certainly there is a paradox that I think we have to resolve in terms of how much leeway we can expect the department to give us. What I am interested in is what your position is on trying to stake out a position for us as historians on trying to make recommendations as historians to the Department of State for dealing with this kind of sensitive material in order that we can get to the basic questions of self-determination and interference in other people's affairs, and then of course to the question you raise of whether we interfere in a progressive or a reactionary way.

*Smith:* I shall respond by saying, first, that I think that some of the New Left writing on the Second World War does ignore the fact that, to use a phrase of the early 1940s, "there was a war on" and that the basic intervention was against Germany, Japan, and Italy. Clearly we are going to intervene in what are the internal affairs of an enemy-occupied country to begin with. Beyond that, I think we get tremendous variety, not a single theme whereby American policy resulted everywhere in the suppression of the left. I just do not think that is an adequate description of what happened at all.

On the other question, this is the basic question of our terms of access as historians to the official records of the government. For the period of the Second World War we now need a personal security clearance to begin with, and then our notes are reviewed. In your case, and I gather in other cases, material is deleted by direction of the department; you must abide by that because you signed an agreement to that effect. I think the only remedy to this is to speak out in every way that we can on behalf of ever more liberal policy on freedom of scholarship for material dated as close to the present as seems reasonable. I hope that someday we can get the unrestricted access period back to twenty years. Obviously, we have difficulties; we are going to have more and more difficulties as we get into the late 1940s. As Bill Franklin indicated this morning, his staff can prepare documents for publication in the *Foreign Relations* series, but this does not mean that the Historical Office will guarantee clearance and publication. I do not know what the answer is, except rational discourse with the powers-that-be in the State Department and with our political representatives.

*Geoffrey Smith, Macalester College:* I would like to ask a question that might be a good point on which to end the discussion. It does not deal directly with the previous subject, but it does touch it indirectly. My question concerns the financial administration of the National Archives: can we expect any largesse on the part of the new administration? Can we expect some consistency in the amount of funds that are given to the National Archives, or do we perhaps face a bit of a retrenchment? [*Laughter.*]

# United States Relations
# with Europe

# How Isolationist Was Nineteenth-Century American Foreign Policy?

## NORMAN A. GRAEBNER

Whether the United States pursued an isolationist foreign policy toward Europe in the nineteenth century depends upon the historian's definition of isolationism. If an active or positive foreign policy toward other nations requires alliances, military commitments, clearly enunciated preferences for some specific order of power, public disapprobation and tension, including a variety of hot and cold wars, United States relations with Europe between 1815 and 1900 were isolationist indeed. But by that definition the great powers of Europe also pursued isolationist foreign policies, for so stable was post-Napoleonic Europe that with few exceptions the major European nations were not concerned with war or preparations for war. If nineteenth-century Europe was scarcely demanding of American financial, physical, and emotional resources, it was hardly more so for the countries of Europe. That was the "British century"; still, the global commitments imposed on Britain were not exacting since that nation faced little opposition to her favored position either in Europe or in the backward and politically inert empire that she controlled. To writers and statesmen alike, the nineteenth century comprised simply the prelude to the twentieth—when peace, liberty, and justice would finally prevail.

For only one brief period in the nineteenth century, 1861 to 1866, did Europe challenge the interests of the United States in the Western Hemisphere. Perhaps even then the threat was not serious. That the United States had become an important and sometimes disturbing element in world politics seemed clear enough. Minister to Russia Cassius Clay wrote in April 1862 that it was "useless to deceive ourselves with the idea that we can isolate ourselves from European interventions. We become in spite of ourselves—the Monroe Doctrine—Washington's farewell—and all that—a part of the 'balance of power.' "[1] At the level of sentiment, much of conservative Europe distrusted the United States because of its youth, energy, and republican institutions. England threatened to become the center of Europe's diplomatic maneuvering during the American Civil War, for England was a powerful maritime rival and possessed major interests in the New World. The French government of Louis Napoleon had designs on Mexico that might be served by a divided and weakened America. Democracy was on trial, and if the American people seemed determined to destroy their great experiment, at least reactionary Europe would encourage the process so that the work of destruction might succeed. Only Russia among the major European powers found in United States power less a danger than a source of stability for maintaining the European balance.

Whatever the sentiments of Europe's statesmen, no nation of Europe had cause to challenge United States sovereignty during a time of civil conflict. Perhaps Secretary of State William H. Seward summarized well the actual status of European diplomacy toward the American Civil War when he wrote to Minister Simon Cameron in Saint Petersburg on August 13, 1862:

There is, as it seems to us, nothing new in the antagonism of European sentiment which you describe. The world sees the same feeling reveal itself anew whenever a nation or people blessed above other nations divides and delivers itself over to civil strife. . . . I cannot believe that any European state will cross the ocean to make war with us without examining the grounds of offence, calculating the results and counting the cost. Whenever any government does this, it will find powerful impulses affecting it in favor of peace and friendship with the United States.[2]

Louis Napoleon's venture into Mexico after 1862 comprised the first and only European defiance of the American interest in Latin America as defined by the Monroe Doctrine. For at least two reasons, however, United States leaders refused to permit the conflict of purpose to reach the state of crisis. First, the Lincoln administration recognized the limitations upon foreign adventures necessitated by the Civil War. Second, both Lincoln and Seward acknowledged from the outset the overcommitment of French policy and predicted accurately the eventual destruction of Napoleon's armies by Mexican guerrillas. Throughout the nineteenth century the realities of power and interest in the Atlantic world protected American preferences in the Western Hemisphere so completely that the United States was never compelled to threaten any European nation with war.

For the Founding Fathers whose words and precepts launched the young Republic on its course in world politics, isolationism was a powerful determinant. But for them isolationism was always more than a response to special geographic factors or the basis of a thoughtless preoccupation with internal concerns and self-sufficient pursuits. The United States never sought the solitude of such hermit nations as Japan and Korea; from its republican beginnings it created and maintained a commercial empire that blanketed much of the globe. American isolationism was always political and military, never commercial or intellectual. In warning the nation against involvement in European affairs, Federalists and Republicans alike reflected a realistic assessment of European power and the conviction that the country would only waste its energies if it engaged in struggles abroad which it could not control. But always, the avoidance of strife was less important than the preserving of the nation's freedom of action in evaluating and defending its own interests. By maintaining a close balance between its commitments and its power, the nation could choose, in Washington's words, "peace or war, as our interest, guided by justice, shall counsel."

If the United States during the wars of the French Revolution maintained its independence of action more successfully than did the powers of Europe, it did not do so because of differences in concept or even because of geographical insulation; rather it was because the precise political conditions of Europe in the late eighteenth century seemed to assure American security. American diplomacy could pursue a policy of isolationism without undermining the country's interests only as long as the European balance of power suited the nation's needs. As Thomas Boylston Adams wrote with remarkable perception in October 1799: "It must always happen, so long as America is an independent Republic or nation, that the balance of power in Europe will continue to be of the utmost importance to her welfare. The moment that France is victorious and Great Britain with her allies depressed, we have cause for alarm ourselves. The same thing is true when the reverse of this happens."[3] That the European balance of power permitted the United States to enjoy a full century of rapid internal expansion, free of the normal demands of international politics, does not deny that this nation's relations with Europe were continuous, generally thoughtful, and often intense.

Perhaps nothing illustrates better the extent of that transatlantic relationship throughout the nineteenth century than does the sheer volume of the diplomatic correspondence. The fact that this correspondence fills thousands of volumes in the National Archives may be less convincing than the fact that the microfilm publication entitled *Diplomatic Instructions of the Department of State, 1801 to 1906* comprises 175 rolls of microfilm. Despatches from Great Britain to 1906 comprise 200 rolls; from Spain, 134 rolls; from France, 128 rolls; from the German states and Germany, 106 rolls; from Russia, 66 rolls; from Austria-Hungary, 51 rolls; and from the Italian states and Italy, 44 rolls. This listing does not include hundreds of rolls of microfilm containing correspondence with the lesser nations of

Europe or with American consuls stationed during the century in all the major cities of Europe. What this volume of correspondence makes immediately clear is the extent to which the history of United States–European relations before 1900, in almost all of its aspects, remains to be written.

Much of this correspondence describes economic and personal questions that never surfaced as matters of major concern. National interests seldom coincide on tariffs or monetary policies; both managed to promote diplomatic exchanges well below the level of open dispute. American legations throughout Europe were involved in the customary requests for passports as well as the protection of the property and claims—no less than the security—of United States citizens against the actions of European governments and authorities. American diplomats engaged in perennial efforts to defend American shipping interests against discriminating regulations in European ports; they negotiated in behalf of American products in the European market. Both in France and in Germany in the late ninteeenth century, American officials worked hard and long to preserve a market for American pork against local accusations that pork shipped from the United States was too heavily laden with trichinae. (Indeed, so voluminous was the correspondence on this question that a student might well convert it into a thesis.)

Among the more pervasive questions of diplomacy were those involving migration, especially from Germany to the United States after 1870. So heavy was this migration that one Pomeranian landholder confided to United States Minister George Bancroft in 1873: "I have the strongest sympathies with the United States, twenty-five per cent of the inhabitants of my district of country have gone to them." German officials readily admitted the advantages in migration for those who chose to move to the United States, although they accepted the loss of population with considerable misgivings. The German government, wrote Bancroft, urged landlords to make life more comfortable and hopeful in Germany, but it made no effort to restrict emigration by law.[4] The problem which disturbed German and United States officials alike was that of preventing German migrants from obtaining United States citizenship and then returning to Germany to escape both the obligations of American citizenship and the burdens of German military duty. Even more obvious among secondary issues were the Alabama Claims controversy with England, 1871–72, and the British-American dispute over sealing in the Bering Sea during the 1890s. Even issues of this lesser magnitude produced ample quantities of correspondence.

Europe's major disturbances of the nineteenth century—its occasional wars and revolutions—scarcely touched the vital interests of the United States. They did, however, invoke the intellectual concern of the American diplomatic corps, which responded with excellent reporting and generally perceptive judgment. United States diplomats probably matched their European counterparts in the accuracy of their observations of men and events during the French revolution of 1848. Richard Rush, for example, kept the Polk administration exceedingly well informed on the developments in Paris. In one despatch Rush summarized the events of February 24: "Scarcely had my dispatch of the 24th of February been folded up, when events the most momentous quickly succeeded each other. Numerous barricades had risen up in the streets; civil war continued; the people were victorious; the palace of the Tuileries was carried; the King abdicated, and fled with all the Royal Family, and the monarchy was overthrown. All this happened in the course of the day—Thursday."[5]

Rush and his successors cataloged with remarkable perception the gradual decline of the Second French Republic and the rise of Louis Napoleon to power between 1848 and 1852. William Cabell Rives, Rush's successor in Paris, reported to Secretary of State Daniel Webster in February 1851: "While the aspect of the future is thus brightening with us, it, every day, grows more and more lowering here, as these people are approaching nearer and nearer, daily, the decisive epoch of 1852. . . . Society is tranquil on the surface, but is deeply agitated within by anxieties and uncertainties respecting the future. The breach between the President and the Assembly seems to be implacable."[6] Two years later American diplomats in London, Paris, and Saint Petersburg maintained a continuous and enlightening commentary on the Crimean War, suggesting on occasion—perhaps too optimistically—that the European war might present a proper occasion wherein the United States might compel concessions from Britain in the region of Central America and elsewhere. Perhaps their expectations were too much for a limited European war; but they, as their European counterparts, were highly conscious of national advantages that accrue from the strife of others.

Bismarck's final and successful efforts to establish the German Empire in 1871 struck a highly responsive chord among American diplomats, for the consolidation of the German states comprised perhaps the major political achievement of the century. Thereafter American officials in Berlin followed the evolution of the German constitutional system and its relationship to the Prussian role in German affairs. Following the Congress of Berlin in 1878, United States diplomats reacted favorably to the establishment of the German alliance system as a source of European stability countering the aggressiveness of Europe's two dissatisfied powers, Russia and France. At the same time, American diplomats in Europe fixed much of their attention on the Balkan question. On July 15, 1878, the American minister in Berlin reported with remarkable precision why the Congress of

Berlin had failed to assure peace in the Balkans and the eastern Mediterranean. As late as 1890 United States officials in Europe placed their hopes for a peaceful continent on the strength of the Triple Alliance that, with England, promised to render the Franco-Russian threat inoperative.

If even the most important events in Europe's nineteenth-century evolution failed to challenge the established order of power, United States diplomats made clear their preferences for liberal democracy, political stability, and property rights as the elements in international life that best represented the interests and ideals of the American people. Richard Rush, alone among the diplomats assigned to Paris, appeared before the French provisional government on February 28, 1848, to compliment that body on the triumph of republicanism in France. Several days later he explained his unusual behavior to Secretary of State James Buchanan:

In recognizing the new state of things as far as I could without your instructions, and in doing it promptly and solemnly, I had the deep conviction that I was stepping forth in aid of the great cause of order in France, and beyond France; and that I was acting in the spirit of my government and country, the interpreter of whose voice it fell upon me suddenly to become. If I erred, I must hope that the motives which swayed me, will be my shield. The Provisional Government needed all the moral support attainable, after a revolutionary hurricane that shook society to its base and left everything at first, portentous and trembling. In such an exigency, hours, moments, were important; and the United States are felt as a power in the world, under the blow that had been struck.[7]

Whatever the American interest in the success of the French Republic—and it soon proved to be negligible—the Polk administration not only lauded Rush on his notable gesture in behalf of republicanism in France but also attempted to assure the triumph of the new government by encouraging it to decentralize governmental power and to establish a bicameral legislature. Despite Rush's urging, French officials rejected the American precedent on both counts. As the French government faltered badly under pressures from right and left, Rush searched for the means whereby the United States, which hoped to avoid any direct involvement in European affairs, might still lend its support to the general march of republicanism now sweeping across Europe. On June 3, 1848, he recommended an American course of action to Buchanan:

I believe that at this most extraordinary epoch in European affairs, when the republican principle is facing the monarchical principle more closely than ever before, the presence of the United States in that sea [the Mediterranean], by a powerful, highly equipped, and highly disciplined squadron, would carry a moral weight for the Republican principle; thus attesting to the world's eye its amazing advance in the Western hemisphere in throwing, in the midst of convulsions, a precautionary shield over American interests and citizens abroad, after raising both to an enviable prosperity by equal laws and equal rights at home.[8]

Rush believed that a United States naval force, by its mere presence in European waters, would demonstrate the advantages of republicanism and thereby bolster its successes in France and elsewhere in Europe. He was still urging this action on Polk and Buchanan when he left France a year later.

United States hopes for Europe included stability as well as republicanism. This preference explained the official United States reaction to the establishment of the German Empire. Historian George Bancroft, representing the United States in Berlin, discounted the danger of German militarism and the Junker aristocracy to the peace of Europe. True, Bismarck's political and military triumphs had challenged the European balance of power, but Bancroft assured Washington that the new empire represented not further change but stability in central Europe. The German army, wrote Bancroft, merely reinforced that stability. Germany, after all, was surrounded by enemies.

If United States officials favored European stability, hopefully through governments based on the American model, they had no interest in socialistic reforms or any assaults on property rights. From the outset of the French Revolution of 1848 Rush opposed the socialist tendencies of the French radicals and their discontent with mere democratic procedures. When early in 1852 Louis Napoleon issued a decree compelling members of the Orleans family to dispose of their property in France and to remove the proceeds from the country, Rives objected strenuously to this disregard for property rights. When Napoleon carried out this decree by transferring jurisdiction from the courts to the Council of State, Rives wrote to Webster deploring the institution of a body whose members were removable at the pleasure of the president. He doubted the security of property under the new system of government.[9] Later when Bismarck dealt ruthlessly with the German socialists, the United States minister in Berlin lauded the German government for defending property rights in Germany and thereby strengthening those rights throughout the Western world.

That the United States maintained generally cordial relations with all the major nations of Europe throughout the nineteenth century seems clear from the ubiquitous examples of goodwill shown both to the American diplomatic corps and to visiting citizens of the United States. Although Americans in Paris had distrusted Louis Napoleon, Rives wrote to Secretary of State John Clayton in November 1849: "Everybody admits now that Louis Napoleon has exhibited far more ability than he had had credit for, and he seems to be gaining popularity daily. His conduct towards us is one of the best proofs of his good sense, and superiority to small things."[10] Following a trip to the Middle East, Bancroft reported to Secretary Hamilton Fish in January 1873: "It gives me pleasure to say that everywhere the name of the American nation stands among the very highest, and its greatness is acknowledged without jealousy or fear."[11] Bancroft noted the widespread expressions of goodwill toward the United States occasioned by the death of William H. Seward that year. United States relations with Germany remained remarkably cordial throughout the final decades of the century. For example, Bayard Taylor reported from Berlin on July 1, 1878: "This evening Prince Bismarck entertains General and Mrs. Grant at a dinner, to which the members of the American legation are also invited. In fact, at so disturbed and excited a period as the present, it would scarcely be possible for the imperial government to show greater and more cordial attentions."[12]

American diplomats generally appear to have thrived in Europe. Perhaps their acceptance diminished with distance; London, Paris, and Berlin facilitated adjustment to life abroad more readily than did Vienna or Saint Petersburg. The observations of Neill S. Brown on the trials of a Western diplomat in Russia during the 1850s remains a classic. Whether American representatives in Europe were men of letters or men of politics, they were often persons of distinction. Most of them served exceedingly well; their reporting was invariably above the minimum demanded of them. If they preferred life in America, they at least recognized the qualities of European life that only tradition can bestow. Rives, for example, anticipated his return to the United States in 1852 with a letter to James M. Mason commenting that "a few months more will see me on our quiet and happier, if less glittering, shores."

American diplomats, no less than many intellectuals, editors, political writers, and politicians, recognized the interrelationship of nations and understood that the affairs of the United States were not being conducted in a power vacuum. They recognized especially the importance of the balance of power principle in preserving the security of the United States and the peace of Europe. They knew that the United States had been the chief beneficiary of that system and that Europe's very stability had permitted the American people to concentrate on domestic concerns. But by the nineties, it seemed clear, complex and powerful pressures rendered the concept of geographic separation obsolete. American interests were becoming too universal, too enmeshed in the affairs of Europe, to be entrusted to the oceans alone. The equilibrium of Europe, moreover, was no longer self-contained. In a narrowly balanced continental system, the policies of such uncommitted nations as England and the United States carried the burden of future peace and security.

Unfortunately, those who viewed America's world relationships in this light could not dispel the illusions created by successive decades of actual noninvolvement in Europe's political and military affairs. The favorable balance, anchored to British power and British diplomacy, was ultimately taken for granted, and its essential contribution to American security was all but forgotten. By the 1890s Americans no longer recognized the nation's vital stake in European politics. The restoration of the continent after the Napoleonic wars created conditions of such stability that the average citizen of the United States, enjoying perennial security at relatively little cost, began to put his faith in the fact of geographic isolation itself. This gradual identification of American security with the Atlantic Ocean rather than with a body of precise political conditions in Europe, which after 1890 were subject to enormous pressures for change, created the foundations for twentieth-century American isolationism. This philosophy viewed mere abstinence from European affairs as the essence of sound policy. Whatever happened in Europe, ran the burgeoning isolationist argument, it could not challenge the historic security of the Amreican people. But such notions, whatever their popularity within the nation, reflected neither the character nor the conceptualization of evolving United States–European relations as embodied in the official record of American diplomacy in the nineteenth century.

## NOTES

1. Clay to Secretary Seward, Apr. 13, 1862, Diplomatic Despatches, Russia, General Records of the Department of State, Record Group 59, National Archives Building, Washington, D.C. This record group is hereafter cited as RG 59, NA.
2. U.S., Department of State, *Papers Relating to Foreign Affairs . . . 1862* (Washington, D.C.: Government Printing Office, 1862), p. 454.
3. Quoted in Norman Graebner, ed., *Ideas and Diplomacy: Readings in the Intellectual Tradition of American Foreign Policy* (New York: Oxford University Press, 1964), p. 79.
4. U.S., Department of State, *Papers Relating to the Foreign Relations of the United States . . . 1873* (Washington, D.C.: Government Printing Office, 1873), pp. 276–77, Bancroft to Secretary Fish, Jan. 25, 1873.
5. Rush to Secretary Buchanan, despatch no. 17, Mar. 4, 1848, Diplomatic Despatches, France, RG 59, NA.

6. Rives to Secretary Webster, Feb. 20, 1851, Diplomatic Despatches, France, RG 59, NA.
7. Rush to Secretary Buchanan, despatch no. 17, Mar. 4, 1848, Diplomatic Despatches, France, RG 59, NA.
8. Rush to Secretary Buchanan, despatch no. 34, June 3, 1848, Diplomatic Despatches, France, RG 59, NA.
9. Rives to Secretary Webster, Jan. 9 and 29, 1852, Diplomatic Despatches, France, RG 59, NA.
10. Rives to Secretary Clayton, Nov. 14, 1849, Diplomatic Despatches, France, RG 59, NA.
11. Despatch of Jan. 21, 1873, in *Papers Relating to the Foreign Relations of the United States . . . 1873*, p. 276.
12. Taylor to Secretary Evarts in U.S., Department of State, *Papers Relating to the Foreign Relations of the United States . . . 1878* (Washington, D.C.: Government Printing Office, 1878), p. 225.

# United States Relations with
# Europe in the Twentieth Century

ROBERT H. FERRELL

The relations of the United States with Europe during the twentieth century constitute the most important topic in the country's entire diplomatic history, next to the eighteenth-century struggle for independence; yet much work has still to be done before a systematic study of the topic can be achieved. How quaint it is to recall now that back in 1904, when the American Historical Association was but twenty years old, Professor Woodrow Wilson, by that time president of Princeton, gave an address at the Saint Louis Exposition in which he announced that the best topics for doctoral dissertations in American history had already been occupied by historians and that only the "high and dry" places remained. Some years later, Samuel Flagg Bemis could take Jay's Treaty as his doctoral thesis at Harvard, secure in the knowledge that when he finished the subject he could turn, without much fear of competition, to Pinckney's Treaty. Meanwhile another young Harvard student, Dexter Perkins, could take the Monroe Doctrine as the subject of his thesis. A quarter century after Wilson had spoken at the exposition, Bemis was searching the European archives on a Carnegie Corporation project to catalog and obtain copies of material relating to American diplomatic history. Two generations of historians have followed him into archival research at home and abroad, and the vein of American diplomatic history is not yet exhausted.

But, one might ask, has not the fraternity of American historians—by the present time grown to huge proportions—so divided up American history that at last Wilson's injunction has begun to hold true? A few years ago Morris Bishop informed the Modern Language Association that it would be just as well to cease research in English because the topics of importance, perhaps even of unimportance, were no longer available. Some of us perhaps at times share the feelings of Bishop as we read the little articles in the

167

proceedings of the association on such subjects as whether Swift's grand-mother was a Catholic. Has the same thing happened to American history? At the present time there are more than seventeen thousand members of the American Historical Association. All of these members have studied at least some American history. If by chance they were to set to work en masse on American history since Columbus, since 1492, there would be a historian for every ten days of American history. To be sure, many of the members of the association are uninterested in American history, or are not working in the field, but if only half of them are—a not impossible guess—then there are plenty of American historians. Have they not finished off American history, the way that Bishop's associates in the field of English have been accused of reducing that field to stubble?

The answer is a resounding no, as anyone may see who peruses the quarterly lists of books published by the Association of American University Presses, not to mention the books published by commercial presses. In recent years, books on American diplomatic history have become so numerous that it is not altogether certain if the Society for Historians of American Foreign Relations, led by the indomitable Joseph P. O'Grady, will be able to find enough diplomatic historians with enough patience to put together a huge new addition to the Bemis and Griffin *Guide to the Diplomatic History of the United States,* which appeared in 1935 and which includes titles published up to that date but bearing only on diplomatic subjects to the year 1921.[1]

New opportunities for research constantly present themselves to the historian of American diplomacy. For example, at the moment the records of the Department of State relating to Europe in the 1930s, and perhaps in earlier years of the twentieth century, are not getting the use they should. So says Patricia Dowling of the National Archives, who presides over those records and ought to know. Dowling says that researchers are fascinated with the department's records for the Far East and Latin America but are neglecting Europe, especially the countries other than Great Britain— that is, Russia, Scandinavia, Germany, France, Spain and Portugal, and eastern Europe. Records for the 1930s are voluminous compared to those for previous decades. And as *Foreign Relations of the United States* pushes past 1945, the records available for Europe are going to increase to an extraordinary, almost catastrophic (for the historian) size. Multiplying the problems of the diplomatic historian of the twentieth century were first, the typewriter and carbon paper, and then the mimeograph. All three of these "records multipliers" were working hard by the 1930s and attained break-neck speeds in the next decade. For records of the 1950s, the Xerox revolution is going to make the researcher's hours not merely longer but heavier.

It is true that a fair part of the State Department's files on Europe in the 1930s are full of reporting rather than announcements of policy or reactions to policy. They nonetheless are rich; and in the 1940s the reporting continued while policy became more important than ever before.

As for specific topics, there are clearly two kinds available concerning the policies of Europe and (for the 1940s and after) the policy of the United States. One category not chosen as frequently as it should be relates to larger topics, sweeping ideas, and interpretations that will gather the monographic work and make sense out of its footwork. An example of this kind of subject is the recently published book by Arnold A. Offner, *American Appeasement,* which brings together American policy during the early and middle 1930s, making full use of available materials in support of its interesting thesis.[2]

The second sort of subject, which is probably more to the taste of the average doctoral student and which in a way is perhaps more justifiable than the sweeping topic, is the thesis relating to an act or event of history: a microcosmic study. Most of our undergraduate students are at the moment in a state of rebellion against history because, they say, we ask them to memorize all the small points, the insignificant details. Their complaints do sometimes have justification. Still, there is much to recommend the small study, so long as it does not self-consciously become a case study and take on all the other repetitive observations of political science. The small study can have large implications, and the right kind of small study can be extraordinarily helpful to the doctoral student. The very processes of history thereby become understandable. Many such studies are possible in the archives of the Department of State relating to twentieth-century Europe. Let me list a few possible topics:

*Consular records.* These records document the trials and minor triumphs of American representatives in other than the legations and embassies. Too frequently, the diplomatic historian assumes the attitude that characterized the members of the old diplomatic service prior to (and even well after) their absorption into the new Foreign Service created by the Rogers Act. Nevertheless, the consuls served too—in several hundred posts, some of them of large importance—and their records have not had a great deal of study.

*American international finance.* The history of this part of American foreign relations has hardly been written. Herbert Feis has written a slim book about policy in the 1920s as he recalled it from his own place of authority during the 1930s.[3] The Moulton and Pasvolsky book on war debts and reparations, published in the early 1930s, was the last book on that important if complicated subject.[4] There have been no histories of the debts-reparations tangle based on the voluminous State Department records, nor of such specific plans or events as the Dawes Plan of 1924, the Young Plan of 1929, and the moratorium of 1931 and the defaulting of 1932–33. Although the lend-lease program occurred at the end of the interwar period, it was analyzed only recently by Warren F. Kimball in his book titled *The Most Unsordid Act*.[5]

*Relations between policy and administration.* There is a great need to look at the internal functioning of the State Department, not simply from the perspective of an organization groping toward an elusive efficiency, but from an awareness of what the problems of organization meant for policy. Consider, for example, a topic such as Sister Rachel West of Indiana University is now undertaking and its possibilities for poignant analysis. She is studying the working of the department at home and in the principal European missions in the years just prior to the outbreak of the world war in 1914, and she is asking why it was that the only warning received from Europe of the impending catastrophe on the continent came from Vice-Consul Frank Mallett in Budapest, and how that warning—because Mallett was afraid to spend the cable money—went by mail. The department had been reorganized in 1906 by the Lodge Act and by an executive order of President Theodore Roosevelt, and Sister Rachel is going to ask what happened from that year until the holocaust in Europe in 1914, and why, including the appointment of Secretary of State William Jennings Bryan in 1913. And there are other possibilities in administrative history. The inquiring doctoral candidate might examine the department under the unkindly ministrations of Secretary Bryan; the effect of the Rogers Act and the Moses-Linthicum Act upon the department's representation in Europe and elsewhere; the department's view of Europe in the crucial years of 1933 and after, while under the secretaryship of Cordell Hull, who always kept his office door open; or, to move back a few years, the department's view of Europe under Secretary Henry L. Stimson, who kept *his* door shut; the effect of Hull's regime on President Franklin D. Roosevelt's disregard for the department, which resulted in, or at least encouraged, the appointment to leading European posts of such bizarre individuals as William C. Bullitt; the effect of the department's administrative inefficiencies upon European policy in subsequent years; or the effect of Edward S. Stettinius, the United Nations man and effervescent organization person, upon the subtle problems of Europe in the closing days of the Second World War. Historians of the near future, when the department's records for the late 1940s and the early 1950s are opened, can consider the condition of the department under Marshall and Acheson, two men of decision and high ability, and ask whether good administration made their good policies toward Europe, or vice versa; or whether Secretary John Foster Dulles's policies toward France and other nations of Europe bore any relation to his well-known attitude toward the administration of his department—to wit, that *he* would deal with policy and someone else could deal with housekeeping. And still later in the twentieth century, some young doctoral student can analyze the effect upon European policy of the "White House State Departments" of the 1960s and, apparently, the early 1970s under "Secretaries" McGeorge Bundy, Walt W. Rostow, and Henry A. Kissinger.

*The department's legal work, in Europe and elsewhere.* This kind of topic has not attracted students, but perhaps it should. Thomas Etzold of Yale is now studying the protection afforded American citizens in Germany during the 1930s.

*The question of peace in Europe.* This topic needs attention; that is, the treaties of arbitration and conciliation and the grand effort of mostly the pre-1914 years to ensure peace. Calvin D. Davis of Duke is studying the Hague Conferences, and someone should look to the various arbitration treaties and also the Bryan conciliation treaties. An excellent article on the Taft treaties by a Canadian scholar appeared recently in the *Journal of American History.*[6] For the Bryan instruments, of which Wilson's first secretary of state was exceedingly proud, historians still cite Merle Curti's study *Bryan and World Peace,* which was not specifically on the conciliation treaties and which, moreover, was published in 1931 without benefit of the department's archives.[7]

*The Paris conference.* Lawrence E. Gelfand has stressed the opportunities for historians to examine the most important peace conference of modern times, the Paris Peace Conference of 1919, both in his publications and at the present conference.

*The conferences of the Second World War.* These are beginning to receive historical analysis; for example, Theodore A. Wilson has published *The First Summit: Roosevelt and Churchill at Placentia Bay, 1941.*[8] Carol Marion has finished a thesis on the Moscow Conference of 1943. No one is doing anything about Casablanca, for which the documents are now available. Nor has Tehran received the attention it deserves, as William M. Franklin has pointed out in a recent article in a *Festschrift* for Reginald C. McGrane.[9]

*Personalities in Europe and European affairs in the twentieth century.* This topic also needs study. Here one speaks of the ministers and ambassadors and also of the deskmen and executive officers of the department. It may be that envoys to Europe have received less attention than other envoys because, somehow, they seem to represent the department more than do the envoys to such distant places as Asia. Diplomatic historians appear to write with the feeling that an Asian envoy of the United States is akin to a viceroy or high commissioner, that his opportunities to make policy are larger than those of his European colleagues. Whatever the reasoning, the European side of American diplomacy has not received the same historical treatment: witness the lack of attention to Ambassadors Harvey, Kellogg, Dawes, Bingham, and Winant in Great Britain; or to Herrick, Mellon, Straus, and Bullitt in France; or to Schurman and Wilson in Germany—to name only the interwar and wartime ambassadors. As for the envoys of the First World War era, Ross Gregory has published an account of Walter Hines Page.[10] Attention is at last being focused on Brand Whitlock, many years after Allan Nevins edited Whitlock's journals. The American ambassador to Italy during the First World War, Thomas Nelson Page, has inspired no historical interest, despite his prominence as a literary figure; nor, for that matter, has that figure of divinity and wartime minister to The Hague, Henry Van Dyke, who, according to Wilbur J. Carr, was the only man Carr knew who could strut sitting down. The administrators in the department have likewise not received their historical due, including such individuals as Leo Pasvolsky, John Hickerson, and Freeman Matthews. It is pleasant to relate that Loy Henderson, who hoped to be present at this conference, is about to become his own historian—and a good one, we may be sure.

It remains to end this commentary on research in department records relating to the United States and Europe with some comments of a critical (I hope not hypercritical) nature about the microfilming of the department's records and what this filming means for historians in general and, for the purposes of this essay, for historians of relations with Europe. In recent years the National Archives has been microfilming its principal twentieth-century and other files in order to prevent the total destruction of those records at—quite literally—the hands of historians. The paper, especially mimeograph paper, of the twentieth century is not of high quality, and without filming the principal files would by now be in sad condition. The idea of selling prints of this film to libraries has caught on in a large way. Diplomatic records on film have been sold to colleges and universities in each of the fifty states and to many countries throughout the world. American colleges and universities are currently using special funds from the Department of Health, Education, and Welfare to purchase the microfilm and to build library resources, which has resulted in a sharp increase in sales. More microfilm is being planned as a result of the Department of State's decision to move the open period forward to the end of 1941, which makes the records of the 1930s available for filming.

What has happened, and what may still happen, because of this microfilm publication program? During the first quarter of 1969 (January–March) the National Archives sold 28,700 rolls of microfilm, and a reliable estimate is that at least a quarter of this film—approximately seventy-two hundred rolls—was related to diplomatic affairs. Average this film at four dollars a roll: that is a cost of about twenty-eight thousand dollars, and only for the first three months of the year. More and more of the scarce library budget money seems to be going into film—or, at least, more and more government money. It is becoming clear that many of the new universities that are inclined to offer the doctorate are stocking up on this film. Other universities are buying film instead of recently published books, and they eventually will have to buy those books at the Johnson Reprint Corporation's prime rate of twenty-five dollars a volume. It is, frankly, a ridiculous situation, and getting more ridiculous.

I end my remarks with a plea that the money used by libraries to purchase diplomatic film—money that this year will run well over one hundred thousand dollars—should be taken away and put into some other fund, whereby researchers in American colleges and universities wishing to study the Department of State's relations with Europe in the twentieth century may have all their expenses paid to Washington and enjoy as well the hospitality of the Manuscript Division of the Library of Congress.

## NOTES

1. Samuel Flagg Bemis and Grace Gardner Griffin, *Guide to the Diplomatic History of the United States, 1775–1921* (Washington, D.C.: Government Printing Office, 1935).
2. Arnold A. Offner, *American Appeasement: United States Foreign Policy and Germany, 1933–1938* (Cambridge: Harvard University Press, Belknap Press, 1969).
3. Herbert Feis, *The Diplomacy of the Dollar: First Era, 1919–1932* (Baltimore: Johns Hopkins Press, 1950).
4. Harold G. Moulton and Leo Pasvolsky, *War Debts and World Prosperity* (New York: Century Co., 1932).
5. Warren F. Kimball, *The Most Unsordid Act: Lend-Lease, 1939–1941* (Baltimore: Johns Hopkins Press, 1969).
6. John P. Campbell, "Taft, Roosevelt, and the Arbitration Treaties of 1911," *Journal of American History* 53 (1966–67): 279–98.
7. Merle E. Curti, *Bryan and World Peace* (Northampton, Mass.: Department of History, Smith College, 1931).
8. Theodore A. Wilson, *The First Summit: Roosevelt and Churchill at Placentia Bay, 1941* (Boston: Houghton Mifflin Co., 1969).
9. William M. Franklin, "Yalta Viewed from Tehran," in Daniel R. Beaver, ed., *Some Pathways in Twentieth-Century History* (Detroit: Wayne State University Press, 1969).
10. Ross Gregory, *Walter Hines Page: Ambassador to the Court of St. James's* (Lexington: University Press of Kentucky, 1970).

# United States Relations with Europe

## DISCUSSION

*William L. Neumann, Goucher College:* Robert Ferrell's third point raises a question I think someone might very profitably pursue. I would like to have some sort of graphic picture of the apportioning of Foreign Service personnel by areas in the nineteenth and twentieth centuries and something similar on the desk officers in the Department of State. I remember once looking into the matter in considering the relationship between the Far East and Europe. A rather interesting shift took place in the twenties and thirties; that is, in the percentage of personnel of the department assigned to these two regions. I think it might have some relevance, to use the word, to the interests of the department and where they thought things were getting hotter and where they were cooling off and how they moved people around. It would not be a very difficult thing to do. It could probably be computerized in some way.

*Robert H. Ferrell:* There is a very interesting section in Henry Villard's memoirs. Do you mean when the department first put people into places, questions like that?

*Neumann:* I mean what percentages of personnel change as one embassy expands or one region expands and another contracts. For example, there was a great expansion of desk officers in the Far Eastern Division in the twenties and somewhat of a shrinking in some other areas.

*Ferrell:* Or the killing of the East European Division.

*Neumann:* Yes. That sort of thing. The renaming of divisions in the department is an interesting topic.

174

*John Davidson, Princeton University:* In regard to Professor Ferrell's reference to Woodrow Wilson, I might add, I suspect that Woodrow Wilson at that time was trying to discourage graduate students rather than to encourage them. He did not really care much for directing graduate students, so perhaps this was his way of discouraging them.

While on the subject of dissertations, I might give some advice about how this problem of at least master's theses was solved by one institution, a teachers' college, years ago. A student from a rural county wrote a master's thesis entitled "The Duties of a Janitor in Wintertime." A year or two later a friend of that same student, from the same county, wrote a companion study. Guess what it was? "The Duties of the Janitor in Summertime." Perhaps if professors who are seeking dissertation topics adopted a policy like this they would find topics easier to get. [*Laughter.*]

*Henry Graff, Columbia University:* As Bob Ferrell read off the list of biographical subjects, I wondered, in light of his reference to the proceedings of the Modern Language Association, whether some of those diplomats whose names he listed would not then make for us in the historical profession an analogue of the list of second-rate poets that the MLA deals with extensively? I wondered whether we will not get into even deeper trouble as a result of working on those biographies.

A second point is how do we know, since we do not have the *Writings on American History* for the last ten years, that these subjects have not already been done?

*Ferrell:* We do have the lists of dissertations, and they are fairly well up to date now. And while a little detective work is necessary to ascertain the people who are not doing theses but who intend to publish somewhere and presumably have degrees, I think one can track down that information. It is always possible, of course, to trace who has been to the Archives—one can ask Pat Dowling who came into her place of business. If no one has consulted the Archives on a specific topic that requires archival research, that fact tends to certify that nothing is being done, I think.

*Graff:* What I really had in mind was that we are more and more depending on a kind of word-of-mouth tradition such as asking an archivist whether anybody has been in recently to look at the papers of, for example, Brand Whitlock and many of the ambassadors particularly. (I think it has always been that way.) Of course I was making light of the persons you mentioned, many of whom were our ambassadors who served for very brief periods. For example, no one has yet done Robert Wagner in Spain. [*Laughter.*]

*Ferrell:* That's for you, Henry.

*Graff:* It occurred to me that possibly articles have been written about some of these people. This is what I am saying. I had a student recently who worked on Frederick Bancroft's brother, the United States ambassador to Japan for a brief period in Coolidge's administration. One sets a student working on such a subject and discovers that the person is as uninteresting as one had feared and that he said almost nothing. There are papers and M.A. theses that get published in journals that we do not regularly read or come upon. I fear that a great deal of diplomatic history is being done, and it is possibly even being done out of this building, that we are not having access to. I am therefore raising the point that this body and others once again press for readier access to the *Writings of American History,* which for a decade now has been languishing in libraries which are more and more difficult to find.

*Norman Graebner:* Actually, Henry, I cannot reply to your comment any better than anyone else in this room can because the problems you have mentioned are universal; we are all aware of them. I can say only that some writing contains insight and some does not. One simply has to make a choice. One can start writing on somebody who turns out to be dull, and there is no intellectual challenge in it at all. If that is true, that is true. One can make a master's thesis out of it and then let it go. It may be that somebody else is studying a superficially even less important person who turns out to be extremely thoughtful. His writings might contain many interesting insights and much information, and they might turn out to be extremely important. All I can say is that one just has to pursue the material as best he can and hope for the best. There is no sure way to tell in advance who is going to be bright and who is not, who is going to have something to say and who is not.

I therefore think that one cannot say a person at one level of the diplomatic corps is rather unimportant and someone at a higher level is necessarily important. Many at the top have had nothing to say, as you know.

*Harold Langley, Catholic University:* I would like to reply to Professor Graff's comment and also perhaps indirectly to some of the comments of the other speakers.

In regard to the availability of this information, I might point out that even when the *Writings of American History* did exist, from time to time Foreign Service officers in the twenties and thirties did see fit to record histories of the posts to which they were assigned. These histories appeared in the *Foreign Service Journal,* but since this journal was a monthly periodical, it was not among those items selected for inclusion in the *Writings.* A publication that appeared frequently was not included in the *Writings* because of the sheer volume.

From time to time there have also been studies done on consular posts in various parts of the world as master's topics, and sometimes beyond. The difficulty with a great many of these studies as far as publication is concerned is that they are too lengthy to be easily reduced into an article, and they are too arcane and perhaps of too minute a focus to be of interest to the normal university outlet.

But one of the difficulties, with all of these discussions, it seems to me, is that there does not seem to be any publishers' representatives around to hear all these calls for additional research and publication.

*Richard W. Leopold, Northwestern University:* I am in a pessimistic mood these days; I think many of us around universities are. As I listen to the calls for additional work on this subject or that, my concern is where the hewers are coming from—I am talking primarily of doctoral-level work now.

I do not know how you feel about this, but I fear the linguistic abilities of our graduate students are declining rapidly to an almost vanishing point. I think the interest in diplomatic history among the current group of graduate students is diminishing. In many of our universities our standards of what we expect of our doctoral candidates are declining. From my own experience and the experiences of some of my friends, I think that some of the students today are avoiding our field because they regard it as the most difficult.

Now I would like to ask of Bob Ferrell or Norman Graebner or anybody else who feels either in agreement with me or in violent disagreement is, if we do have a limited number of doctoral candidates or a limited number of first-rate doctoral candidates, what are the subjects we want to encourage them to work on. I think we have to cut down our list of possibilities. What should be our priorities for someone who feels that there are still important things to be said about isolationism in the nineteenth century or problems of the twentieth century?

Now maybe my pessimism is not shared, but I am really alarmed at the tendencies in our graduate schools and the feeling that a student can write on any number of subjects without doing the sort of work that we have traditionally required of our own graduate students and, certainly in this group, that we have traditionally required of ourselves.

*Graebner:* No two of us agree on what we regard to be important. I am concerned with insight, just what kinds of studies help one better understand the nature, the quality of American foreign relations. And I think we look in different places for that insight.

Now, I spoke today about nineteenth-century diplomatic history. I have an interest in it, but that does not mean that I know a great deal about it. But I do know that some good work has been done in that field. I know a lot has not been done. I am interested in it, and for that reason I had our library buy the whole set of the microfilm I read out to you today, 750 reels. (If anyone wants to use it, he should visit Charlottesville; it is right there.)

I intend to put at least some of my students who are inclined that way onto the subject of United States–German relations. Much of the United States–British relations have already been done well by Brad Perkins, and I suspect he is going to do some more. But I think the topic of United States–German relations is wide open.

Blumenthal's book on United States–French relations deals with part of the subject, but not all. And there is the whole question of American thought—again, I am concerned with the quality of the thought. I think there is a lot of extremely good thought coming out of this kind of diplomatic correspondence in the nineteenth century. In other words, I am looking for the thing that transcends the immediate. A good idea is a good idea. I do not know where one finds it or where one applies it. But the diplomatic correspondence of the nineteenth century is replete with very shrewd observations of what foreign affairs is all about.

Therefore, to the extent that my students care to go through the nineteenth-century diplomatic correspondence and look for this material I say the more power to them. And they will come up with something. They are not going to search everything, that is certain, but the volume is there, and most of it has been untouched. And I think that after it has been done people will say that maybe this was isolationism in a certain sense. But, after all, I try to make it clear that one cannot define that term. Are relations today with Panama isolationist or not? We are not going to war. How does one define that? We had relations with Europe, plenty of them. I therefore do not regard that as isolationist, necessarily. There is a lot of thought in this material that is worth ferreting out.

*Ferrell:* I would like to say just a word. I am not as pessimistic as Dick Leopold; I agree with Norman Graebner. I had an experience with the

Turner Prize contest of the Organization of American Historians last year. I am no longer on the committee, so I guess I can say this. We had fifty-five manuscripts, and it usually worked out that one in seven or eight was good. But the good ones, I think, are better than I remember the manuscripts of twenty years ago.

Diplomatic history seems to be a favorite. I think that of the six we took, three were in diplomatic, and the three that we took had that remarkable quality which, if I may say so, I think Barbara Tuchman told us about at the New York meeting two or three years ago. If I recall correctly it is what she describes as the ability to control materials. A marvelous sense of control, and this is encouraging.

Now, sure, there is a lot of poor material still coming out, and I do not like the spreading of the Ph.D. As you know, the number is almost double from the tradition of about 60 institutions granting the degree up to about 120 now. This is one of the stupidities of our age. And the quicker that is rolled back, the better. But our learned societies are too timid to do anything about the situation. I do not mean to make a speech about this. Despite this discouraging quality of the present scene, I think the best of the research in our field is much better than what was done twenty years ago.

*S. Everett Gleason, Department of State:* I was particularly struck with one suggestion of the study of individual diplomats, the suggestion of looking into the careers of Freeman Matthews and Jack Hickerson in the European Division, particularly, I think, from the point of view of the tension between two very experienced and dedicated Foreign Service officers and the White House in the Roosevelt years. Some of the tension is apparent in the formal memorandums, many of which, of course, we publish in *Foreign Relations*. But I think to get at the heart of it one would have to see and talk to these people before they have forgotten all of the tension. The same proposition, of course, would apply also to Loy Henderson, but happily he will be doing something about it himself.

*Stuart Bernath, California State College at Long Beach:* I think we are all quite pleased that we do have microfilm available for purchase and in some of the major universities around the country. But I think there are many colleges, small colleges generally, that do not have the funds necessary to acquire the microfilm materials that we do have. I wonder how feasible it might be to have these things available from the National Archives on an interlibrary loan basis?

*Albert H. Leisinger, Jr., National Archives and Records Service:* I wonder how many of you are aware of the fact that the Archives for the last few years has been trying to finance the placing of each set of our microfilm in the regional archives branches throughout the country. This would give us a million rolls scattered in ten archives branches. This is one of the ways we think that this enormous mass of film can be made more readily available to scholars. We know that as the size of the mass grows it is virtually impossible for any one university to collect all we have published.

Professor Ferrell proposed using the proceeds from microfilm sales that are now used to prepare other film to finance the trip of graduate students to Washington. The only trouble with this, Professor Ferrell, is that I am afraid the number of graduate students who would come to Washington would in effect result in a continual drop in scholarly production, for example, in nineteenth-century history.

I do think, though, that one of your ideas is very fine, and that is the idea of getting funds together to hold seminars here in Washington. A group working in the field of diplomatic history could be brought to Washington for about a week to spend some time at the State Department, the National Archives, and the Library of Congress. I think this would give them an excellent feel, and then they could return home and work with the microfilm and the documents published in *Foreign Relations.*

I want to conclude with a story about an incident that occurred quite a few years ago. A prominent scholar from Minnesota was working here at the National Archives on United States relations with China and other Far Eastern countries. I met him after he had been here for two months, and he was using all the original materials. I said to him, "By the way, I don't mean to be personal, but how much have you spent thus far on your visit to Washington?" He replied, "About fifteen hundred dollars." I said, "Did you know that for the sum of $1,000 your university could have purchased film copies of everything you have used?" He was furious. No one had told him about this. He went back, and a year and a half later we got a whopping order for film. That is the moral of my story.

*G. Bernard Noble, former Director, Historical Office, Department of State:* I would like to say how I appreciate the work that the National Archives has done in promoting the discussion not merely of the Archives but of these new approaches to history. The discussion has been very profitable. And you probably know that Mr. Ferrell has a textbook on foreign policy and that he is revising it. I suppose we can look forward to some of these new methods appearing in that revision. [*Laughter.*] Dick Leopold I know is being pressed also to revise his, and I am sure we can look forward to the new edition. And particularly there will probably be no further revisions of Samuel Bemis's valuable text, which some have indicated had some gaps in it from the point of view of what we have been discussing. And so it will be a competition, I suppose, as to who will fill that gap.

As to subject matter, as we know there has been a great deal written in the past few years about the cold war. And I would like to ask Mr. Ferrell and also Professor Graebner how profitable they think that subject is for theses and what profit there can be in promoting studies in that field, particularly on the cold war.

*Graebner:* The cold war is extremely important and extremely complex. The literature on it is becoming so huge now that one can hardly follow it any longer. And nobody seems to agree with anybody else. That fact makes the subject very difficult. I did a long bibliographical essay on it for the *Journal of Conflict Resolution* this spring and went through some twenty-five books on the origins of the cold war, and it is hard to tell just exactly what happened. But I think the real difficulty now is that we cannot get at all the sources. We still write on the topic—and I am guilty of that, too—but one has to do it, of course, realizing that whatever one does has got to be very imperfect.

We talked this morning about opening the files from 1945 to 1950; as long as they are not open, it just may be that we are not getting any good answers yet. On the other hand, it may be that we are doing rather well. One can always overemphasize the importance of getting these last bits of facts, because as they are being exposed on the World War II period, they are not introducing so much that is so different from what we knew earlier. Certainly we get a certain amount of detail, but it does not make that much difference, and maybe it is that we are not doing as badly with the cold war as I sometimes think we are. But I think it is a subject of tremendous importance, and I would encourage people to study it. My only feeling is I think we have got to wait a few years until some of those archives are opened for the period since 1945.

*Robert Wolfe, National Archives and Records Service:* This series of conferences has as one of its major purposes getting your advice to us. Assuming that the lack of dissent or lack of comment might imply assent, I wonder if you are really suggesting to the National Archives or giving the National Archives the advice that we ought to stop selling you microfilm. Now of course, this would not include my own bailiwick of the captured records. We do not have the original records—they are in Europe—so mine would be sold and disseminated anyway. But unless I hear a great deal of comment otherwise, I have to assume that you really want us to continue to at least sell the microfilm we have already made. We would like you to write us if you think otherwise.

# United States Relations
# with Latin America

# The National Archives and United States–Latin American Relations in the Nineteenth Century: Resources and Problems

DAVID M. PLETCHER

The research field of United States–Latin American relations is one in which the resources of the National Archives assume unusually great importance for the scholar. This is true for a number of reasons. First, it is a relatively undeveloped field, at least compared to that of United States–European relations. Second, with a few exceptions, Latin American scholars have paid little attention to the field, leaving us in the United States to tell their side of the story as well as our own. Third and most important, Latin American diplomatic archives are generally unreliable as sources of research materials, uncertain of access by United States scholars, and often incomplete or partly disorganized. More than one Latin American scholar has turned to the National Archives and Records Service as his principal source of information on United States–Latin American relations.

In examining the first part of this research field, I shall define the nineteenth century as extending to the first reorganization of the State Department records in 1906. I am most familiar with materials on United States–Mexican relations through my own research activity, but I shall try to distribute illustrations throughout the hemisphere with the aid of John P. Harrison's indispensable *Guide to Materials on Latin America in the National Archives*.[1] I shall first survey briefly the types of National Archives materials which I have found most useful. Then I shall mention a few outside archival and other manuscript materials which ought to be consulted along with those stored in the National Archives. I shall suggest topics on which I feel that the National Archives can make significant contributions.

Obviously the largest and most immediately important body of material on United States–Latin American relations is the mass of diplomatic and consular correspondence which passed between the State Department and its officers in the field. This correspondence is valuable for scholarship in two ways. First, it shows American government policy in most questions that arose, how this policy was carried out, and—in a much vaguer, less satisfactory manner—how it was formed. Second, the correspondence presents a great deal of narrative, descriptive, and sometimes analytical material about conditions in Latin America. The correspondence in the first category, that pertaining to American policy, is mostly available in published form. From Latin American independence to 1860 it appears in two comprehensive series edited by William R. Manning.[2] After 1860 some of it is included in the annual volumes of *Foreign Relations of the United States*.[3] Manning's volumes are well edited and seldom omit really significant despatches; but, as anyone who has used the nineteenth-century volumes of *Foreign Relations* knows, they are a grab-bag full of trivia along with some but not all of the major documents.

Although these volumes provide the scholar with an initial core of usable material, he must eventually come to the National Archives. For eyewitness reports on Latin American conditions by American diplomats it is usually necessary to start at the Archives, for Manning carefully weeded most of these out of his series, and the early volumes of *Foreign Relations* include only enough to be tantalizing. To be sure, in addition to *Foreign Relations,* a companion set, *Commercial Relations of the United States,* furnishes reports on economic conditions; in 1880 the government also began to publish the *Consular Reports of the United States*. Neither of these economic series, however, includes more than part of the manuscript consular correspondence in the National Archives.

The quantity and quality of these eyewitness reports vary greatly, for the American government usually sent out diplomatic amateurs. If they proved to be keen observers with a flair for pithy writing, this was due to an earlier career, most often journalism. The best American reports are full of valuable material. For example, Joel Poinsett's initial observations on Mexico attracted so much attention that they soon appeared in book form,[4] and his later account of his running feud with the British minister gave a very colorful picture of Mexican politics in the 1820s. A similarly acute observer of about fifty years later—and a much better diplomat—was John W. Foster, an experienced journalist. Between Poinsett and Foster and toward the end of the century passed a succession of ministerial observers—good, bad, and indifferent—and a few special missions, such as that of William M. Churchwell, who reported at length on Mexican conditions during the War of Reform.

Meanwhile consuls were providing economic data, sometimes plentiful but seldom well coordinated. Thus it is possible to trace the economic development of some parts of Mexico individually, but it is usually difficult to make comparisons between one consular district and another on the basis of State Department documents alone. Once in a while Washington did call for parallel reports. For example, in 1869 and 1870 nearly all consuls in Mexico returned long accounts answering specific questions. Taken together, these provide a valuable panorama of economic and social conditions in Mexico just after the French intervention and before the inrush of American capital.

Diplomatic and consular observations on the Caribbean islands and Central America are less consistent than those on Mexico. Generally speaking, the richest materials appear in correspondence from Havana, Panama, and Nicaragua, in about that order, because of American territorial and economic ambitions for Cuba and American interest in isthmian transit problems. For South America the quantity of reporting is somewhat smaller because of the lesser American interest and the smaller diplomatic and consular corps sent there. Some of the best reporting comes from the years during and immediately after Latin American independence, such as the special missions of Poinsett in southern South America or Baptis Irvine in Venezuela and the regular consular tour of William Tudor in Peru. Lacking the focus of the independence movement, later ministers and consuls all too often slumped into routine or colored their reports to suit their business interests or the political goals of their closest friends in the host government.

Before leaving State Department materials I should mention two types of documents that can be of special value for quite different reasons. One is the Reports of Bureau Officers, containing memorandums and summaries of despatches which were used in the process of deciding policy. These memorandums are not nearly so plentiful as we should like—the British do this sort of thing better—but when some methodical soul such as Alvey A. Adee was on hand to pull the facts together, he occasionally produced a revealing analysis of official thinking to bridge the gap between incoming despatches and outgoing instructions.

The other special type of material is documents on claims. The largest collections of these were gathered for special commissions such as the one between the United States and Mexico in the early 1840s or under a special convention such as that of 1868 between the same countries. Sizeable collections of claims documents exist for Mexico, Brazil, Chile, Colombia, Venezuela, and Spain, and smaller amounts exist for several other countries. In themselves the great majority of claims cases now seem insignificant, of course, but the supporting documents provide invaluable facts—often the only ones available—about nineteenth-century American residents and economic interests in Latin America.

Other executive departments of the United States government offer less grist for the Latin Americanist than the State Department. War Department files contain many valuable series on activities along the Texas-Mexican border and on the Mexican War, but until the Cuban occupation of 1898 to 1902 the United States Army stayed pretty much out of other Latin American countries. The Navy Department, however, is quite another story; Latin America has a long coastline, and much of its early economic activity was concentrated in its seaports. This means that the nineteenth-century files of reports from captains, squadron commanders, and officers commanding special expeditions are full of political, economic and quasi-diplomatic materials, to say nothing of logbooks and private journals or letterbooks. All of these categories are well represented in the National Archives. Most naval activity in the early part of the period was concentrated in the Caribbean, but beginning in the 1840s the Pacific became a focus of activity, and in the 1850s the steamer *Water Witch* even explored the Paraná system, yielding reports on interior areas of Argentina, Brazil, and Paraguay.

Occasionally naval officers doubled as diplomats—for example, Commo. Robert F. Stockton during the last phases of Texan annexation and many ship captains in South American waters during the independence period. Like most of the State Department officials, these naval officers were amateurs in foreign affairs, and sometimes their reports gained in color for the lack of diplomatic restraint. For example, Capt. Charles Stewart called San Martín and Lord Cochrane "two of the greatest rogues existing," and the commander of the *Water Witch* characterized Brazil as "that *miserable* worse than contemptible government. . . . grasping and *worse* than Chinese in her exclusive policy."[5]

It would not be enough to summarize National Archives resources on nineteenth-century Latin America without giving some indication of collateral, outside materials that can be used with them. Obviously one type of outside resource is the manuscript collections of the Library of Congress and other archives throughout the country. While presidential papers and those of the various secretaries of state occasionally contain Latin American materials, I have special reference to the private papers of ministers, consuls, and naval officers who spent part of their careers in or around the area. Many of these men combined diplomacy and business. No one dealing with the Tehuantepec isthmian question can ignore the papers of Commo. (later Adm.) Robert W. Shufeldt, who also represented the United States in Cuba during a brief but significant period. As recent research has shown, the papers of William L. Scruggs provide significant background for the Venezuelan crisis of 1895. The correspondence of such men as Joseph W.

Fabens, Chauncey F. Black, and D. R. Keim assist—or complicate—our understanding of the Dominican question of the 1860s and 1870s. The diplomat-promoter Edward Lee Plumb left official reports in the State Department archives dealing with Mexico and Cuba during the late 1860s. But his private papers contain closely related correspondence on business ventures both before and after his official tours of duty, along with evidence of his work in Washington as lobbyist for the Juárez government during the French intervention. The Plumb papers are divided between the Library of Congress and Stanford University, with an outgoing letter draft sometimes in one place and the incoming reply in the other.

One particularly valuable source of descriptions and analyses concerning Latin American conditions is to be found in European diplomatic despatches, especially those of the British Foreign Office. Often when the American minister or consul was unobservant, the British despatches furnish a better picture of American interests and actions than those received in Washington. Usually the American and British diplomats were working at cross-purposes, but if one makes proper allowances for bias and exaggeration, the American and British accounts can provide a kind of stereoscopic view over a Latin American situation or series of events. This is true to a lesser degree of French, Spanish, and even Prussian reports. For example, the British and Spanish accounts of Mexico City before and during the Mexican War go far to clarify Mexican thoughts and actions which greatly puzzled the American agents.

The existence of these European diplomatic records may help to resolve a dilemma which confronts many researchers in United States–Latin American relations. It is becoming increasingly difficult to publish a monograph on American foreign relations based on United States materials alone. Some specialized journals such as the *Hispanic American Historical Review* are reluctant to accept articles on United States–Latin American relations derived from such unilateral sources. This fact means that after the researcher has exhausted American resources, he must try to obtain access to the archives of the Latin American country or countries in which he is interested. But all too often these records are in a state of disarray or perhaps closed entirely to research. In this case the correspondence of a British or French minister may be a godsend, adding a new dimension to the American materials and rescuing an otherwise worthy monograph from overdependence on a single point of view or source of information.

What is to be done with the researcher's mass of facts and opinions? What topics on United States–Latin American relations of the nineteenth century need study? The answer is bound to be encyclopedic, for the field is relatively undeveloped. What can the National Archives contribute to such a study? One can hardly imagine a topic in the field for which its resources will not be useful. The following survey makes no pretense of completeness; it is intended to be suggestive rather than exhaustive.

The most obvious form of writing on United States–Latin American relations is the monograph on bilateral relations with a single country; yet with a few exceptions this form is low on the priority list. For some major countries, such as Argentina, we have recent adequate surveys. We do badly need an up-to-date study of United States–Mexican relations from Mexican independence to the present. Even though a short account by Lester D. Langley has recently been published,[6] a one-volume work on United States–Cuban relations would be helpful. Although a much-acclaimed monograph of Fredrick B. Pike on United States—Chilean relations presents an enlightening picture of Chilean politics and hemispheric *Anschauung*,[7] there is still room for a study of United States–Chilean diplomatic and economic relations drawing more deeply from American sources. When one goes beyond these countries, however, the need for comprehensive bilateral studies falls off sharply. Either scholarly studies exist, at least for the nineteenth century, or the relations of the United States with the country in question have been fragmentary and devoted to petty quarrels, without any discernible overarching trends to hold them together. I see little point in monographs on United States relations with Ecuador, Paraguay, or individual nations of Central America.

If I were to seek a model for studies of United States–Latin American relations, I should turn to that great collaborative project of the 1930s and 1940s, *The Relations of Canada and the United States,* edited by James T. Shotwell and published by the Yale University Press. I have sometimes wondered why someone did not start up a counterpart series for Latin America. The time may now be past for such a mammoth unified undertaking, but anyone scanning the list of titles in the Shotwell series must be struck by the ease with which many of them could be rephrased to embrace some phase of United States–Latin American relations.

Let me indicate a few large-scale topics which the Shotwell series has suggested to me. Rather than studying bilateral relations between the United States and a Latin American country, why not deal comprehensively with a geographic area, such as the Plata Basin? To be sure, British influences were paramount here during most of the nineteenth century, but those of the United States were not always negligible. The same is true for the countries of the west coast of South America, especially after the early 1880s. Perhaps we already have adequate studies of United States diplomacy and the War of the Pacific, but the period after that war is little studied, especially for Peru, Bolivia, and Ecuador. In each case the study should cross national lines, dealing with a geographic area, rather than with a single Latin American government. It should fuse diplomacy, politics, economics, and the kind of Latin American *Anschauung* described by Pike for Chile. Such studies might also discuss the role of the United States in maintaining or disturbing the regional balance of power, perhaps using ideas from Robert N. Burr's recent monograph on Chile and the Pacific balance.[8]

It is not necessary, of course, to organize international topics by limited geographic areas. We still need a comprehensive analysis of the origins and early years of the Pan-American movement. Outside the formal Pan-American system, the resources of the National Archives can contribute much to surveys of the United States role as mediator of boundary and other quarrels in Latin America. Such surveys should not be confined to the legal cases and bases of judgment but should also include the political repercussions in Latin America and the role of interest groups, if any, in the United States.

In studying United States foreign policy of the nineteenth century we have all too often neglected the agents who sometimes inspired and usually had to carry out that policy—the ministers, chargés, and consuls. Casually appointed for political services, they often had little preparation for their role and were more inclined to use plain speaking than diplomatic protocol in dealing with the host government or the better-trained European rivals. We need at least one volume presenting a cross section of these American diplomatic careers in Latin America all the way from the aforementioned John W. Foster, who worked long and skillfully to smooth out a war crisis with Mexico, to James Watson Webb, minister to Brazil in the 1860s, who left behind him a trail of misunderstandings, petty quarrels, and chicanery. Many of these careers are suitable for vignettes, diverting in themselves. A collection of them would also serve the useful purposes of demonstrating American diplomatic techniques before the era of quick communications with Washington and of testing the Jacksonian proposition that common sense was often more valuable than expertise in carrying out the business of a simple, God-fearing republic.

The field of economic relations between the United States and Latin America provides varied topics for articles or books of almost any size. A good example is the movement for reciprocal trade and the counterpull of economic nationalism toward protective tariffs, both in the United States and in Latin America. The whole problem is developed with profuse examples in the reports of a commission that President Arthur sent around Latin America in the mid-1880s. These reports, most of them published soon after they were submitted, led directly to some of the questions discussed at the Pan-American Conference of 1889–90, but a survey of consular reports for twenty or thirty years before that ought to show that the dilemma of hemispheric trade was a chronic problem of the nineteenth century.

In addition to trade, we need books on the most important industries for which the United States furnished capital, technology, and markets. An obvious example would be silver mining in Mexico, whose study has been opened up but not exhausted by Marvin D. Bernstein.[9] Perhaps even more difficult and provocative would be an examination of the United States relationship to the sugar industry of the Caribbean area—an economic force which increasingly shaped United States policies in northern Latin America during the late nineteenth century as well as the internal development of a half-dozen Latin American countries. The spread of American machinery and business techniques to Latin America should provide many case studies: farm implements, commercial law, and various types of insurance, to name a few examples.

Not only economic but also social topics in United States–Latin American relations might be developed with the aid of National Archives materials. During the nineteenth century there was no "mingling of peoples" as is described in one volume of the Shotwell series on United States relations with Canada. The great Mexican, Cuban, and Puerto Rican migrations to the United States came in the twentieth century. But the composition, attitudes, and activities of American "colonies" in Latin America would reward study. Some of these were isolated settlements such as the Mormons in northern Mexico or the Confederates in Brazil. It seems to me, however, that the merchants, artisans, and other Americans who lived in Mexico City, Havana, and the principal Central and South American capitals are more significant, for they contributed more directly to the national economies, while furnishing Latin Americans with living, breathing examples of the otherwise faraway Yanqui.

Related to the study of United States residents in Latin America is the whole problem of Latin American reactions to the United States. Latin American historians themselves should take the lead in this field, but until they do, we must fill the gap as best we can—and it is an enormous gap. In my own study of the Mexican War I have been impressed with the complex "love-hate" relationship which seemed to be developing between mid-nineteenth-century Mexicans and the United States. Charles A. Hale has briefly analyzed and explained this phenomenon in his recent monograph on Mexican liberalism;[10] it will reward further examination. One of the most fascinating subjects for such a study ought to be Argentina, which became a focus for Yankeephobia in the early twentieth century, although its formal diplomatic contact with the United States had been slight. Thomas F. McGann has opened up this subject with his analysis of the Argentine ruling class and its relationship to the early Pan-American movement.[11] Works such as those of Hale and McGann and that of Pike on Chile ought to attract others to a subject as pervasive as fog and just about as difficult to pin down.

Another topic of broad scope which overlaps many mentioned so far is the triangular nature of United States relations with Latin America in the nineteenth century. For the Shotwell series on Canada J. B. Brebner wrote a general diplomatic survey entitled *The North Atlantic Triangle,* which presented the now axiomatic thesis that United States–Canadian relations cannot be understood apart from Anglo-American relations and relations within the British Empire. I would submit that the same thesis should be applied to United States–Latin American relations of the same period. Any study of United States activities in the Plata area or on the Pacific coast makes it clear that wherever the Americans went in South America, they found that the British had been there first. Any diplomatic account of United States relations with Mexico or Central America must consider Britain as an active political force down to the mid-1860s. Economic rivalries, of course, survived well into the twentieth century. Indeed, nineteenth-century Latin America might be studied as one of the great arenas of that Anglo-American global rivalry, a rivalry that furnished a relatively peaceful century with a substitute for the world wars of the eighteenth and twentieth centuries.

The triangular nature of United States–Latin American relations reinforces what I have already said about the importance of multiarchival research. A good rule of thumb about archives is: "The more, the better." When Latin American materials are not available, the records of European legations in Latin America may help to fill the gap. Even when Latin American documents are available, the correspondence of the British or French minister will usually add breadth and depth, and when a major crisis is concerned, despatches from European diplomats in Washington as well may shed additional light on American policy.

The Mexican War is an excellent example of this complex, triangular relationship. Before the war the Mexicans' vision of British support helped influence their intransigence toward the United States. At the same time the disdain of the British for Mexican misgovernment and Britain's desire for peace and prosperous trade with the United States reduced the likelihood of British aid to Mexico. After the war began, the Mexicans still hoped against hope for British loans or warships, while the British did their best to mediate and somehow end the war before the war ended Mexico. One cannot fully understand the long, drawn-out peace negotiations without recognizing the contributions of British diplomats in Mexico, reluctantly respecting American strength while trying to minimize American conquests by speeding these negotiations. The Mexican War was far more than a mere family quarrel in the Western Hemisphere. It was also an incident in Anglo-American relations almost as important as the Oregon question, and it was an incident in Anglo-Mexican relations leading toward the tripartite treaty of 1861 and the British recognition of Maximilian.

In this paper I have discussed relatively finite, specific topics and also lifetime projects as broad as all outdoors. But of course it is not difficult to slice up the most comprehensive concept into monographs and articles. I can foresee a catalog drawer full of dissertation titles proceeding out of these broad topics titles such as "Anglo-American Rivalry in the Plata and Its Influences on Latin American Nationalism," "American Merchants in Mexico City, 1821–1848," "The Sugar Tariff in United States–Latin American Relations, 1865–1900," and many others. At the moment I am directing one dissertation on Commodore Shufeldt and another on Texan influences in United States–Mexican border relationships after the Civil War. I hope to encourage other projects on similar subjects as the occasions present themselves—unless, of course, other thesis directors beat me to them.

In all this directed activity and in my own future research plans the National Archives will play a major role. It is literally the first step on the researcher's itinerary after he emerges from his own university stacks clutching a tentative bibliography and a bundle of notes on secondary sources. Since the advent of microfilm, the archives have been somewhat dispersed. By using film, however, one may postpone but cannot obviate the eventual visit to this building for materials too bulky or too fragmentary to photograph effectively. In the field of United States–Latin American relations of the nineteenth century the resources of the Archives are varied and plentiful. So are the topics awaiting study. All we need are a battalion or two of scholars to bring them together, for this task, alas, is beyond the powers of the most ingenious Recordak or Xerox machine yet invented.

## NOTES

1. U.S., National Archives and Records Service, *Guide to Materials on Latin America in the National Archives,* by John P. Harrison (Washington, D.C.: Government Printing Office, 1961). George S. Ulibarri is now preparing a revision of this guide.
2. William R. Manning, ed., *Diplomatic Correspondence of the United States concerning the Independence of the Latin-American Nations,* 3 vols. (New York: Oxford University Press, 1925); idem, ed., *Diplomatic Correspond-*

ence of the United States: Inter-American Affairs, 1831–1860,* 12 vols. (Washington, D.C.: Carnegie Endowment for International Peace, 1932–39).

3. For a discussion of the *Foreign Relations* series, see William M. Franklin's article in the present volume.
4. Joel Roberts Poinsett, *Notes on Mexico . . .* (Philadelphia: H. C. Carey and I. Lea, 1824).
5. Quoted in *Guide to Materials on Latin America in the National Archives,* pp. 184, 230.
6. Lester D. Langley, *The Cuban Policy of the United States: A Brief History* (New York: Wiley, 1968).
7. Fredrick B. Pike, *Chile and the United States, 1880–1962: The Emergence of Chile's Social Crisis and the Challenge to United States Diplomacy* (Notre Dame, Ind.: University of Notre Dame Press, 1963).
8. Robert N. Burr, *By Reason or Force: Chile and the Balancing of Power in South America, 1830–1905* (Berkeley and Los Angeles: University of California Press, 1965).
9. Marvin D. Bernstein, *The Mexican Mining Industry, 1890–1950: A Study of the Interaction of Politics, Economics, and Technology* (Albany: State University of New York, 1964).
10. Charles A. Hale, *Mexican Liberalism in the Age of Mora, 1821–1853* (New Haven: Yale University Press, 1968).
11. Thomas F. McGann, *Argentina, the United States, and the Inter-American System, 1880–1914* (Cambridge: Harvard University Press, 1957).

# The Archival Record and United States–Latin American Relations in the Twentieth Century

ROBERT FREEMAN SMITH

## EXAMINING THE ARCHIVAL RECORD

To some students of United States foreign relations, archival research deal-ing with Latin America may appear to be a somewhat boring and perhaps even an irrelevant experience. After all, one cannot expect to find major revelations concerning either the causes of United States participation in world wars and cold wars or the behind-the-scenes maneuvers at conferences designed to rearrange other parts of the world. Yet, Latin America is that part of the underdeveloped (or Third) world with which the United States has been the most intimately and consistently associated during the twenti-eth century. The relations between the United States and Latin America may not be characterized by highly dramatic events, but they provide impor-tant insights into both the overall United States role in the underdeveloped world and the development of various tactics of informal empire (or world order) as these have been shaped by the push for hegemony in the Western Hemisphere.

The low-key revelations are in the archival record. One could point to such things as Theodore Roosevelt's secret approaches to Colombia in 1906, offering possible monetary balm for the Panamanian episode; or to the 1928 investigation which disproved the story of German attempts to secure canal rights in Nicaragua in 1914; or to Woodrow Wilson's secret preparations in 1920 for the possible occupation of Cuba and Mexico City; or to the "informal" landing of armed forces in various parts of Cuba during the 1933 Revolution; or to the completely serious proposal made by staff members of Nelson Rockefeller's Office of Inter-American Affairs in 1942 to use blond, female operators to seduce various Latin American statesmen. In all probability, when the archives for the post–World War II period are open we will find a considerable number of such revelations. My speculation in this regard is stimulated by several factors. I recall a discussion with a State Department official concerning the role of the Central Intelligence Agency in Latin America; his final comment (after several drinks) was that if I really knew what was going on I would indeed have cause for concern. On another occasion I speculated in an article that the CIA deliberately created the situation which led to the elimination of the left-wing Cuban underground movement at the time of the Bay of Pigs invasion in 1961. I have since learned that the intelligence course for army officer candidates teaches this as established fact and accepted doctrine.

But such archival revelations or key documents that provide *the* explanation for crucial events are only a small part of the basic task of archival research. The in-depth understanding comes only with the sometimes tedious, always time-consuming job of examining the voluminous collection of memorandums, correspondence, and other material collected by various governmental agencies. It is the role of the historian to go through these collections, assemble the important pieces, and then integrate these into a coherent pattern. There will be contradictions, loose ends, and conflicts between individuals and groups in this pattern. But the totality of such steady research into the day-by-day accumulations of material will provide a more accurate and fundamental understanding of the elements of continuity and change in United States–Latin American relations. Within such a research background the so-called key documents may be more effectively evaluated and the rhetoric of political leaders more accurately criticized.

A good example of the use and misuse of a key document is *Memorandum on the Monroe Doctrine,* written by Undersecretary of State J. Reuben Clark in 1928 and published in 1930. Many historians cite this document and develop an interpretation based upon the statements contained therein. I have seen very few references to the covering letter which Clark sent with the memorandum and which considerably modifies (or clarifies) the pronouncements on intervention. The memorandum was not written as a declaration ending armed intervention or interference in the affairs of Latin American nations, but as an explanation separating such actions from the Monroe Doctrine.

These two documents can be understood completely only against the background of official concern over the reputation of the Monroe Doctrine. This concern originated early in the 1920s. Over a period of several years diplomats in Latin America were requested to send to the State Department all newspaper and governmental statements concerning the doctrine. In addition, officials in the field and in Washington submitted numerous memorandums concerning the interpretation of the doctrine and the impact of

Latin America opinions as to its meaning upon United States relations with various countries. These documents also reveal the conflict between officials over the tactics of United States policy, and this conflict was in part responsible for the delay in publishing the Clark Memorandum. Some officials advocated the "God Save Our Marines" approach (a term used by Arthur Bliss Lane to describe a fellow official who was also one of the leading historians in the field), while others advocated nonmilitary means of influence. The administration of Herbert Hoover strengthened the latter position and provided in practice a less interventionist interpretation for the memorandum than Clark had intended. In any event, the Clark Memorandum must be interpreted within a framework provided by detailed archival research for the pre-1933 period. It may be regarded as a kind of symbol of the development of a less military-oriented policy, but it was not a declaration ending United States intervention in the affairs of its neighbors.

Detailed archival research has given a new perspective to other events and developments. For Cuba, recent scholarship has demonstrated the various tactics utilized in the attempt to "Americanize" the island after the granting of formal independence in 1902. The archival record also reveals the effect of this upon the intensification of Cuban nationalism in the twentieth century. State Department officials, however, often pointed to the Cuban policy of the United States as a kind of model to be applied to other Latin American nations, and the verb *Cubanize* was created to define succinctly this process of pacification and Americanization.

Army officers played an important role in the elaboration of the basic strategy and the development of some of the tactics. In fact, some officers had a better understanding of the fundamental problems of Cuba than the civilian officials. During the 1906–9 occupation several officers stated (almost prophetically) that the political and economic problems of the island could be solved only as a result of basic socioeconomic reform.

Archival research also has shown that the United States military (especially the Marine Corps) was directly concerned with problems of pacification and counterinsurgency warfare during the first quarter of the century. An important part of this involvement was the establishment of native internal security forces to prevent revolution in Cuba, Haiti, the Dominican Republic, Nicaragua, and Panama. All of these forces eventually deviated from their original roles and became conventional, parade-ground armies. This type of military involvement was dropped in the late 1920s, only to be revived in the early 1960s. Some scholar in the future will have the interesting job of investigating whether the military planners of the 1960s made any use of these earlier precedents.

For Mexico, recent archival research has revealed that in 1907 some

United States officials believed that Mexico was ready to assume the role of auxiliary policeman in Central America, and even to assert protectorates under United States guidance. This view quickly changed when Porfirio Díaz acted independently in the case of Nicaragua. The revolution which began in 1910 profoundly altered the course of United States–Mexican relations, and historical scholarship has only recently begun to probe the complexities of the United States response. For many years Wilsonian rhetoric was the major source for interpretations of United States policy between 1913 and 1921—even for those who opposed Woodrow Wilson. The archival record, however, reveals that after 1915 one of the major concerns of the State Department was to prevent the implementation by Mexico of the Calvo Clause, which was essentially designed to assert national control over foreign enterprises. Specifically, this became a fight against Article 27 of the Mexican Constitution of 1917. During World War I, Wilson may have paid little attention to Mexico, but the State Department worked consistently to prevent President Venustiano Carranza from implementing Article 27. After the removal of Carranza in May 1920, Wilson refused to recognize any new government unless it signed a treaty which in effect would eliminate this article.

A detailed study of the archival record for the years 1913–30 shows how consistently this contest was waged and how central it was to United States–Mexican relations. A perceptive State Department official, writing in 1926, stated that his study of the record of United States–Mexican relations from 1913 revealed a consistently tense situation, and he concluded that "this state of affairs has resulted from the persistent efforts of Carranza and succeeding executives of Mexico to deprive American citizens of properties legally acquired by them under Mexican laws in effect at the time of purchase, and from the fact that the Government of the United States has consistently opposed such efforts." In addition, the archival record shows the important negotiating role played by business groups during the 1920s, especially the International Committee of Bankers on Mexico headed by Thomas Lamont. In part these negotiations laid the foundations for the accomplishments of Dwight W. Morrow.

During the 1920s and early 1930s United States policy toward Latin America cannot be described as "isolationist" in either economic or political terms. Officials believed that what the United States did or did not do in Latin America had a direct relationship to relations with Europe and East Asia. Secretary of State Henry L. Stimson was reluctant to use military force in Central America, in part because he thought that this would undermine the treaty system for maintaining the Open Door in Manchuria. Similarly, Cordell Hull viewed the Reciprocal Trade Agreements and Export-Import

Bank arrangements with Latin American nations as part of a broader, economic-ideological system.

Archival research on the Good Neighbor policy has provided an understanding of the goals and tactics of the Franklin Roosevelt administration which goes far beyond the rhetoric of Pan-American Day speeches. Improving United States–Latin American relations was an important factor, but this cannot be interpreted properly apart from the economic and ideological elements of United States policy. The president of Haiti discovered this in 1933 when he specifically appealed to the Good Neighbor policy as the reason the United States should terminate its supervision of Haitian customs. He was informed that the "new" policy in no way changed the obligation of the United States government to protect the interests of those who had invested in Haitian bonds. The customs receivership was finally abrogated in 1941. For additional research I would suggest the concept that the reputation of the Good Neighbor policy in the latter 1930s had a direct relationship to the activities of Germany and Japan.

My own study of the archival record of United States–Latin American relations in the twentieth century (combined with those of numerous other scholars) has convinced me that these have been characterized by a preponderant consistency and continuity in United States goals. The historian may stress the political, economic, or ideological factors involved; but regardless of emphasis, the consistency clearly emerges from the record. Looking at one component of these goals, one could cite the minister to Cuba writing in 1904 that the terms of the Reciprocity Act of 1903 "are not sufficiently favorable to enable us to secure control of the Cuban market—a control which would be so advantageous from a political as well as a commercial point of view." In 1918, Secretary of State Robert Lansing noted in regard to rivalry with Britain over construction of steel and armament facilities in Brazil that "it is of the utmost importance to our interests in Brazil that no other than an American company should eventually secure it [the concession] and the vast amount of trade it would control." Sumner Welles reported in 1933 that a proposed reciprocal trade agreement with Cuba would "give us practical control of a market we have been steadily losing for the past ten years." Officials of the Office of Inter-American Affairs speculated in 1941 that postwar loans to Latin America could be utilized "to seek abandonment or reduction of tariffs for protection of the more uneconomic industries, adoption of a policy of selective immigration, greater willingness to participate in commodity agreements, better treatment of American investments, and acceleration of the process of adjusting defaulting debts." It is interesting to note that President Roosevelt defined the goal of "selective immigration" as the development of "a virile, democracy-loving *white* population." In a similar vein, United States officials earlier in the century had expressed the hope that United States influence would lead to a "whitening" of the Cuban population, which they believed would contribute to the proper stabilization of the island.

The major controversies over United States policy toward Latin America have concerned the tactics, or the means, of reaching the goals. This is especially noticeable in regard to the use of military force and the question of how to influence the South American countries and Mexico. Different kinds of nonmilitary tactics have been developed during the century, but even here there is much consistency. The Export-Import Bank and the Alliance for Progress are much more sophisticated than the "dollar diplomacy" of Taft and Knox, but the basic ideas involved are quite similar. The Hickenlooper Amendment represents the same kind of economic pressure which was used against Cuba in 1918 and in Mexico from 1917 to 1921. This list could be vastly extended. During the 1950s and 1960s the United States government (especially the CIA) became deeply involved in the internal politics of various Latin American nations. But the scholar can find archival evidence that Woodrow Wilson in 1916 secretly channelled funds to the American Federation of Labor for the purpose of helping that organization influence the Mexican labor movement and Mexican politics. Similarly, during World War I the Chilean assistant minister of war was secretly employed by the United States government.

The tactics of military intervention have become more highly refined (although the Dominican Republic intervention of 1965 was something of a massive regression) and have been extended beyond the Central American and Caribbean countries. But the Green Berets, operating with the armies of Bolivia and Guatemala, could recognize as historical colleagues the marine advisors who helped the Nicaraguan army pursue Augusto Sandino from 1928 to 1932.

This brief resumé of what I consider to be some of the major themes of recent archival research does not do full justice to the arguments, personal differences, and other complexities involved in policy making. These have indeed influenced the kinds of tactics used by various administrations, the degrees of flexibility involved, and the countries which have received primary attention. Changes in Latin America have produced new problems and intensified old ones. Some officials have proposed bold, new departures to cope with these. The Alliance for Progress initially seemed to fit into this category. Yet the Clay Committee's definitions of the alliance in 1963 could have been made by General Wood in 1901 when he defined stability as "money at six percent."

## RESOURCES OF THE NATIONAL ARCHIVES

The starting point for archival research in United States–Latin American relations should be several very useful publications. John P. Harrison's *Guide to Materials on Latin America in the National Archives* is indispensable.[1] In addition, the Archives has published a number of preliminary inventories that provide relatively detailed annotations for the files contained in the record groups surveyed. Several lesser-known (and used) record groups have been surveyed and have proved to be very helpful for tracking material which is not filed in the country sections of the decimal file of the State Department. The *Foreign Relations* series is another starting point, especially for pinpointing file numbers.[2] The documentary coverage for Latin America, however, tends to be somewhat erratic and at times even deceptive. The National Archives microfilm series for Latin America is progressing; to date, records from the decimal file (1910–29) relating to political relations between the United States and the specific country, the political relations between that country and other states, and internal affairs, have been filmed for Mexico, Cuba, Argentina, Brazil, Chile, Costa Rica, El Salvador, Haiti, Nicaragua, Panama, and Central America. One or two of these series have been filmed for Bolivia, Peru, the Dominican Republic, Guatemala, and Honduras.

Most archival research on United States–Latin American relations has concentrated on the General Records of the Deparment of State, Record Group 59. For the period 1900–1906, the historian must consult a variety of files such as the Diplomatic Instructions (1791–1906) and the Diplomatic Despatches (1789–1906). Most of this material is filed by subject for the period after 1906—in the numerical file from 1906–10 and the decimal file after 1910. This record group also contains the Consular Trade Reports (1925–50), the Consular Political Reports (1925–35), the Foreign Service Inspection Reports (1925–37), and a file of correspondence between President Wilson and Secretary of State Bryan between 1913 and 1915.

Additional collections not part of the central files of particular relevance for United States–Latin American relations are Francis White's Files, 1921–33, and two Latin American Division Files, 1905–48. During World War II over three thousand lot files (unindexed) were created, and in all probability some of these contain relevant material.

But there are several other record groups which are of great value not only for studying relations with specific countries but also for their coverage of broader aspects of United States relations. These are as follows:

1. Records of Boundary and Claims Commissions and Arbitrations,

Record Group 76. In this group the historian will find the records of the Mexican–United States Claims Commission, established in 1923; the Costa Rica–Panama Boundary Arbitration, 1910–13; and the Tacna-Arica Plebiscite, 1925–26.

2. Records of International Conferences, Commissions, and Expositions, Record Group 43. This group contains the records of the American and Mexican Joint Commission, 1916; the Inter-American High Commission, 1916–33 (the economic wing of the Pan-American Union); the Conference on Central American Affairs (1922–23); the Buenos Aires Conference of 1936; and other, more specialized conferences.

3. Records of the Foreign Service Posts of the Department, Record Group 84. This group contains the field records for both diplomatic and consular posts.

The Archives also contains a variety of material from other governmental departments and agencies that have played a role in United States–Latin American relations. In addition to the general records, most of these have special files. The War Department archives contains the Records of the Panama Canal, Record Group 185, the Military Government of Cuba, Record Group 140, the Military Government of Veracruz, Record Group 141, and the American Expeditionary Forces (World War I), 1917–23, Record Group 120. The records of the Punititive Expedition to Mexico (1916–17) are contained in the latter. The Navy Department archives include the records of the Military Government of Santo Domingo, 1916–24 as part of the Records of the Office of the Chief of Naval Operations, Record Group 38. The archival records of the departments of Treasury and Commerce also contain relevant material (especially the records of the Bureau of Foreign and Domestic Commerce, which became a quasi-State Department under Herbert Hoover). There are archival records for the Congress, but these are most useful for evidence of pressure group activity.

I would like to point out several other record groups which quite often represent compilations of materials from several agencies and departments. (In some cases the responsibilities were transferred from one department to another.) These are as follows:

1. Records of the Office of Inter-American Affairs, Record Group 229, 1941–46. Many of the roots of the Alliance for Progress can be found in this agency.

2. Records of the Bureau of Insular Affairs, Record Group 350, 1902–39. This agency was in some respects the United States equivalent of the European offices of colonial administration. For Latin

America, the bureau archives contain material on Cuba, Puerto Rico, the Panama Canal, the Dominican Republic, and the Haitian Customs Receivership.

3. Records of the Office of Territories, Record Group 126. This agency took over many of the responsibilities of the Bureau of Insular Affairs in 1939 when it was transferred from the War Department to the Interior Department, where it was consolidated with the Division of Territories and Island Possessions. For Latin America, its record holdings deal with Puerto Rico and the Virgin Islands.

4. Records of the Foreign Economic Administration, Record Group 169, 1939–45. The records of the Pan-American Division are relevant to any study of United States–Latin American relations during World War II.

5. Records of the Puerto Rico Reconstruction Administration, Record Group 323, 1935–50. This agency was especially important for its attempts to rehabilitate the economy of the island after years of official neglect and in the light of rising Puerto Rican nationalism.

6. Records of the Government of the Virgin Islands, Record Group 55, 1917–50. This is the primary collection for this subject.

This brief survey of the multiplicity of archival sources for the study of United States–Latin American relations conveys something of the variety and volume of material which is available. For more detailed analyses the student should consult the publications cited at the beginning of this section. I have not mentioned several other agencies (most of post–World War II origin), but at some future date the historian will need to see the records of the Export-Import Bank, the International Bank for Reconstruction and Development, the Peace Corps, the Agency for International Development, and (with tongue in cheek) the Central Intelligence Agency.

## PROBLEMS ENCOUNTERED IN ARCHIVAL RESEARCH

At this point I would like to consider some of the problems involved in archival research and the historian's utilization of archival resources. Some of these, of course, apply to such research in any field.

The problem caused by the increasing volume of records can only be solved by detailed finding aids. In this regard, it would be especially helpful to have guides to the central files which point out material relevant to various countries that is contained in other files; for example, material concerning Mexico contained in the files dealing with Great Britain, Japan, and other nations.

A particularly annoying problem is that of material that has been filed out of date either through carelessness or because it was made available only at a later time. For example, some important material dealing with the negotiations of the Joint American-Mexican Commission (1916) was filed at random during 1919 and 1920. Closely related is the problem of missing documents. I recall my anguish while going through one file on Mexico, to find that numerous documents (especially the ones I had noted from the purport book) had been sent back to the State Department. In some cases the removal card indicated that they had been removed more than five years previously. In other cases, documents are simply gone and no one knows where they are. Sometimes, however, the lost document is found. Albert B. Fall removed from the files of the Interior Department numerous letters dealing with the Joint American-Mexican Commission negotiations in 1916, especially letters between President Wilson and Secretary of the Interior Franklin K. Lane. These can be found in the Fall papers at the Huntington Library.

Another major problem facing the scholar is the wide distribution of material in private manuscript collections dispersed across the country. This problem has been exacerbated by the proliferation of those "vanity" monuments known as presidential libraries; whether they be housed in the rather modest dwelling at Hyde Park or the citadel (dubbed by students as "Montezuma's Mausoleum") which is currently arising on the hills overlooking Austin, Texas. It would be of much value if some organization concerned with Latin American or foreign relations history compiled a combined guide to relevant material in all depositories. One such project is under way. Prof. Berta Ulloa Ortíz, of the Colégio de México, is compiling a guide to archival and manuscript collections dealing with United States–Mexican relations. This will be an annotated guide covering materials located in both the United States and Mexico.

Historians in this field have tended to concentrate their archival research on United States relations with a limited number of Latin American countries. Mexico, Cuba, and some of the Central American nations have received the most study. There are signs, however, that historians are broadening the scope of their research both in terms of countries and activities which are multinational in scope. We also need more studies of the role of less-publicized governmental agencies (such as the Inter-American High Commission) and of private organizations such as corporations, religious groups, and foundations.

Another problem of historical research in this field has been the tendency of historians to stick rather closely to the main State Department political files. In the case of Mexico this has meant a great concentration on the 812.00 files, with much less attention being given to the 812.50 files on economic matters, or the 812.6363 file on petroleum. Documents must also be sought in various topical files. Material on the Jenkins Case and Mexico (1919) is located, in large part, in files 125.61383 and 125.61383J41. Vital material on United States commercial relations with Cuba is located in files 611.373 and 611.3731. General material on United States trade relations with Latin America is located in such files as 611.001 (general conditions affecting trade), 610.4017 (commercial methods of Europe affecting United States trade with Latin America), and 611.033 (tariff). Relatively little attention has been given to file 710.11 (the Monroe Doctrine and relations between the United States and Latin America). This file contains various important memorandums which document the continuity in United States goals.

Another problem facing the historian doing research in the United States archives is the tendency to absorb the thinking of United States officials, and to write the story from the perspective of United States policy makers. Total immersion in official sources for an extended period has the effect of subtly shaping one's approach to a particular issue, but this has produced unduly harsh and even inaccurate interpretations of Latin American leaders and their policies. A case in point is the portrayal of United States–Mexican relations during the administration of Venustiano Carranza. The Mexican president was a determined nationalist, but to assert that his policies were based simply on the desire to harass the United States (whether from motives of political expediency or true hatred for the Yankee) is a distortion of the Mexican position. Likewise, some scholars have written that the Carranza government intended to "nationalize" (by expropriation or confiscation) the oil industry, and that Carranza pushed Wilson because he knew that the United States president would not go to war with Mexico. All of these views were repeatedly expounded in the correspondence and memorandums of the State Department. From my own research in both United States and Mexican sources I am convinced that the Carranza government did not want to nationalize the oil industry, and it did fear that the deep penetration of the Pershing Expedition was the prelude to all-out intervention. The purported unwillingness of the Carranza government to cooperate with the United States was not simply due to anti-Yankee feeling. Mexican officials, however, believed that cooperation was possible only if the United States respected Mexican sovereignty, and they regarded the Veracruz occupation, the Punitive Expedition, and the repeated attempts to alter the Constitution of 1917 as something less than such respect.

In some cases, the United States archives contain material which gives the needed perspective to the official views. Secretary Lansing and Ambassador Henry P. Fletcher frequently denounced the anti-United States feelings they ascribed to Carranza and cited the Carranza Doctrine as conclusive evidence. Yet, these men vastly distorted the general set of principles that were called the Carranza Doctrine. The United States archives contain several Mexican publications (including the most elaborate explication, *La Doctrina Carranza y el Acercamiento Indo-Latino,* by Hermila Galindo), and these documents show that the Mexican government was willing to accept the Monroe Doctrine, encourage foreign investment, and even cooperate with the United States, provided the United States in fact accepted the full sovereignty of Mexico and the right of a country to exercise control over its natural resources.

Perspective can also be gained by the use of various private manuscript collections and foreign archival sources. Scholars have begun to utilize the archives of Great Britain and Germany, but the use of twentieth-century materials in Latin American archives is still difficult.[3] My own experience in trying to see post 1915 material in the archives of the Mexican Foreign Office is an example. The main document catalog is classified "secret," and the regulations for use of the archives are difficult to obtain. Prof. Daniel Cosío Villegas is working to improve this situation, and it was through his intervention that I was allowed to see documents in one record group. Limited as this was, I was still able to ascertain that Mexican officials were much better informed about United States policy, pressures within the United States, and the activities of various private groups than historians have assumed. Their reactions to United States actions were at least as well informed (if not more so) than United States reactions to Mexican policy.

Basically, I am arguing that one of the main problems of United States studies of relations with Latin America is the difficulty of United States scholars in getting out of their own "national skins" and seeing these relations from the perspective of Latin Americans. They are not peculiar in this respect. But that fact is still no defense for writing about United States–Latin American relations without some real attempt to understand the cultural values, the political complexities, the socioeconomic conditions, and the views of national interest of Latin America. The least we can do in this regard is to read, and seriously consider, the evidence and interpretations of Latin American scholars. United States policy towards Latin America produces reactions which must be understood within the context of the countries concerned. For too many years United States scholars virtually ignored what Cuban historians were writing about United States–Cuban relations, and as a result the impact of Cuban scholars on modern Cuban nationalism shocked many people in the years after 1959.

Archival research and reading the works of Latin Americans will not automatically remedy the problem of an ethnocentric interpretation of United States–Latin American relations. Some United States scholars are not very receptive to the idea of giving serious, and even sympathetic, consideration to perspectives which stand outside of their country's view of national interests. Some recent reviews in United States journals of Gordon Connell-Smith's *The Inter-American System* attest to this fact. This situation is changing as more scholars are giving serious consideration to the legitimate aspirations, fears, and national endeavors of Latin Americans, and the relationship of these to inter-American relations. Why this situation has not changed more rapidly is beyond the scope of this paper. Prof. Richard Morse has suggested that:

Despite sometimes useful or even handsome accomplishments, Latin-American studies have, since the 1920's, been a faintly ridiculous tail to a politico-commercial kite. In the groves of Academe the scholar lies down in darkness with the former diplomat, the casual pundit, the entrepreneur.

I would include the study of United States–Latin American relations in the twentieth century as a part of the above-mentioned Latin American studies. In this inclusion and the growing coordination of insights between specialists in foreign relations and internal Latin American conditions lies the best hope for a history of these relations which has broader perspective and seeks understanding not as a vehicle of manipulation but as a foundation for the development of an authentic nonintervention policy for the United States. Scholars in the field of twentieth-century United States–Latin American relations must seriously face the challenge presented by Dr. Manfred Max-Neef, a Chilean sociologist and economist, in his critique of the pseudo-scholarly Project Camelot:

Your country is reaching the highest possible limit of historically permissible arrogance in foreign relations. I hope that you, as responsible citizens, will become conscious of this fact, and will want to react to it with strength, with honor and without fear.

I hope that archival research in United States–Latin American relations, blended with the right kind of *simpatico,* will help create the responsible reaction requested by Dr. Max-Neef. At times I am pessimistic, but as a scholar I would like to believe that Prof. Cosío Villegas was correct when he wrote: "Research by professors and students into the present-day life or the history of the two countries [Mexico and the United States] is perhaps the surest way to understanding."

NOTES

1. U.S., National Archives and Records Service, *Guide to Materials on Latin America in the National Archives,* by John P. Harrison (Washington, D.C.: Government Printing Office, 1961). George S. Ulibarri is now preparing a revision of this guide.
2. For a discussion of the *Foreign Relations* series, see William M. Franklin's article in the present volume.
3. For some Latin American archival resources see: Roscoe R. Hill, *Los archivos nacionales de la América latina* (Havana, Cuba: Publication 19 of the Archivo Nacional de Cuba, 1948); Joaquín Llaverías, *Historia de los archivos de Cuba,* 2d ed. (Havana, Cuba, 1949); idem, "Memoria de los trabajos realizados en el Archivo Nacional," *Boletín del Archivo Nacional* (Cuba, 1932); Berta Ulloa, "La revolución en relaciones," *Historia Mexicana* (Jan.–Mar. 1961), which lists relevant files for the study of United States–Mexican relations; idem, ed., *Revolución Mexicana, 1910–1920* (México: Secretaría de Relaciones Exteriores, 1963), a guide to record group 119.

# United States Relations with Latin America

DISCUSSION

*Wilkins B. Winn, East Carolina University:* I have two questions, the first directed to Dr. Pletcher. I am interested in your United States–British rivalry in Latin American thesis, in particular the religious rivalry of these two countries in Latin America. I know there was a rivalry when they were trying to secure religious provisions in commercial treaties, but I would like you to comment on what light the archives shed on other types of religious rivalries of these two countries in Latin America.

*David M. Pletcher:* That is a subject I really do not know very much about. I think that you would find a certain amount of religious cooperation as well as religious rivalry since they were both operating (at least the citizens of both countries) as small minorities within an overwhelming Roman Catholic majority. But beyond that I cannot really give you much enlightenment, because it is a subject which I have not found mentioned very often in the diplomatic archives that I have examined. There is a little bit in the early period. As you know, we made an effort to establish freedom of worship in our early relations, in early commercial treaties with Mexico and some other countries, and the British were trying to do much the same thing. I think in both cases the religious efforts were greatly subordinated to the economic efforts; the desire was to establish free trade and free commerce with these countries, and this assumed more importance to both the British and the Americans. That is about all I can say on the subject.

*Winn:* I have one other question. It might be redundant, but I think since there was a Protestant missionary movement in the last part of the nineteenth century, not only worldwide but within Latin America, I would like to address a question to both of you. What light might the Archives shed on efforts of religious organizations in the United States, both Roman Catholic and Protestant, to influence the policy of the United States toward Latin America?

*Robert Freeman Smith:* I have found material—I hesitate to say considerable, but there certainly is material there. For example, some of the most important groups that wrote to the State Department, to Woodrow Wilson, and to Secretary of War Newton D. Baker to protest against any possible intervention in Mexico were religious organizations. They were either specifically denominational organizations or groups like that led by Dr. Samuel Guy Inman, which was basically not connected with any one church but was sort of an intergroup organization—the Committee for Cooperation on Latin America, I think it was called. This kind of contact continued, certainly. Religious groups seemed particularly to surface at times of crisis. As Wayne Cole said in an earlier session, measuring the impact of such groups on policy is an extremely difficult thing to do. I do believe that in some cases it can be established they had some impact. Now it may have been that this was because the particular official concerned happened to agree with the position and offered the letters as support for his position, as in the case of Newton D. Baker, who was basically against military intervention in Latin America for the most part, particularly during the agitation of 1919. I think that one can say at least it made up part of the baggage of those officials who opposed military action. I happen to know more about this in the case of Mexico because I know that Baker particularly liked to call these communications to the attention of President Wilson.

In the 1920s, especially when things seemed to be heating up in late 1926 and in early 1927, once more there was a tendency of religious groups to petition, to send letters, petitions to the State Department. In terms of Roman Catholic pressure, here I have found, of course, some communications, primarily from laymen, but occasionally from ranking clerics. Here again the tendency, while not specifically calling for intervention, tends to be rather anti-Mexican. I have always pondered the very peculiar irony that perhaps the strength of anti-Catholicism in the United States in the first part of the twentieth century was one of the factors that helped prevent intervention on one or two occasions. It was not the only factor by any means. But certainly some Roman Catholics did become rather excited and, not only in public but in their communications with the government, called for some kind of stern stand against bloody Mexico. This action in turn provoked a Protestant reaction. Not to color this too much, but certainly in 1927 and 1928 there is also evidence in the Archives that a group of Roman Catholic clerics in particular decided that really this was going too far and that the Knights of Columbus were really stirring up a reaction against all Roman

Catholics. They began to work with Dwight Morrow, as an example, for a solution to the religious controversy. A lot of this information can be found in communications in the Archives; there is material there.

*Geoffrey Smith, Macalester College:* I would like to direct this question to Professor Smith. With regard to the work of men such as John Gerassi and James Petras with which you are probably familiar, I have felt that there is developing in Latin American history a germ of a New Left revisionism that is attempting to do what you have suggested yet at the expense of ignoring some of the archival materials that are available. In other words, more emotion than archival competency. Could you perhaps comment on this historiographical trend, if it is a trend?

*Smith:* I must say I do have a certain antipathy for categorization like this. I know the general group you are discussing. I think, however, that this group is part of a longer, broader, and older tradition. I think perhaps one might argue that for a while the tradition lapsed, but certainly the Vanguard series of the 1920s presented a variety of books by men who at that time were young scholars in the field. I think J. Fred Rippy wrote one. There is one on bananas in Central America, for example. I think this is a long tradition that to a certain extent fell into disuse from the latter 1930s. Perhaps one can argue that in a general sense there has been a revival of this tradition. Certainly my own interest in approaching history from perhaps this perspective antedates the creation of the term "New Left" and is influenced quite a bit by Prof. Fred Harvey Harrington of the University of Wisconsin. Quite frankly, I would also have to give some credit to the historical influence of men like Charles A. Beard and the Vanguard writers of the 1920s—particularly, of course, to the influence of Beard's idea of national interest, not specifically his books about the origin of the Second World War.

So I think there has been certainly a revival, and I would hesitate to call it completely a New Left phenomenon. Certainly people that might be generally classified that way have taken a great interest in Latin American history; unfortunately, a lot or at least some of this work has not been based on archival resources. I think that this is the poorest kind of critical approach. There is, unfortunately, anti-intellectualism among various academic groups, whether New Left, New Right, or even New Center. I certainly know that those who are concerned with the idea of a broader perspective do know that archival research is very basic. Now, of course, Jim Petras writes primarily in the area of domestic history. You may be aware of his recent book on the sociology of Chilean politics. Again, I happen to know John Gerassi, and again I think his is primarily the kind of work to which you are referring, particularly his introductory chapter in the book recently published by Random House on Latin American radicalism. This is a view that is shared by many Latin Americans. Here I would certainly agree with you that any kind of critical approach must be bound on very detailed archival research.

Now another development is the broadening of the whole concept of the field of foreign relations. I think this broadening is evident in some of the works that Professor Pletcher mentioned, and it certainly applies throughout the whole perspective, whether the nineteenth or twentieth century. This development goes beyond multiarchival research. United States policy produces reactions within the context of the particular Latin American country, and it is understanding what that does, why this happens. In other words, one cannot simply write the history of United States foreign relations from the perspective of the United States. I think very much that we have to achieve a balanced analysis also of the internal situation of, in this case, the particular Latin American country. I referred earlier to Cuban nationalism and the impact of a variety of things on Cuban scholars, particularly from the 1920s on. We should understand, for example, what they were saying, for they wrote the textbooks that young Cubans were reading in the universities. I could cite other examples, but I think that this is also an approach I hope we will see taken much more. In one sense Fred Pike did some of this in his book on Chile. I think Tom McGann and the authors of the books that were mentioned have certainly laid out in many cases the legitimate Latin American criticisms of United States policy toward their country and the reasons for the criticism.

I would therefore say that again the situation is more complex than just what might be called New Left revisionism. That is involved, but I think many other things are also involved. I do not think one can separate oneself from the context of one's own time. I would like to trace my own intellectual evolution, beginning with the ideas with which I identified and which I held at the time I started graduate school. Then I would like to see how and why I have changed these ideas. The context of the times is important, this is true; yet we all must be aware about being purely reactive to the times. I cannot deny, however, that the times in which I have lived have had an impact on the changes in my ideas, but I must also add that I think my own archival research has been just as important. How one mixes the two factors is something else again.

*Milton O. Gustafson, National Archives and Records Service:* I would like to mention for this particular group one of the items I discussed this morning. I think the Francis White file in the National Archives would be of special interest to Latin American historians in the twentieth century. This group of records has been almost completely unused. The only person who has done any extensive work with the file to my knowledge is Dana Munro. The file is an extremely rich source, containing items such as the private correspondence between White as Munro's superior in the State Department and Munro, who was the minister in Haiti, commenting on the instructions that had just been sent as official instructions of the department—on what they really meant and what Munro was supposed to do in terms of those instructions. I hope that someone will give White the attention he deserves, whether by biography or by using these papers. I certainly commend them to the people here.

*David F. Trask, State University of New York at Stony Brook:* I would like very briefly to accent what has been said this morning and, I think, this afternoon about the importance of European archives, particularly the recently opened British archives. Professor Smith, for example, should (and I am sure this will be good news to him) spend a very great amount of time in London. If he does not his book will be improperly documented because the material in this collection is certainly far more important for a study of United States and Latin American relations regarding Mexico than the material in the National Archives, simply because there was a much more extensive and competent diplomatic service from Great Britain in Latin America than from this country. Walt Scholes, among other historians, is already delving into this information. I do not know if any others here have been in those archives, but I cannot imagine any research topic that I have heard mentioned at this conference with regard to Latin America that would not benefit very greatly from that collection of material.

The question I would like to address to the panel is whether the National Archives has in its possession any information that is really of Latin American derivation. I am thinking of material comparable to the captured or seized records of Germany and Italy.

*Robert Smith:* The only items that come to my mind are the documents that were reputedly seized by the Pershing Expedition and which are supposedly part of the Villa archives. I cannot offhand think of any large volume of material in any way comparable to the collections that have been described earlier. As far as I know, during the military occupations of Cuba the records were either left or destroyed and not brought to the United States. In fact, even some of the records of the United States Military Government were left in Cuba. So that would have been an opportunity, for example, to have photographed (at the time impossible) the Cuban archives, but this action, of course, would have undermined the whole idea of independence.

The only thing I can think of are certain Mexican documents. Then there is the 1928 flurry over the purportedly forged documents—the collection of documents sent to the State Department, reputedly gathered by some agent from certain Mexican offices. There is a controversy as to whether these are authentic or whether they are forgeries. To the best of my knowledge this has never been fully established; the argument still goes on. Perhaps there are other materials, but these are the only examples that come to mind.

*Gustafson:* The only other group I can think of is something of rather obscure origin that we call the Library Collection. That is a collection of photostats of documents from the Cuban archives relating to early American history. But we regard this as library material rather than as archives.

*Pletcher:* I can give you one or two answers to your question. Not this but a rival institution, the Library of Congress, has quite a collection of photostats of Mexican documents. They are very rich for the 1840s and 1850s; they extend to as late as the 1860s, and some reach back to 1830s. But I think also in answer to this sort of question that what has already been mentioned earlier in this conference ought to be reemphasized. The State Department despatches from Latin America contain a great many inserted newspapers and fliers that are extremely valuable for studying Latin America in the nineteenth century. These are not documents, but often they are one of a kind and are selected for some particular article or some particular editorial of interest. The diplomat who prepared the despatch has often done part of the work for the researcher by culling articles from newspapers.

*Jerry Israel, University of Texas at El Paso:* I would like to ask Professor Smith a rather thorny question. Both Professors Pletcher and Trask have emphasized that multiarchival research in this field is essential, and yet your published work reflects (if I may take the liberty) more of the kind of thing Professors DeConde and Cole were talking about yesterday—domestic influences on the structure of United States policy. I wonder whether you will comment or whether you are in full agreement with Professors Pletcher and Trask's comment as to whether that kind of work no longer has any utility and that one must use British and other sources in order to study this field from a United States position.

*Robert Smith:* Quite frankly, I feel it is of the essence to study domestic pressures. Here again, granted the use of multiarchival resources, these people are still dealing at purely the diplomatic level. In the case of Mexico after 1917, the British, of course, had no relations until approximately the mid-1920s, when they requested the United States to help them reestablish relations. They had a chargé d'affaires and perhaps some spies, and they had the oil companies and other things that appear in the papers of Sir William Wiseman, who was head of British intelligence in the United States.

I certainly feel that to understand the formulation of United States policy, as differentiated from what the policy produced in the field or what a particular United States diplomat did in the field under specific circumstances, it is essential that one consider the various domestic groups a prime factor. I am not arguing that this is the only aspect of foreign relations. Certainly the field is considerably broader. For certain aspects of it I certainly agree that one has to get perspective. If one could get it from the Mexican archives as much as possible, that would be helpful. For example, one will find copies of United States correspondence in the Mexican archives.

The Mexicans had a very good spy system, by the way. Even though at one time they had to hire a private detective agency to conduct their intelligence work in the United States before they really got the thing organized. But here, again, I still think my approach is more basically oriented to the domestic influences shaping policy decisions. I am not arguing the unimportance of other aspects; this is simply my response to the question, and I do not mean to denigrate other approaches.

*William Beezley, State University of New York College at Plattsburg:* I would like to request an answer to one comment Dr. Smith made about the detective agency in the United States he mentioned. Was he referring to the Furlong Agency, and if so has he been able to find out anything about that agency?

*Smith:* My information comes from some limited material available in the one record group that I saw in Mexico last summer. I think (and here I would have to check my records) in the official Mexican documents they did not tend to identify the detective agency by name. I think, though, that this is the one. I would really have to check and refresh my memory on the name of the agency, but it was operating in 1917 and 1918. There is reference to such activity in United States archival sources but certainly with not much precision of information since the Mexicans were trying to organize their own foreign intelligence service. My primary exposure to it has been through the various reports, some of which have the tops clipped off and simply contain the essence of the report or maybe a distillation of the report. The Mexican archives, at least the record group that I saw, in certain ways are rather different from what we are accustomed to finding in United States archives. I found in this one record group, for example, relatively little correspondence but material such as I have described.

# United States Relations with East Asia

# The Study of Sino–American Relations: Where Are We Now and Where Must We Go from Here?

WARREN I. COHEN

In large part, the task before me and Professor Heinrichs has been made easier by the self-styled pundit among pooh-bahs, John King Fairbank, in his presidential address to the American Historical Association in December 1968. Professor Fairbank urged upon us as an assignment for the 1970s the study of American–East Asian relations. He offered a number of pressing reasons for undertaking this assignment, and he outlined the difficulties which impede us.

To those of us who are caught up in concern over the current follies of American policy toward China, whether it be the moment's furor over an ABM system to defend ourselves against Chinese missiles or the longer-endured horrors of the effort to contain China in Vietnam, the myth of an aggressive China is indeed oppressive. To those of us who are students of the broader scope of relations between the United States and China, there exists a host of other myths which we cannot blame on Dean Rusk or Lyndon Johnson or Melvin Laird or even the CIA. Although these gentlemen and that organization constitute an impressive array of myth makers, they cannot compete, in that capacity, with those who gave us the myth of the China market, the myth of a friendly China, the myth of a democratic China, and, of course, the myth of American altruism toward China.

At the 1968 AHA meeting, Ernest May, pleading for earlier access to materials on American foreign policy, sought to justify his request by explaining that with this material the historian might be able to help the policy maker avoid certain pitfalls and make better decisions. Hans Morgenthau, commenting on May's paper, insisted that what policy makers needed was not a more up-to-date record of the national experience, but "wisdom." Though I do not share May's optimistic estimate of the salutary results of more rapid analysis of the recent past, I know of no way to produce wiser statesmen than through analysis of the past—if not to provide lessons, then at least to destroy myths. If this process cannot guarantee an improvement in American policy, surely it allows for more hope than does a policy based upon false or at best unfounded assumptions.

The most obvious problem confronting the student who would like to set straight the record of Sino-American relations is the difficulty of the Chinese language. To be sure, there is much useful work to be done on the American side, in English-language sources, but there is infinitely more to be done on the Chinese side. For example, in addition to the broader works of Tyler Dennett and A. Whitney Griswold, we have numerous works on the formulation and meaning of the Open Door notes—but we have yet to study their impact on China and the formulation of Chinese policy. We have a host of careful analyses of Henry L. Stimson's every move during the Manchurian crisis and are increasingly well informed on every decision made within the Roosevelt administration prior to Pearl Harbor, but we know little, if anything, of what the Chinese were up to. Of course, part of this problem has nothing to do with language. I doubt if we will ever have available to us any meaningful collection of the papers of Chiang Kai-shek or T. V. Soong or of the Wai Chiao Pu. Even the existing records of the Wai Chiao Pu for the pre-Kuomintang period, theoretically available at the Academia Sinica, have been carefully, if not too efficiently, ransacked. Nonetheless, there are valuable Chinese sources in the Ch'ing documents such as were translated by Earl Swisher for the period from 1840 to 1860 and in a variety of published documents, memoirs, and newspapers available in the United States as well as in Japan, Hong Kong, and the Republic of China.

By using these sources, we might learn something about China's American policy, of the significance of the United States to China, of the perception of American policy among the Chinese. But to use these sources, we have to be able to read Chinese. And as John Fairbank declared, to my relief, "no one can simply 'read Chinese.' " Without quoting his elaboration, the point is that there are many different kinds of Chinese and even the number of natives who can read classical Chinese is rapidly declining—as I learned trying to find a research assistant in Taiwan. At the peak of my ability to read Chinese, I was limited to political writings from the 1920s to the Korean War—and I could not do so well today. Certainly, I cannot deny the difficulty of learning the language.

But what are the alternatives? Few indeed are those with the language skill who, like Earl Swisher, would sacrifice the time for the relatively thankless task of translating important sources for us. American students of Chinese history who are able to use the language, though not reluctant to offer criticism of contemporary American policy, have generally ignored the history of Sino-American relations. One alternative is to rely on Chinese scholars—not those like Li Ting-i who write in Chinese, but rather like Te-kong Tong and Tang Tsou who have performed valuable services with volumes in English. Even better results have been obtained by Akira Iriye, a Japanese scholar trained at Harvard who is able to utilize American, Chinese, Japanese, and Russian sources to write the kind of international history within which Ernest May has long argued that the history of recent American policy belongs. Regrettably, these Asian scholars frequently lack an understanding of the domestic context in which American policy is formulated.

Another alternative is the establishment of extensive contacts between students of American diplomacy and students of Chinese history, in the hope that in frequent conferences a useful exchange of information will emerge. Certainly we, in our attempts to understand internal Chinese affairs and their influence on American policy, can benefit from such contacts. In addition, students of Chinese history may yet concede that we, in our study of consular reports, of the State Department decimal files in particular, may have something to teach them about Chinese history.

For ourselves, these alternatives will have to suffice. Few among us have a choice. But I must insist that our students be allowed a choice, that they be pushed into Chinese language studies, that we demand of them a reading knowledge of Chinese as we would demand a knowledge of Spanish or French or German for those concerned with American relations with the nations of Europe and Latin America. Even so limited a language ability as my own can permit contributions—as in my articles on Chinese Communist attitudes towards the United States prior to the establishment of the People's Republic—and our schools are filled with students with far greater aptitude for language study than my own. Short of training American diplomatic historians who can use Chinese material themselves—that short we must always be of bringing the study of Sino-American relations up to the standards Profs. Robert E. Quirk and David M. Pletcher are requiring for United States–Latin American studies at Indiana or Prof. Bradford Perkins has done with his own work in Anglo-American relations. The task is a difficult one, but it is by no means impossible to accomplish. The AHA Committee on American–East Asian relations may provide some help, but we must all decide the standards upon which we will insist. Surely American relations with China are not likely to become less important in our lifetime.

But for those of us over thirty, too old to be retooled, working with students unable to use any but English language sources, there are a few questions yet to be answered, and in the National Archives lie clues to the solution of these and to questions yet unasked. Obviously most of these questions relate to the formulation of policy. Within this category, we might well begin by studying the sources of information available to the men making policy—and in the process perhaps we can determine who *they* are—their attitudes toward China and their perception of American interests in China and of the role of the United States in East Asia. Of course, for the followers of George Kennan or William Appleman Williams, who seem to agree that the United States pursued a single policy toward China, at least between 1899 and 1941, what I propose may seem irrelevant. But just as Raymond Esthus has raised questions about the meaning of the Open Door to various policy makers in the first few years of this century, I would suggest that close examination of successive administrations will allow far less complacency about the continuity of American policy. I do not mean to deny the possibility of generalization, but merely to question the reliability of generalizations which precede research. Moreover, I readily concede the value of such generalizations as stimuli for the research of others.

Scholars familiar with the basic literature on the policy of the United States toward China—at least with the works of Tyler Dennett and A. Whitney Griswold, both published before the Second World War—and familiar with much that has appeared in the *Foreign Relations* series—are aware of constant references to the Open Door, to the protection of American interests in China as the basis of policy. Now it is time for us to determine just what each administration understood these interests to be and just what the Open Door meant to a succession of presidents, secretaries of state, and lesser functionaries. Continuity of rhetoric provides no assurance of continuity of policy or even of intention. Certainly Dorothy Borg, in her study of the first six years of FDR's Far Eastern policy (*The United States and the Far Eastern Crisis of 1933–1938* . . . [Cambridge: Harvard University Press, 1964] ) has given cause to question theories of continuity. Both Dennett and Griswold found cycles in the American concern for the territorial integrity of China, and my own research confirms the existence of cycles in American attitudes toward China as well as in policy—cycles not predictable in terms of time or the political complexion of the administration. In fact, I suspect that these cycles are not generally dependent on Far Eastern considerations but are rather lesser arcs following the sinuations of American foreign policy in general.

In the presidential libraries, in the records of the Department of State, and in the less frequently used records of other departments and bureaus of the executive branch, there are countless estimates of developments in China, analyses of American interests there, arguments for and against various possible roles the United States might play in China. These are all important for an understanding of American perception of the Chinese condition, but these records may also provide insight into the process of policy formulation. A number of scholars, some inspired by the thought of William Appleman Williams, have demonstrated the importance of the Department of Commerce or the Treasury Department as formulators of policy independent of the Department of State. In Sino-American relations, this fact was particularly important from 1935 to 1941—as Dorothy Borg has shown and as Lloyd Gardner confirms. Surely our students will have to learn to look beyond the State Department decimal file, particularly to learn more about relations with a country in which American interests appear to have been largely commercial in the nineteenth and early twentieth centuries.

And what of the military services? Some of us have long used military intelligence reports as one means of learning about events in China—the most famous report being that on the Chinese Communist movement reissued in 1968 by Stanford University Press after being edited by Lyman P. Van Slyke. It is time that we examined the role of the military in the formulation of policy in China. Did the troops we stationed in China simply guard the legation or did their presence affect not only China's response to the United States, but also the nature of American policy—as, for example, in the face of Japanese military operations in China after 1937? What of the navy—my own favorite branch? What of the Asiatic fleet—what role did it play in the formulation of American policy? We all recall that naval officers in the nineteenth century were not above making their own foreign policy decisions. What of the fleet the United States kept in Chinese waters? We all recall the *Panay* incident, but there was a host of other less famous incidents in which hostile actions occurred between the Chinese and the vessels of the American Yangtze Patrol. Some of these operations were against "Communist bandits." Might these be meaningful to an analysis of Chinese policy then and now or of the total effect of American policy, regardless of what the president or secretary of state believed was American policy? When, toward the end of the Second World War, the navy equipped and trained forces under the control of the Chinese Nationalist leader responsible for anti-Communist operations, to what avail were the efforts of the Department of State to remain out of the KMT-CCP conflict?

Another influence on American policy toward China which has been neglected is Congress. No one who has been reading the papers during the last few years can doubt that congressional pressures have closed in on the executive branch's freewheeling policy in East Asia. Surely no student of history is unaware of the tremendous importance of Congress in the formulation of policy in the years between the Paris Peace Conference and the Japanese attack on Pearl Harbor. We are familiar with frequent references to the China Lobby which, functioning through Congress, is alleged to have thwarted the Truman administration's efforts to extricate itself from interference in the Chinese civil war. Has not the time come to investigate the role of Congress in Sino–American relations? In the files of the congressional committees concerned with foreign and the presumably separate military affairs, there may be a wealth of valuable material. Supplemented by evidence extracted from hearings and the correspondence of various congressmen which can be found in the State Department decimal file and presidential archives, these files may provide new and important insights relevant to our questions of *who* was making policy decisions and to what end.

Most researchers are aware of the limitations of exclusive use of the holdings of these archives, of the need to supplement materials available in the Archives Building and other material under control of the National Archives and Records Service with manuscript materials in a host of other libraries and attics all over the country. Let me emphasize the importance of the obvious corollary: the importance of supplementing manuscript research with materials available in the National Archives. To illustrate, let me begin with the problem of the role of the American missionary in Sino-American relations. John Fairbank has long urged the use of missionary archives which have time and again proved to be useful sources of information about events in China. In the State Department decimal file, in the files of congressional committees, in the presidential archives, there are countless examples of efforts by individual missionaries to influence policy decisions. Paul Varg has, of course, used many of these in his work. Of greater interest to me, however, has been the existence of evidence which sustains Chinese charges that missionaries served as agents of the government of the United States. I have been struck by the number of missionaries who sought political activity, who offered themselves to the government as sources of information, as "inside dopesters," or who worked for the Chinese government, seeking and achieving prestige not available to them at home. My favorite case is that of an American Catholic missionary who accepted a commission as a major general in the forces under the command of Tai Li, head of the Nationalist government's notorious "Blueshirts." During World War II, this man of God operated an intelligence network—spying not on the Japanese, but rather on the Chinese Communists for the benefit of the most reactionary elements in the Chinese Nationalist regime.

Similarly, a study of the role of journalists, from the familiar Thomas Milliard, Theodore White, George Sokolsky, and Edgar Snow, to the less well known case of Earl Leaf, while necessarily based on other manuscripts, would be greatly enhanced by evidence of their activities in the State Department decimal file, military intelligence reports, and perhaps other files in the Archives. These men not only served as sources of information for the American public, but for the government as well. Some of them served simultaneously as advisors to the Chinese government or lobbyists in Washington, and at least one came back to the United States to run a propaganda agency financed by the Chinese government.

In this realm of the influence of private groups on relations between the United States and China, we have done well in our study of segments of the business community, but in the process we have greatly exaggerated the influence of business interests on policy simply by *understudying* and ultimately underestimating the importance of other private influences, such as missionary and other church organizations and the American peace movement. In these areas basic research must be done in collections elsewhere, but in my own work I have found much of value (in the State Department decimal file and, thanks to Wayne Cole, in the files of congressional committee) which was not available in the files of the organizations I studied. This material on occasion indicated the importance or lack of importance of various individuals and organizations in the eyes of those men presumably formulating policy.

In sum, there is no shortage of work to be done on the American side. And again, the past has shown that valuable contributions have been made by scholars who had no other options: by Griswold who knew little of Asian history, and more recently in the excellent work by Dorothy Borg, Paul Varg, and Marilyn Young, written without benefit of Chinese language training, though not without Chinese sources. Borg and Young in particular have performed perhaps the most important task of the student of American policy toward China—and that is to place this policy within the larger context of American foreign policy. Their work has indicated the extent to which the domestic influences and impulses affecting policy toward China were the same impulses affecting policy toward other parts of the world and has indicated the relative significance of China in American policy considerations.

And so, as I see the assignment for the seventies, it is to produce young scholars not only capable of work of the quality of the Borgs, Vargs, and Youngs but also capable of applying such magnificent talent to *both* sides of the historic relationship between China and the United States.

# Progress and Opportunity in the Field of Japanese–American Relations

WALDO H. HEINRICHS, JR.

This paper has three purposes: to report on how the study of Japanese-American relations is doing at the moment; to describe how scholars are currently approaching the subject; and to sketch briefly what they are saying.

The second topic—how historians are approaching the subject—receives most attention because we know a great deal more at the moment about how we are searching than what altogether we are finding. The history of American foreign relations and Japanese-American relations in particular is in a state of flux. New materials, new methods, new perspectives are providing a bewildering variety of triangulations on the past. The older frameworks and reference points no longer seem valid. Many otherwise sound studies answer questions we no longer are asking. The past seems to be assuming new form but in patches, for we lack new syntheses. Like the blind man and the elephant we have a lively sense of what is beneath our touch but little sense of the whole.

The study of Japanese-American relations is a vigorous and thriving enterprise. A growing number of good scholars are using archival and presidential library materials and publications relating to Japan. They are attracted partly by current interest in Japan. Whether avowedly or not, historians are always influenced and affected by the present in what they seek of the past, and East Asia bears heavily on our consciousness. Japan itself has a growing significance. We are all familiar with this extraordinary nation's leap from prostration in 1945 to present material prosperity and first-class economic power. Thus far Japan's growing power has been largely masked by her identification with the United States for security purposes, but that condition is changing. More and more she will seek her own identity and become a distinct unit in international politics. We hope and trust that the two nations can establish a permanent partnership, but it would be unrealistic to expect her attachment to us for all purposes. Inevitably Japan will pursue a course in some degree independent.

As Japan moves out from the umbrella of American protection she will assume a more interesting role to the student of international political history. Questions will be asked that have been asked in an earlier period of Japanese history. The modern history of Japan falls into three periods. The first, from the opening of Japan in 1854 to the Sino-Japanese War of 1894, was a time when Japan was learning from the West to strengthen herself against the West. It offers a fascinating story of modernization and cultural mediation but has less significance from the point of view of diplomacy because of Japan's subordinate role as a pupil nation. In the second period, from 1895 to 1945, Japan sought in various ways that became increasingly desperate and ultimately tragic to find a suitable role as a great power. The third period, from 1945 to the present, found Japan once again under the tutelage of the West. Now that her American interlude appears to be ending, she must once again face the perils of an island nation sandwiched between great powers. Will Japan find an acceptable role as leader of the East, or will she act as agent of the West in the East, or as mediator between East and West? Or will she try to play all these roles? These are questions Japan also faced in the second period.

This second period is especially rich in historical materials. We can now see State Department records to the end of World War II. The microfilm publication of the 1910–29 State Department decimal file as well as the publication of the Roosevelt papers relating to foreign affairs simplify research by bringing materials on campus. The presidential library system bulks ever larger in research plans, for the papers of upper- and middle-echelon foreign affairs officials as well as for the central collections. But scattering the libraries from Massachusetts to California and Texas to Iowa poses a severe problem. In meeting presidential and local desires, the added financial burden on the scholar tends to be forgotten. History is not necessarily divisible by presidential administrations, and the careers of the officials whose papers repose in the libraries span many decades, so we must crisscross the nation. Would it not be possible for the presidential libraries to set up a joint fund for travel grants to match grants of universities and foundations?

Documentation on the Japanese side is formidable. Scholarship on the 1930s began as a Western enterprise with the proceedings and translated documents of the Tokyo war crimes trials, but in the sixties young Japanese historians began moving with increasing confidence and success to recover their past. The multivolume *Road to the Pacific War,* a group effort, has been judged an impressive achievement and is in the process of translation to English.[1] Another group of Japanese historians has recently published a seven-volume collection of documents which they claim virtually exhausts the basic materials on the thirties.[2] Archival materials are available for earlier decades as well, and young American scholars trained in university East Asian centers are in Japan making use of them. Still more are needed, and a committee of the American Historical Association is seeking funds to assist graduate students as well as senior historians who want to make the effort to cross the East Asian language barrier.

This summer a dozen or so American historians ventured forth to Japan for a unique historical gathering. They met for four days with an equal number of Japanese scholars and by way of simultaneous translation discussed papers they had previously prepared and exchanged. These papers seek to reconstruct, brick by brick, the history of American-Japanese relations in the decade before Pearl Harbor. Each American historian has been assigned one element in the policy-making and opinion-forming process: the president, the State Department, Congress and political parties, the American embassy in Tokyo, the Navy, War, Commerce, and Treasury Departments, business, private groups, the press, and historians. Furthermore, each American is paired with a Japanese historian who has been assigned the rough Japanese equivalent. The papers will soon be published in English and Japanese. Next winter at another conference sixteen historians will present papers on the entire course of American-East relations with the object of making an inventory on what has been done and what needs to be done. In this case participants will generally take a narrow time span to deal with exhaustively. All these efforts should start a major restructuring of the history of American-Japanese relations and make this a lively field in the next few years, both for archivists and for historians.

Note the emphasis in all these efforts on team history. This group approach testifies to the extraordinary complexity of the subject, arising as much from the fact that we expect more of our explanations as from inherent difficulty. The student of American-Japanese relations may cast his topic in four different frames of reference. Not all will necessarily apply to a given event, but all will apply sooner or later.

First the student must consider the East Asian framework, including at times Southeast Asia. This was a distinct diplomatic arena with its own stakes and actors. The actors might be Western powers, but they moved under constraints imposed by the region's geography and problems as well as the policies of the other powers. In other words, there was a separate, though changing, international power structure for East Asia which strongly conditioned activities of Japan and the United States. No one has done more to give us a sense of this East Asian dimension than Prof. Akira Iriye of the

University of Chicago. Born in Japan in 1934 and trained in the United States, Iriye is one of the few historians equipped to work in the languages of all major nations active in the Far East. He represents, according to Prof. John K. Fairbank, a "new generation of international scholarship . . . composed of young researchers who are not culture-bound, who have a world view that encompasses the various cultures and uses the social sciences, and who are unafraid to put the interest of the human race above that of any particular nation as they look at the historical record."[3] Iriye's first book, *After Imperialism,* is a study of how the Soviet Union, Japan, and the United States dealt with the problem of revolutionary nationalism in China in the twenties.[4] More recently he has brilliantly reconstructed the American-Chinese-Japanese triangle from the beginning until the present in a book entitled *Across the Pacific,* which also provides an excellent introduction to recent thought on American–East Asian relations.[5]

A purely East Asian framework by no means suffices, however. At times that sphere was distinct, at other times not. For Theodore Roosevelt, diplomacy was a single global game, and we will gain a fuller appreciation of his 1905 mediation of the Russo-Japanese War if we view it as part of a skillfully orchestrated program to maintain peace among the great powers. Similarly, an explanation of Woodrow Wilson's decisions at Paris respecting China and Japan is incomplete unless placed within the context of an immensely complex world settlement. In the thirties and forties policy makers in the United States, as well as in Britain and the Soviet Union, had to weigh interests and risks in East Asia against those in Europe. As a result, American Asian policy was often the reciprocal of American European policy; it was a "large policy" when European problems were small, and vice versa. Caution succeeded boldness in Wilson's handling of Japan's demands on China when war began with Germany. Boldness succeeded caution in Franklin Roosevelt's handling of Japan in 1941, after Germany's attack on Russia relieved fears for Britain's survival. The broad history of American foreign relations has much to contribute to the East Asian specialist.

A third frame of reference has to do with what nations consider acceptable international conduct. Most of the twentieth century seems to lack standards, but at times certain norms prevailed. At the turn of the century great powers acted according to a set of assumptions we cover with the term "diplomacy of imperialism." This involved various types of control—colonialism, spheres of influence, concessions—over lesser powers and so-called backward areas, as well as forms of understanding and adjustment between great powers. Japan and the United States both more or less accepted these norms, and this common sense of what was acceptable facilitated adjustment of differences. Thus Theodore Roosevelt had no qualms, indeed found positive advantage, in accepting Japanese expansion on the mainland at Korea's, China's, or Russia's expense. By the same token, when Wilson changed the rules of the game, as he did in introducing the New Diplomacy, he placed an added burden on Japanese-American relations. And again, this strain was relieved when Japan came to accept the new pattern of conduct at the Washington Conference of 1921–22. The point is that implicit international sanctions cannot be ignored in describing Japanese-American relations.

There remains one more framework of analysis, the domestic scene. Foreign policy decisions reflect the complex internal interests, perspectives, and political pressures of any national decision. The pressures are broader and more diffuse in a democratic system, but political power is rarely absolute, and initiatives abroad must be weighed against domestic needs and capacities. We are not ignoring internal factors. For example, Charles E. Neu's *Uncertain Friendship* shows how the internationalist framework chopped off a good part of the story of Roosevelt's handling of Japanese problems in the years 1906 to 1909.[6] He sees the president responding sensitively to domestic factors in foreign relations.

It is apparent that the history of American foreign relations is greatly enlarging its perspectives, to the point where it is difficult to describe it as a distinct field of history. What the foreign minister said to the ambassador and the ambassador said in return is only part of the story. We shall be exploring records that on the surface bear not the remotest relation to our topics. Yet all these circumambulations eventually will lead us back to the traditional goal of the diplomatic historian, the explanation of events in the intercourse of nations. The same diversification exists in the kinds of data historians select and the way they use them. Let me offer five examples of methodological innovation as they may apply to Japanese-American relations.

First, biography will continue to be a useful historical medium. Foreign affairs biography will not be immune to advances in the technique of probing the inner man. Prof. Betty Glad has applied a certain psychological typology to the personality of Charles Evans Hughes as secretary of state.[7] Her study is suggestive, but we are still a long way from Freudian diplomacy. More pedestrian but immediately useful would be group biographies. We need to know a great deal more about Americans in eastern Asia—missionaries, businessmen, and old China hands as well as old Japan hands in the Foreign Service. Aside from personal and official papers much can be learned about their socioeconomic backgrounds and careers through quantitative methods, as behavioralists in sociology, political science, and history have shown. The difficulty is that Foreign Service personnel records, which may contain a great deal of such information, are confidential, and properly so. Yet, since the type of information the historian seeks is not individual but aggregate and numerical, it seems to me that some method could be found to gather the data without violating the privacy of the records.

Second, the economic factor should receive closer scrutiny. The extent to which economic interest determines foreign policy is a much-debated question, and the case of Japanese-American relations is complex. Competition in the China market was certainly productive of tension, but the American trade and investment stake in Japan was always greater than in China, and occasionally American businessmen sought to exert a restraining influence on both Japanese and American governments. On the other hand, expectation if not reality made the China trade important, and for every business friend of Japan in America there were business enemies whose goods were undersold by Japanese imports. With all these plusses and minuses it is difficult to determine the net effect on Japanese-American relations. We need more detailed trade analyses and entrepreneurial case studies showing market strategy, political influence, profits and losses, and relations with Japanese counterparts. Toy, notion, and silk importers, cotton exporters, oil companies, and investment houses would all merit studies. Records of business firms will be important, as well as records of the Bureau of Foreign and Domestic Commerce, consular reports, and embassy economic reports.

Third, public opinion will regain attention, but with a new mode of inquiry. We have shied away from it because results seemed impressionistic and haphazard. Now Ernest May's essay on American attitudes toward imperialism suggests methods for grappling with it more effectively.[8] Using the techniques of communications researchers and other social scientists, May has narrowed the scope of inquiry to public opinion that counts; that is, to those Americans who were interested in foreign affairs and community opinion leaders whose views they respected. His results are gross and speculative, he admits, but he does open the way to a methodical assessment of the very important factor of American public attitudes toward Japan. The influence of the press is also ripe for analysis. After all, the world of policy makers has to a great extent been the one pictured in the *New York Times*. Furthermore, valuable estimates of what policy makers believed the public was thinking are to be found in State Department records and presidential collections. Occasionally, in the most unlikely places, we run into collections of what John Q. Citizen was saying. For example, in the 1900–1910 files of the Adjutant General of the Army is a fascinating group of letters from Americans who were worrying about a Japanese invasion. The provenance of the letters suggests that anti-Japanese feeling was not restricted to the Pacific slope but was felt in all parts of the country.

Fourth, we shall read more about bureaucratic processes as they affect foreign policy, and I use the word "bureaucratic" in a descriptive and not pejorative sense. We have tended to assume that national decisions are reached by some orderly sifting of rational alternatives, yet political scientists and sociologists tell us this is not necessarily so. Roberta Wohlstetter's book, *Pearl Harbor: Warning and Decision,* gives us a startling look at government sliced open.[9] We see that in the mass of information feeding into the agencies dealing with foreign affairs, there existed critical data that pointed to a Japanese attack on Pearl Harbor but that procedures for handling and disseminating information and the preconceptions, or mindsets, of evaluators resulted in these "signals" being ignored. The Wohlstetter book shows us the inner workings of government at a moment in time, but more can be learned by studying them over time. Organization theory tells us that bureaucracies have their own patterns of behavior, their own goals, priorities, and procedures. Above all, each bureaucracy has a need to survive and enlarge itself if possible. If we conceive of government as a conglomeration of bureaucracies, then foreign policy decisions become compromises among those concerned with foreign affairs, the State Department, the military services, and so forth, each proceeding according to its inner dictates. By directing our attention to these subunits of government and learning their organizational habits and needs, we discover a great deal. Where the topography of policy had seemed flat, it is now full of hills and valleys.

It is easy to assume, for example, that the more active China policy of the Taft administration, particularly in countering Japanese influence in Manchuria, was simply a response to business pressure for overseas trade and investment opportunities. Yet the diplomat-financier Willard Straight encouraged a more active policy for the additional reason that it would arouse favorable sentiment among businessmen for reform and enlargement of the diplomatic and consular services.[10] So we need to consider the bureaucratic needs of the State Department as well. Government was the handmaid of business expansion, true, but it would also appear that business was the handmaid of government expansion.

Another example is War Plan Orange. On the face of it this is typical staffing by the military services against the contingency of war with Japan. Yet the story must be more complex if we credit the following excerpt of a letter of 1940 from the commander in chief of the United States fleet, Adm. J. O. Richardson:

It is the general conception that the Plan had its inception primarily in the desirability of having a guiding directive for the development of the Naval Establishment to meet any international situation that might be thrust upon it. It is my belief that the impracticabilities of the ORANGE Plan, in the absence of a better one, have been periodically overlooked in order that the Department might have for budget purposes and presentation to Congress the maximum justification for the necessary enlargement of the Navy.[11]

Richardson had been the budget officer of the navy. What he said suggests that in terms of the bureaucratic imperatives of the navy, this basic strategic policy appears less as a sailing plan than as a building plan.

Fifth, greater attention is being paid to foreign relations as intellectual history. It should be self-evident that men who make policy are much affected by their view of what past policy has been, by their perception of what role their nation should play, and by their images of other nations—in short, by their ideas. Among Americans interested in East Asia, public and private, we can discern shifting constellations of ideas about East Asia, and by delineating these patterns of thought, we can grasp the underpinnings of policy. A great virtue of Iriye's *Across the Pacific* is his depiction of the images which Chinese, Japanese, and Americans held of one another and his contrasting of image and reality. For example, Americans, in groping for an understanding of Japanese, drew upon their own experiences and views of themselves in projecting an image of Japan, and Chinese and Japanese did the same in reverse. The resultant myth and misunderstanding found its way into policy. Iriye calls for study of the past to relieve ourselves of the burden of the past. "Only when American–East Asian relations are seen as an intellectual problem," he says, ". . . will it become possible to transcend the past and look toward a more peaceful Pacific."[12]

With such a variety of approaches, obviously no historian will be able to command the whole field of Japanese-American relations. Each will tackle some part of it according to his interests and background. The archivist may find requests for his assistance perplexing in their variety, but he will know his sources are being put to ever-greater use.

To turn to what historians are learning, we find emphasis on the discontinuities of this turbulent century. When each decade is examined on its own terms, rather than burdened with later events, the picture of monolithic Japanese expansionism stretching back to the nineteenth century falls to pieces. The coincidental emergence of Japan and the United States as great powers and rivals in the Pacific and East Asia created strains and antagonism, but the relationship to 1909 was characterized less by the tensions than by the generally satisfactory adjustment of differences, and what is more, the expectation of adjustment. The following dozen years to 1921 is the most obscure period of the relationship and begs study. It witnessed a parting of ways, primarily over Japanese expansion on the mainland, as the result of opportunities created by the war in Europe. It is noteworthy that Japan displayed a marked sensitivity to the reactions of the United States and an eagerness to make her gains acceptable or, if unacceptable, to scale them down. Furthermore, adjustment was not so easy as before because the United States was taking a new interest in what it liked to conceive as an emergent democracy in China and was revolutionizing the rules of international conduct in denouncing the old diplomacy and demanding equality of nations and self-determination. Suddenly alliances, concessions, and spheres of influence were evil. Nevertheless Japan adjusted to the new style while maintaining intact the core of her influence on the mainland. The decade of the twenties was peaceable but not internationalist as we had supposed. Japan did not adopt the cooperative approach to East Asian problems implicit in the Washington Treaty framework, but neither did the other signatories, including the United States. Rather each nation went its own way. As of 1931 Japan and the United States had failed to establish any intimacy or any habit or system of cooperation. Considerable suspicion and antagonism had taken root and naval and economic rivalry persisted. Nothing in the relationship assured peace, yet nothing precluded it.

Postwar writing on the decade before Pearl Harbor has been generally in accord with the judgment of the Tokyo war crimes trials that Japan was in the grip of a militarist conspiracy that executed a carefully planned program of totalitarianism, war, and empire. That view seems to be passing. Recent revisionists would not contend that Japan was a peace-loving, law-abiding nation; on the contrary, in the new view this was an exceedingly dangerous nation, but not so much from intent as the absence of careful calculation and ordered purpose. The Japanese military services anticipated that Japan could never find security except through self-sufficiency and her own strong arm, and they anticipated total war. But war with whom and when, and what constituted an adequacy of resources and territory, were subjects of shifting opinion and constant dispute. No central authority existed to rationalize the aims of the services with Japan's capabilities. As a result Japan blundered into full-scale war in China when anticipating war with the Soviet Union and blundered into the southward advance partly to extricate itself from the morass of the China war and partly to seize the resources required for war with the United States, which seemed inevitable only upon the seizure of these resources. Looking backward, the Greater East Asia Co-Prosperity Sphere seems the fulfillment of a step-by-step program of conquest; looking forward it seems an ever more desperate and neurotic search for security. In this disoriented condition Japan was very much at the mercy of world events and moves by other powers. What the United States did or did not do made a great deal of difference. Thus the road to Pearl Harbor is full of twists and turns.

Why did war come then? Let me mention three factors that seem important in the answer. I would stress the importance of world events. The economic crisis in the early thirties had a profound impact on Japan, as did the German triumph in Europe. Second, the Kennan critique of legalism and moralism in American policy is still pertinent, but more as an explanation for the failure of initiatives for compromise and negotiation on the China question than as an explanation for American initiatives to halt the Japanese advance.[13] As Dorothy Borg has shown, the United States took care to avoid any provocation of Japan in the 1933 to 1938 period.[14] It was the Indochina not the China advance of Japan that triggered a confrontation. Third, there is one significant continuity in American–East Asian relations of the twentieth century, and that is the persistent American idea of the United States as an Asian power. It was a collapsible and expansible idea; its locus shifted from group to group and agency to agency; the kind of role the United States might play varied over time. But the concept remained and had much to do with establishing in the American mind this nation's quality as a world power. Japan's threat to foreclose that role, I think, was very significant in determining American policy in the last years of peace.

There is much research and writing to be done. We feel free of cast-iron assumptions and conclusions. We are dissatisfied, restless and curious, and that is a healthy sign for the study of American-Japanese relations.

## NOTES

1. See review article by Akire Iriye, "Japanese Imperialism and Aggression: Reconsiderations II," *Journal of Asian Studies* 23 (Nov. 1963): 103–13.
2. See review article by Akira Iriye, "Japan's Foreign Policies between World Wars—Sources and Interpretations," ibid. 26 (Aug. 1967): 677–82.
3. John K. Fairbank, introduction to Akira Iriye, *Across the Pacific: An Inner History of American–East Asian Relations* (New York: Harcourt, Brace & World, 1967), p. x.
4. Akira Iriye, *After Imperialism: The Search for a New Order in the Far East, 1921–1931* (Cambridge: Harvard University Press, 1965).
5. See note 3.
6. Charles E. Neu, *An Uncertain Friendship: Theodore Roosevelt and Japan, 1906–1909* (Cambridge: Harvard University Press, 1967).
7. Betty Glad, *Charles Evans Hughes and the Illusions of Innocence: A Study in American Diplomacy* (Urbana: University of Illinois Press, 1966).

8. Ernest R. May, *American Imperialism: A Speculative Essay* (New York: Atheneum, 1968).
9. Roberta Wohlstetter, *Pearl Harbor: Warning and Decision* (Stanford: Stanford University Press, 1962).
10. Straight to Wilbur J. Carr, Aug. 6, 1909, Papers of Wilbur J. Carr, Library of Congress, Washington, D.C.
11. U.S., Congress, Joint Committee on the Investigation of the Pearl Harbor Attack, *Hearings*, 79th Cong., 1st sess., 1946, 39 pts., 14:968.
12. Iriye, *Across the Pacific*, p. 329.
13. George F. Kennan, *American Diplomacy, 1900–1950* (Chicago: University of Chicago Press, 1951).
14. Dorothy Borg, *The United States and the Far Eastern Crisis of 1933–1938: From the Manchurian Incident through the Initial Stage of the Undeclared Sino-Japanese War* (Cambridge: Harvard University Press, 1964).

# United States Relations with East Asia

## DISCUSSION

*James W. Moore, National Archives and Records Service:* To begin, I think I had better answer to the best of my ability Professor Heinrich's question regarding presidential library grants. During the past nine years the Truman Library Institute has given 125 grants for travel. I do know that the Hoover Library Association is considering doing something similar; I do not know about the others. Thus grants are being made, but it is highly unlikely that we will ever have funds appropriated by Congress to use for this purpose; they would have to come from another source.

*Barbara Tuchman:* I am fascinated by both of these presentations. I am working on United States–China relations myself at the moment. I think one word that I want to pick up was Professor Cohen's use of the word *wisdom,* which seems to be in a sense a key to one of the problems of diplomatic history. Perhaps what we all want to see and what we are working toward is the development of wisdom in policy making. I think that in our current history, in the experience of Vietnam, we know (at least I believe) that this policy could have been avoided by understanding our previous relations with East Asia. That is, by the application of wisdom. It seems to me the subject historians should be approaching is how policy is made in the larger sense. What happens to it, who makes it, how it develops, why wisdom is absent. So many of the things I have heard at this conference come together in this question of what subject matter we all should be trying to find and the question of the uses of history. In this field these are extremely urgent because of the connection with the formation of policy. The question of subject matter and the approach to it has been dramatically emphasized in the last decade, in the last five years, by the contrast with the Vietnam policy and what we ought to have known about our relations with Asia before our involvement in Vietnam.

*Warren I. Cohen:* Well, I think we are all agreed on the value of wisdom to our policy makers and I think we all have to agree that how we are going to impart this wisdom to them is a problem. As historians, I think we are committed to a particular technique. Now I think what we have failed to do and failed to consider is how we are to make policy makers read the things we write. In the years I have spent at the Fletcher School of International Law and Diplomacy and in dealing with diplomats in my years in Taiwan, with friends in the Foreign Service, and with other unmentionable agencies in the American government, I myself have been appalled by their ignorance of the literature in the fields in which they were making policy decisions, appalled by the fact the people responsible for making these tremendous decisions every day knew far less about what was in the archives of the Department of State than I did, in their own specialty.

This, I suppose, is the problem. I fear that for imparting wisdom, Professor Morganthau would have had us read *The Idea of National Interest* and stop there. I think our own technique for revealing the past is the only one that I can come up with. Perhaps Professor Heinrichs can think of some way to induce policy makers to read about the past.

# United States Relations
# with the
# Middle East and Africa

# Researching American Relations with the Middle East: The State of the Art, 1970

JOHN A. DeNOVO

President John Quincy Adams sent young William Brown Hodgson to Algiers in the summer of 1825 to study oriental languages, because "we were in this country so destitute of persons versed in the Oriental languages that we could not even procure a translation of any paper which occasionally came to us in Arabic."[1] It comes as a surprise to discover that another president encountered similar difficulties as late as World War II. Several weeks elapsed on one occasion before Franklin D. Roosevelt received a translation of a personal letter from King Ibn Saud of Saudi Arabia, which the Department of State had farmed out to a legal consultant of the Veterans Administration. Some months later, Roosevelt complained when one of his secretaries presented him with another letter in Arabic from Ibn Saud. "Will you please let me know," he objected, "where and when you think I learned to read and translate Arabic? Please take pity on me and have this translated and any similar Arabic letters that come in the future, before sending them to me."[2]

Official Washington's apparent dearth of competent Arabic translators was a token of the larger national neglect of Middle Eastern studies in the United States prior to the mid-twentieth century. There had been, of course, a tradition of scholarship concerned with the ancient Near East, notably the biblical lands, and those universities offering oriental languages usually did so in connection wtih curriculums in theology, archaeology, and ancient history. Only during the past quarter century have comprehensive centers developed for study of the modern Middle East. Not until 1946, when the newly established Middle East Institute inaugurated the *Middle East Journal,* was there a major American journal dedicated to that entire region; and there was no strictly professional association until the formation of the Middle East Studies Association of North America in 1967.[3]

243

Although historians of American foreign relations had devoted considerable attention to relations with Latin America, the Far East, and Europe prior to the 1940s, they had virtually ignored the past connections with the lands between the Eastern Mediterranean and the Persian Gulf.[4] The first reasonably comprehensive study from the American side was Leland J. Gordon's *American Relations with Turkey, 1830–1930: An Economic Interpretation,* published in 1932.[5] Notwithstanding his intended economic emphasis, Gordon introduced the diplomatic and cultural aspects of the connection. His remained the only notable monograph in the field for a generation.

Momentum gathered slowly after World War II. In 1947 a book appeared that claimed by its title to treat American relations with the region. This was Ephraim A. Speiser's *The United States and the Near East,* a commendable but slim volume in the American Foreign Policy Library, a series aimed particularly at providing American readers with area background and only incidentally at supplying a few miscellaneous details about past American activities in the area. A companion volume in the same series, covering Turkey and Iran, appeared in 1951.[6] To illuminate contemporary policy issues at mid-twentieth century, Jacob C. Hurewitz's valuable *Middle East Dilemmas: The Background of United States Policy* employed substantial historical flashbacks.[7]

As the area became an arena of the cold war and while the Arab-Israeli conflict remained unsettled and Western Europe relied increasingly on Persian Gulf oil, the writing issued in the 1950s often reflected the continuing contemporary crises. Historians and political scientists published books between 1952 and 1960 manifesting those current concerns. In *The Middle East in World Affairs,* George Lenczowski touched on the role of the United States, which John C. Campbell treated more expansively in his *Defense of the Middle East: Problems of American Policy.*[8] Several solid monographs detailing the history of Middle Eastern oil appeared during the 1950s, many of them authored by Americans. Those of Stephen H. Longrigg (an Englishman), Benjamin Shwadran, and David H. Finnie are still standard volumes on this important subject.[9] American activities in Iran were the subject of books by T. H. Vail Motter and Abraham Yeselson.[10] Several doctoral dissertations and master's theses completed during the decade and a half following World War II have formed the basis for books that have appeared only recently or are forthcoming.[11]

What was missing in this early postwar output was a sufficient foundation of basic monographs exploring in depth American contacts with the Middle East since the eighteenth century. Reasons for the relative neglect of an eastern orientation are not difficult to suggest, for Americans had long looked westward and southward. Preoccupation with the westward movement, stimulated by Frederick Jackson Turner's insights and the assiduous labors of his disciples since the 1890s, coincided with the parallel projection of American interests across the Pacific on an unprecedented scale, even though the United States had been a Pacific power for at least half a century. What had largely receded from memory was that there had been an early Mediterranean trade paralleling and related to the early China trade; that the treaty of 1830 with the Ottoman Empire was followed by Edmund Roberts's treaty with the sultan of Muscat and Oman in 1833, both agreements antedating Caleb Cushing's Treaty of Wanghia with China and Commo. Matthew Perry's "opening" of Japan; and that a small, but colorful array of private Americans had engaged in missionary, advisory, and other functions.[12]

Two notable recent books that have done much to record the activities of Americans in the Mediterranean and Middle East during the nation's first century are David H. Finnie's *Pioneers East: The Early American Experience in the Middle East* and, more comprehensively and explicitly, James A. Field, Jr., *America and the Mediterranean World, 1776–1882*. Finnie dealt episodically with a varied assortment of Americans who experienced the Middle East firsthand prior to 1850. During those years, "a constant procession of essentially nonpolitical Americans [journeyed] to the Middle East: missionaries, of course, but also merchants, engineers, inventors, promoters, and artisans; scientists, scholars, and literary figures; philanthropists, adventurers, tourists, and eccentrics; naval officers and sailors; and even a farmer or two." Finnie arranged his narrative around the travels of the young adventurer John Lloyd Stephens, who "was characteristically American in his conviction that human energy and enterprise could bring about beneficial change. The frontier experience seemed to prove precisely this." The author contended that these eastward pioneers "gave the New World its first direct exposure to what is still in many ways a remote and difficult culture and society. The lives they led, the reports they brought home, and the books they published—even if largely forgotten now— awakened Americans of their own and succeeding generations to the romantic inscrutability of the Middle East and to its importance and challenge as well." Today's Americans in the Middle East, Finnie suggests, "are not all so different from some of the early ones."[13]

The idea of Americans' "pioneering" in the Middle East, carried in Finnie's title and intermittently in his narrative, has been developed more fully into a sophisticated thesis by Field, whose book represents the most striking advance in the state of the art during recent years. While muting the traditional emphases on the Atlantic moat and westward expansion, he accentuates maritime and ideological frontiers, thereby raising to their proper importance the neglected subjects of early foreign commerce and missions.

The United States, Field believes, established its conception of its relationship to the world in the Mediterranean during the nineteenth century. Americans searched "for the better world through (1) the fostering of a mutually profitable and civilizing commerce; (2) the support of self-determination and the rights of small nations and subject peoples; (3) modernization, whether in religion or secular terms." By the mid-twentieth century, these aspects of policy "had become generalized and ecumenical." He suggests that the anti-European bias inherent in Washington's Farewell Address, in the Monroe Doctrine, and even in Frederick Jackson Turner's writings "is really an anti-power bias. The government declined [political] entanglement, but no merchant or missionary or naval officer ever drew a line down the middle of the Atlantic; equally the dimensions and the behavior of Europe at any given time are important in influencing the thrust of American activity." From these ideas, he infers that "the history of the last century of American foreign relations, like that of American internal development, is in large part one of the shift of function from private to public sector (e.g., privateer into naval officer, missionary into Peace Corps operative, etc.)." "The long run shift [also] involves . . . the problems that develop for those committed to an anti-power ideology when they find that they are powerful."[14]

A third well-researched and illuminating book about nineteenth-century activities of Americans, specifically those finding outlets for their religious and educational predilections in the region of Greater Syria, has come from the pen of A. L. Tibawi.[15] Included in his study are illuminating comparisons and contrasts of American efforts with those of counterparts from several European nations. The issue of the Turkish straits, so central to the international diplomacy of the Eastern Question, was the subject of an article by Harry N. Howard, while Lenoir C. Wright's new book scrutinizes in detail relationships with Egypt before 1914.[16] Much new information about the humanitarian impulse appears in Robert L. Daniel's recently published *American Philanthropy in the Near East, 1820–1960*.[17]

No scholar has yet been brave (or foolhardy) enough to write a comprehensive survey of American contacts with the Middle East from the late eighteenth century to the present. Field's *America and the Mediterranean World* serves admirably for the segment from 1776 to 1882 and even sketches subsequent developments briefly in an epilogue. But there is a gap for most of the 1880s and the 1890s. These decades deserve the attention of a competent scholar who can portray the Middle Eastern relationships in terms of both the internal and external dynamics influencing American foreign relations.

For the first four decades of the twentieth century there is my attempt to provide a comprehensive synthesis.[18] I developed the plan for that book in 1957 in the face of the prevailing wisdom holding that there was little worth researching, except perhaps the period of Wilsonian concern during the Paris Peace Conference. Certainly there was only a scanty foundation of previous scholarship on which to build, but it turned out that the scope and extent of American connections during those forty years taxed the capabilities of a single researcher. Even the extensive research in unpublished archives of the Department of State fell short of being "exhaustive." I assuaged the frustrations generated by my inability to follow all the leads by hoping that the offering would encourage others to expand and, where necessary, revise my findings.

This is exactly what has been happening as several scholars have been assiduously probing the relationships during World War I and its aftermath, currently the most intensively examined chronological segment. Recent or impending studies take up the grand themes of relief for hard-pressed minorities of the Ottoman Empire and the Wilsonian concern with national self-determination that made the American president a symbol of world leadership attracting such aspiring national groups as Syrians, Zionists, and Egyptians.[19] Near East relief and related subjects receive attention in Daniel's *American Philanthropy*. The Armenian question has been explored in depth by James B. Gidney in *A Mandate for Armenia* and in a series of articles by Thomas A. Bryson, who is also completing studies of Walter George Smith and the Armenian Question.[20] Harry N. Howard published in 1963 the definitive monograph on the King-Crane Commission.[21] Currently in press is Joseph L. Grabill's *Protestant Diplomacy and the Near East: Missionary Influence on American Policy, 1810–1927,* based on extensive research in archives and manuscript collections. Grabill concentrates on the intercultural and political role of missionaries and philanthropists from 1914 to 1920, presenting them as the chief lobbying influences in Wilsonian support for Syrian and Armenian self-determination.[22] "Wilson and Near East Nationalism" is the theme of a book being completed by Leon E. Boothe.[23] In his *United States Policy and the Partition of Turkey, 1914–1924,* Laurence Evans approached the final decade of the Ottoman Empire as a series of problems related to American political interest in the war against the Central Powers and postwar goals for Central Europe and the Balkans.[24] Although there is no full account of the career of Adm. Mark A. Bristol as high commissioner at Constantinople between 1919 and 1927, we can look forward to the monograph Peter M. Buzanski is preparing.

After the Senate rejected American membership in the League of Nations and a proposed mandate for Armenia, the United States rapidly retreated from its flirtation with the politics of the Eastern Question. Needed were policies designed to protect the interests of American nationals in missions, schools, colleges, and archaeology, not to mention their expanding economic aspirations, notably in petroleum development. The notion of the Open Door served as Washington's rallying cry to guard American rights and privileges without undertaking major responsibilities for contributing to political stability. My *American Interests and Policies* approached the interwar years in terms of accommodations made by the United States government and private interests to the intense nationalism of the New Turks under Kemal Atatürk and Iran under Reza Shah. In the Arab East, the British and French still dominated through their mandates for Iraq, Transjordan, Palestine, Syria, and Lebanon; and the British remained influential in Egyptian affairs despite the nominal independence granted Egypt in 1922. Profs. L. C. Wright and Leon Boothe have independently prepared articles, not yet published, on Woodrow Wilson and Egyptian nationalism.[25] Now in press is Roger R. Trask's *The United States Response to Turkish Nationalism and Reform,* a major contribution. His monograph and several articles are especially valuable for understanding the kinds of adjustments Americans had to make to the first of the significant postwar revolutions in the Middle East.[26]

Petroleum was probably the most significant new element in United States relations with the Middle East between the wars, and the books previously cited signify the attention scholars have given to this development.[27] And, although Zionism had not gained its fullest momentum before 1939, American concern for Palestine has attracted some scholarly attention. We now look forward to Selig Adler's study of Franklin D. Roosevelt and the Palestine issue.[28]

The period of World War II and the years following present special impediments for researchers. The problem of recency alone makes some hesitate, and the reluctance is often compounded by difficulties in gaining access and clearance for certain kinds of archival and manuscript materials. There is the dual difficulty of unavailability of crucial material and too much material to sift. My present project makes me particularly sensitive to these problems. What initially seemed a workable research plan for a book on American relations between 1939 and 1950 has been revised because exploration of the war years revealed developments of sufficient significance to merit an entire volume. World War II proved to be a catalyst moving the Middle East from the periphery of American foreign policy closer to the center. The United States government was by 1945 asserting an unprecedented political and strategic stake in the area and playing a major role both in the international politics of the Eastern Question and in the region's internal affairs.[29] Just to treat the subject of *Greece and the Great Powers, 1944–1947: Prelude to the "Truman Doctrine,"* Stephen Xydis needed a very long book, for which he used important Greek sources. Xydis's book illustrates that serious work on the postwar era is feasible in some cases.[30] Nearly completed is Prof. T. Cuyler Young's *The United States Involvement in Iran since World War II* (tentative title), anticipated because of the author's talents both as an orientalist and as a practitioner of American foreign policy.[31]

Most of the fairly sizable new literature dealing with recent years is, however, "policy" oriented or of a reportorial character. Among them are many worthy books, and no slight is intended to authors not included among the four singled out for mention. *The United States and the Middle East,* a study sponsored by the American Assembly, contains essays by several specialists on area problems related to American foreign policy.[32] Two complementary volumes in the American Foreign Policy Library series are Nadav Safran's *The United States and Israel* and William R. Polk's *The United States and the Arab World.*[33] Finally, there is John S. Badeau's stimulating analysis, *The American Approach to the Arab World,* sponsored by the Council on Foreign Relations.[34] Most of these authors combine academic expertise with firsthand experience gained through government service or with private agencies. They testify to the enlarged reservoir of talent now available in the United States.

What have we learned from this output of recent years rapidly surveyed above? Certainly outmoded is the old view that American connections with the Middle East before World War II were too inconsequential to merit serious attention from professional historians. Though the idea that inquiries into cultural endeavors are mere "antiquarianism" dies hard in some quarters, it no longer seems legitimate to fault studies of missionaries, educators, philanthropists, archaeologists, and other private persons and organizations as evidence of ethnocentrism. James A. Field, Jr., has amply demonstrated how such inquiry can illuminate important strains in the American national character and conceptions of "mission" overseas. Field, Finnie, and Tibawi, among others, by enlightening us about the rich variety of Americans who had contacts with the Middle East in the nineteenth century, have also demonstrated the value of a cultural and intellectual approach to American foreign relations. Connections with the area during and since the Wilson years are now much better comprehended and are rapidly being related to such themes as the twentieth-century social revolutions, anticolonialism, and self-determination. Much concrete detail is now available about the way private American groups and the United States government adjusted to the zealous nationalism of the Middle East between the two world wars, particularly to the transformation wrought under the New Turks. More is known about the international politics and economics of oil than about any other aspect of the Middle East commanding American attention. Zionism has been closely studied, both in its international and its domestic political aspects. There is abundant documentation showing how this special interest group has functioned to rally support from American Jews and other sympathizers.[35]

To build on the promising advances which have partially corrected the previous neglect of American connections with the Middle East, perhaps some suggestions for future research are in order, arranged for convenience into three groups: first, further examination of American interest groups; second, studies of international interplay, especially among the powers; and third, cross-cultural explorations. Particular studies should, of course, often intersect the lines of these categories.

Notwithstanding the books and articles using the "interest group" approach, noted above, we have not exhausted the possibilities even for missionaries, educators, and others of humanitarian bent.[36] Some critics of recent foreign policy have taken a jaundiced view of a secularized "missionary impulse" as leading the United States into unwise foreign interventions.[37] Little has been published about the commercial and trade enterprises of Americans, oil excepted. The full history of the early trade in opium, figs, dates, and nuts remains to be written;[38] so does the marketing of such disparate products as Singer sewing machines and Coca Cola; and little is known about shipping arrangements over the years. In fact, the entire field of communications, including aviation, needs scholarly attention. Press reporting and, for more recent years, radio and television reporting from the Middle East bear closer scrutiny; so does the impact of American movies in the area. For a group as important as archaeologists, we have had only a few suggestive references until John A. Wilson's recent book on American Egyptology; but for other areas we can say figuratively that only the surface has been scratched.[39] Nor should we overlook such organizations as the American Geographic Society and the Metropolitan Museum, which have helped to integrate the Near Eastern past into the larger cosmopolitan culture.

Scholars also need to bring up to date the history of the American colleges, for no full history of Robert College or the American University of Cairo has been published, and the standard account of the American University of Beirut (AUB) carries only into the early stages of World War II.[40] As the alma mater of an airplane hijacker (Leila Khaled) and Arab

guerrillas, the AUB of 1970 continues, sometimes inadvertently, to stimulate the Arab awakening, reminding one of the earlier intimate connection
of Robert College with modern Bulgarian nationalism.

Except as Robert L. Daniel covered the subject in his recent book, the
philanthropic work of American foundations is still largely unexamined by
historians.[41] The enormous operations carried on over the years by the
Rockefeller, Ford, and other foundations in such fields as medicine, public
health, education, and agriculture have accelerated since World War II.

Systematic studies of how Americans have been trained for specialization
in Middle Eastern affairs remains to be undertaken. Existing studies of
Middle Eastern immigration to the United States are inadequate. Needed
are modern studies by historians with backgrounds in sociology and anthropology to portray the acculturating effects of population movements. The
phenomena of Armenians, Syrians, Lebanese, and others returning to their
homelands after residence in the United States should yield some fascinating
studies.[42]

The international aspects of American involvement can be studied only
incompletely and imperfectly as long as access to records of major European powers is severely restricted; especially for the recent period, the
researcher has to make do with scattered public documents and whatever
collateral sources can be located.[43] But we have been able to accomplish
much from the American side, thanks in no small part to the relatively generous access policies of the United States government. Within limits, we can
move forward slowly to further serious examination of the post-World War
II years as the publication of the *Foreign Relations* series inches ahead and
the archives become available for the corresponding years.[44] As an introduction to the major subjects arising in our official overseas operations, we will
continue to lean heavily on that series, which provides invaluable clues to
file numbers to be examined in the unpublished archives. Since it is impossible to search through all the unpublished material on any but the nar-
rowest themes, one can never be certain that he has located the "right" or
the "best" files for his subject. Let me illustrate from personal experience.
If it had not been for the lead in *Foreign Relations,* I might have overlooked
file 800.24, bearing the unpromising title "Equipment and Supplies." This
file contains many of the policy documents for United States operations in
the Middle East during World War II, basic material on lend-lease and on
the Middle East Supply Center, which was the Anglo-American agency for
coordinating regional supply problems.

Incidentally, one sometimes comes upon useful files in the most unex-
pected way. While at the Library of Congress examining the papers of
William Jardine, minister to Egypt during the early 1930s, I found a copy

of a document from Department of State file 811.5031 Near East. When it was checked at the National Archives, this file yielded annual reports from all the consulates, summarizing American interests in each consular district under such headings as numbers of United States citizens (classified as native born and naturalized); capital invested in businesses, missions, or other enterprises; and listings of American missionary, cultural, and philanthropic agencies. This data, albeit imperfect, furnished priceless evidence of a kind difficult to locate.

It would ease the researcher's inevitable confrontation with the unknown if the Historical Office of the State Department would publish a little guide showing how its *Foreign Relations* staff organizes and conducts its search when compiling the annual volumes. The Department of State classification guide, now available on microfilm, is helpful but not sufficient.[45] It would also facilitate research if the National Archives could add to such existing, useful aids as Elizabeth Buck's *Materials in the National Archives Relating to the Middle East*.[46] There is also the special problem of the so-called "lot files" of the State Department, which are not incorporated into the decimal filing system. For these, the researcher must make special arrangements— provided he learns of their existence.[47]

Also among the rich archival records not yet adequately exploited are the post records. They are difficult to use, and for broad studies covering many themes or long periods a researcher can probably do little more than sample. It would help if the National Archives could construct guides to the individual post records. As it stands now, the researcher wastes too much time in ascertaining the exact contents of the files for particular embassies, legations, and consulates.[48] There are inviting possibilities for studies in depth of particular posts. In the area of my special concern, for instance, one thinks of how much could be learned from detailed studies of the Beirut, Cairo, and Constantinople stations concerning not only the operation of the field staffs in their relationships with Washington and the host governments but also the interaction (or lack of it) of the American community with the peoples of the region.[49]

With our broadened conception of the scope of foreign relations, Department of State records do not by themselves provide an adequate base even for official research. This is especially true for the 1940s and thereafter, years characterized by the monumental proliferation of departments and agencies concerned with implementing foreign policy. Depending on his themes, the scholar will need to consult records of the Army,[50] Navy, Treasury, and Agriculture Departments, and perhaps others. Anyone who has tried to find his way through the maze of World War II records can testify to the effort required simply in ascertaining what records exist, locating them, and becoming acquainted with the varying complex rules for access and clearance.[51] For graduate students, in particular, the access and clearance obstacles are especially severe. If a student discerns that his degree may be delayed unduly because he must wait for notes or manuscript to be cleared, he will, perforce, for practical reasons often turn to a subject perhaps intrinsically less worthwhile. The beleaguered scholar, graduate student or otherwise, can only applaud Walter Rundell's suggestion calling for a central governmental agency in Washington for research guidance and clearance of all the records.[52]

Cross-cultural studies, suggested as a third category for further research, are the least developed and most demanding.[53] The record, while not completely barren, bears evidence of "muddling through," characteristic of developing phases of scholarship. One defect, however, has been over-indulgence of the urge to filiopietistic and nationalistic writing about the minorities of the Ottoman Empire and its successors; thus, the strong and volatile emotions aroused by religion and nationalism have marred some treatments of the Turks, Armenians, Greeks, Nestorians, Arabs, and Jews. Many studies reflect the traditional Christian denigration of Islam, apparent since the Crusades but exacerbated by the travails of the Armenians in the late nineteenth and early twentieth centuries.

Unless we also temper the tendency to overstress "American" activities and influences, we may sacrifice accuracy, fairness, and balance to ethnocentrism. Ernest R. May has observed that "neither Americans nor Englishmen seem usually to realize how odd and improbable a field of study is the diplomatic history of one country. Yet the assumption that international relations can be viewed as aspects of one nation's history underlies much of the writing about past American foreign affairs."[54] While his stricture deserves respectful attention, we need not conclude (nor does May) that we should abandon the study of *American* diplomatic history. The remedy lies in broadening our approach. Toward this end, a conceptual framework recently proposed by James A. Field, Jr., offers guidance. The nation-state, he writes, has been only one of the elements in international affairs: "much—perhaps most—of the work was 'transnational' in nature, reaching across state boundaries and initiated by or acting upon private individuals and groups." To support this thesis, he adduces a learned array of historical examples that illustrate how the growing mobility of men, machines, and ideas influenced such realms as political theory, scientific and technological innovation, and economic intercourse.[55]

The transnational approach opens promising vistas to the student of American relations with the Middle East. Although our knowledge of missionaries, educators, philanthropists, archaeologists, and business men has—probably unavoidably—been filtered through predominantly American sources and lenses, we should not unduly separate these activities from the total impact of the West. We also need to know more about Middle Eastern reactions to American ideas, goals, and methods; and these responses should be placed alongside the self-images Americans have had of themselves. We have some hard data, but too often only "impressions" of the influence of Americans on government, political thought, education, science, technology, economic development, and social change.[56]

The plea for more sophisticated comparative cultural analyses rests, of course, on the premise that historians of American foreign relations should illuminate the total reciprocal relationships of nations and peoples.[57] Yet all cannot be done in a day, and a proper seedbed must contain several elements. Progress has been made in providing three of the essentials: a foundation of monographic blocks and comprehensive narratives presenting the basic facts of the relationship from the vast American sources; comprehensive Middle Eastern studies training centers; and theories of political, economic, and social change derived from the approaches of such related disciplines as political science, economics, anthropology, and sociology.

Unfortunately, our disciplinary compartmentalization has militated against a satisfactory collaboration among specialists. There seems to be a presumption that the historian of foreign relations must take the initiaitve in drawing on area and other experts. And so he must. But maximum achievement will not come until Middle East area specialists assign a higher priority to studies of reciprocal relations between the United States and the Middle East. Fortunately, some scholars concentrating on the Middle East have been aware of both American influences and Middle Eastern responses. A few random examples will illustrate the kinds of leads they provide. Roderic H. Davison has alluded to the contributions of American educators and missionaries among the minorities during the nineteenth century and observed how they "often went counter to Ottoman interests." John Joseph has noted how Western influences in the nineteenth century made the Nestorians of Persia feel superior to their Muslim neighbors and how the Muslim world has come to identify Christianity with Western imperialism.[58] Writing about contemporary Turkey, Kemal H. Karpat has remarked that "since the second World War, American ideas have made a general impact on the country and have replaced some of the previous influences." The foreign aid program under the Truman Doctrine and NATO have stimulated modernization, specifically by imparting technological skills to certain elements of the military. Professor Karpat is probing these influences in his continuing research on postwar Turkey.[59] Not surprisingly, oil development in the Middle East has elicited studies detailing local attitudes toward foreign developers and the impact of oil on regional development.[60]

Clearly, a variety of talents must devise cooperative arrangements to develop a new breed of specialist, one trained both in American history and in Middle Eastern civilizations. Any concerted effort should also draw heavily on scholars in the Middle East, because they are uniquely situated to analyze the relationships from their perspectives, drawing on their local sources.[61] They can make a large contribution to answering some pertinent questions. How, for example, were Middle Easterners' reactions to American activities differentiated on the basis of ethnic backgrounds, social groupings, and economic strata? Did American political ideas and efforts to induce economic and social change produce discernible results? How did the reactions compare or contrast with those produced by parallel activities of other Westerners? Complex research techniques may be required to develop these themes.

This inquiry into the state of research on American connections with the Middle East has attempted to survey past accomplishments, to assess the current situation (which may be summed up as developing, but still immature), and to speculate both on some subjects for future inquiry and the need for enormous cooperative efforts among American historians, area experts, and disciplinary specialists. It is abundantly clear that the staff and facilities of the National Archives, which have already contributed handsomely to advancing the scholarship of American foreign relations, including the Middle Eastern aspect, can play an even larger role in the future.

## NOTES

I wish to express my appreciation to Professors James A. Field, Jr., of Swarthmore College and Kemal H. Karpat of the University of Wisconsin for their helpful, detailed comments on an earlier draft of this essay. I also wish to thank Professors Harry N. Howard of American University, Roger R. Trask of Macalester College, Leon E. Boothe of George Mason College, Thomas A. Bryson of West Georgia College, and Joseph L. Grabill of Illinois State University for their suggestions and corrections.

1. Diary entry, Jan. 16, 1830, John Quincy Adams, *Memoirs of John Quincy Adams, Comprising Portions of His Diary from 1795 to 1848,* ed. Charles Francis Adams, 12 vols. (Philadelphia: J. B. Lippincott & Co., 1874–77), 8:170. Prior to going to Algiers, Hodgson "had already made some progress in the Hebrew, Arabic and Persian," and while there he "acquired the Arabic, Turkish, the Lingua Franca, and the Berber." See also Morroe Berger, "Middle Eastern and North African Studies: Development and

Needs," *Middle East Studies Association Bulletin* 1 (Nov. 15, 1967):
1–2; David H. Finnie, *Pioneers East: The Early American Experience in the Middle East* (Cambridge: Harvard University Press, 1967), p. 11; and Van Wyck Brooks, *The Flowering of New England, 1815–1865* (n.p.: E. P. Dutton & Co., 1936), pp. 69–70. Prof. Thomas A. Bryson of West Georgia College has begun a study of Hodgson's career.

2. James S. Moose (minister in Jiddah, Saudi Arabia) to Cordell Hull, June 26, 1943, transmitting a sealed letter from King Ibn Saud to President Franklin D. Roosevelt, June 8, 1943; Stanley Woodward to Grace Tully, July 10, 1943; W. X. Black, chief clerk, Veterans' Administration, to the Department of State, July 27, 1943—all in OF 3500, Franklin D. Roosevelt Papers, Franklin D. Roosevelt Library, Hyde Park, New York. Memorandum, Roosevelt to George Summerlin, Apr. 25, 1944, OF 3500, summary from PPF 7960, ibid.

3. *Muslim World,* a quarterly journal established in 1911, has traditionally stressed the study of Islam and the Christian-Muslim relationship, past and present. Hence, its scope has been less eclectic than that of the *Middle East Journal,* which concerns itself with history, culture, and political and economic affairs.

4. For an earlier historiographical assessment, see John A. DeNovo, "American Relations with the Middle East: Some Unfinished Business," in *Issues and Conflicts: Studies in Twentieth-Century American Diplomacy,* ed. George L. Anderson (Lawrence, Kans.: University of Kansas Press, 1959), pp. 63–98. Hereafter cited as DeNovo, "Unfinished Business." This earlier essay should be consulted for many references not repeated here. For example, for autobiographies and memoirs, see ibid., nn. 12, 14–19, 29, 42, 44, 56, 60, 68, 76, 78, 81, 83, 85–87. See also Lewis Einstein, *A Diplomat Looks Back,* ed. Lawrence E. Gelfand (New Haven: Yale University Press, 1968), pp. 25–82, 118–43; and Missionary Research Library, *Missionary Biography: An Initial Bibliography* (New York: Missionary Research Library, 1965).

5. Leland J. Gordon, *American Relations with Turkey, 1830–1930: An Economic Interpretation* (Philadelphia: University of Pennsylvania Press, 1932). Not to be overlooked are the occasional major books published in the United States between the world wars dealing with themes from the Ottoman and Arab past. Among them are several that touched incidentally on United States relations as appropriate to their themes: Edward M. Earle, *Turkey, the Great Powers, and the Bagdad Railway: A Study in Imperialism* (New York: Macmillan Co., 1923); Harry N. Howard, *The Partition of Turkey: A Diplomatic History, 1913–1923* (Norman: University of Oklahoma Press, 1931); Nasim Sousa, *The Capitulatory Régime of Turkey: Its History, Origins, and Nature* (Baltimore: Johns Hopkins Press, 1933); George Antonius, *The Arab Awakening: The Story of the Arab National Movement* (Philadelphia: J. B. Lippincott Co., 1939). Harry N. Howard, Edward M. Earle, and Albert Lybyer also published journal and periodical articles during the interwar years. For a recent survey, see Harry N. Howard, "Turkish Studies in the United States," *Balkan Studies* 5 (1964): 311–22. For a generation, Professor Howard has been

one of the most active American scholars writing on the international relations of the Middle East; many younger scholars have benefited from his generous advice and encouragement.

6. Ephraim M. Speiser, *The United States and the Near East* (Cambridge: Harvard University Press, 1947; rev. ed. 1950). Lewis V. Thomas and Richard N. Frye, *The United States and Turkey and Iran* (Cambridge: Harvard University Press, 1951).

7. Jacob C. Hurewitz, *Middle East Dilemmas: The Background of United States Policy* (New York: Harper & Bros., 1953). Hurewitz had already published *The Struggle for Palestine* (New York: W. W. Norton & Co., 1950). A pioneering volume on this theme was Frank E. Manuel, *The Realities of American-Palestine Relations* (Washington, D.C.: Public Affairs Press, 1949).

8. George Lenczowski, *The Middle East in World Affairs* (Ithaca: Cornell University Press, 1952; rev. eds. 1958 and 1962). Lenczowski had previously published *Russia and the West in Iran, 1918–1948: A Study of Big-Power Rivalry* (Ithaca: Cornell University Press, 1949). John C. Campbell, *Defense of the Middle East: Problems of American Policy* (New York: Harper & Bros., 1958; rev. ed. in paperback, New York: Frederick A. Praeger, 1960). See also Halford L. Hoskins, *The Middle East: Problem Area in World Politics* (New York: Macmillan Co., 1954).

9. Stephen H. Longrigg, *Oil in the Middle East: Its Discovery and Development* (New York: Oxford University Press, 1954; 2d ed. 1961; 3d ed. 1968); Benjamin Shwadran, *The Middle East, Oil, and the Great Powers* (New York: Frederick A. Praeger, 1955; 2d rev. ed., New York: Council for Middle Eastern Affairs Press, 1959); David H. Finnie, *Desert Enterprise: The Middle East Oil Industry in Its Local Environment* (Cambridge: Harvard University Press, 1958). See also Raymond F. Mikesell and Hollis B. Chenery, *Arabian Oil: America's Stake in the Middle East* (Chapel Hill: University of North Carolina Press, 1949).

10. T. H. Vail Motter, *The Persian Corridor and Aid to Russia* (Washington, D.C.: Government Printing Office, 1952); Abraham Yeselson, *United States-Persian Diplomatic Relations, 1883–1921* (New Brunswick, N.J.: Rutgers University Press, 1950).

11. For citations to dissertations and theses of that vintage, see Freeland K. Abbott, Elizabeth Allison, Ralph E. Cook, John A. DeNovo, Rosaline D. Edwards, Thomas H. Galbraith, Mustafa N. Kazdal, Roger R. Trask, Joseph W. Walt, and Lenoir C. Wright, listed in John A. DeNovo, *American Interests and Policies in the Middle East, 1900–1939* (Minneapolis: University of Minnesota Press, 1963), pp. 404–8; and Howard M. Sachar, Howard J. Kerner, George P. McDonough, Mustafa N. Kazdal, and Irwin Oder, cited in DeNovo "Unfinished Business," pp. 95–96. See also Robert L. Daniel, "From Relief to Technical Assistance in the Near East; A Case Study: Near East Relief and Near East Foundation" (Ph.D. diss., University of Wisconsin, 1953); Peter M. Buzanski, "Admiral Mark L. Bristol and Turkish-American Relations, 1919–1922" (Ph.D. diss., University of California, 1960); and Edward A. Raleigh, "An Inquiry into the Influ-

ence of American Democracy on the Arab Middle East, 1819–1958"
(Ph.D. diss., College of the Pacific, 1960).

12. This theme is developed in James A. Field, Jr., *America and the Mediter-
    ranean World, 1776–1882* (Princeton: Princeton University Press, 1969),
    pp. 442–44 and passim. Field has observed "that treaty-making outside
    Europe and the Americas proceeded in the sequence of (1) Mediter-
    ranean, (2) Indian Ocean, (3) Pacific. There is a double point here: that
    government relations expanded eastwardly rather than westwardly, and that
    the Mediterranean was in some sense the school for other new relation-
    ships." He calls attention to Prof. John K. Fairbank's point that the tours
    of duty of naval officers (Biddle, Read, Kearny, Perry) in the Mediter-
    ranean preceded their tours in the Far East. Memorandum, Field to John
    A. DeNovo, Nov. 10, 1970.

13. Finnie, *Pioneers East,* pp. 3, 272, 276–277, 275.

14. Memorandums, James A. Field, Jr., to John A. DeNovo, Mar. 12, 1969,
    and Nov. 10, 1970; Field, *America and the Mediterranean World,* pp. x,
    439 ff., and passim.

15. A. L. Tibawi, *American Interests in Syria, 1800–1901: A Study of Edu-
    cational, Literary, and Religious Work* (Oxford: Oxford University Press,
    1966).

16. Harry N. Howard, "The United States and the Problem of the Turkish
    Straits: The Foundations of American Policy (1830–1914)," *Balkan
    Studies* 3 (1962): 1–28. See also idem, "The United States and Turkey:
    American Policy in the Straits Question (1914–1963)," ibid. 4 (1963):
    225–50; idem, "The Turkish Straits after World War II: Problems and
    Prospects," ibid. 11 (1970): 35–60. Professor Howard is revising a book-
    length monograph on the entire history of the United States and the straits.
    Note also idem, "President Lincoln's Minister Resident to the Sublime
    Porte: Edward Joy Morris (1861–1870)," *Balkan Studies* 5 (1964):
    205–20. Lenoir C. Wright, *United States Policy toward Egypt, 1830–
    1914* (New York: Exposition Press, 1969). Wright is now preparing a
    sequel to carry the theme from 1914 to 1939.

17. Robert L. Daniel, *American Philanthropy in the Near East, 1820–1960*
    (Athens, Ohio: Ohio University Press, 1970).

18. DeNovo, *American Interests and Policies.*

19. The Society of Historians for American Foreign Relations sponsored a joint
    session entitled "A Search for an American Near East Policy" at the South-
    ern Historical Association meeting in Louisville, Kentucky, November
    1970. Thomas A. Bryson presented a paper called "The Merchant's Search:
    Admiral Mark L. Bristol, an Open Door Diplomat"; Joseph L. Grabill a
    paper entitled "The Missionaries' Search for an American Policy on the
    Arabs, 1914–1923"; and Leon E. Boothe, "The Zionist Search for Policy,
    1917."

20. James B. Gidney, *A Mandate for Armenia* (Athens, Ohio: Ohio Univer-
    sity Press, 1967). Thomas A. Bryson, "An American Mandate for Ar-
    menia: A Link in British Near Eastern Policy," *Armenian Review* 21
    (Summer 1968): 23–41; idem, "Woodrow Wilson and the Armenian Man-
    date: A Reassessment," ibid. (Autumn 1968): 10–29; idem, "Mark Lam-

bert Bristol, U.S. Navy, Admiral-Diplomat: His Influence on the Armenian Question," ibid. (Winter 1968): 3–22; and idem, "Walter George Smith and the Armenian Question at the Paris Peace Conference, 1919," *Records of the American Catholic Historical Society of Philadelphia* 81 (Mar. 1970): 3–26. Bryson has completed editing Smith's travel journal, which will appear in several installments in the *Armenian Review*. As part of his projected biography of Smith, he has prepared a paper on Smith and the Armenian-American Society, showing that in representing the church interest Smith was contesting with the American merchant interest for the right to influence Near Eastern policy. Bryson has an article on John Sharp Williams and the Armenian question scheduled for publication in the *Journal of Mississippi History*. See also Robert L. Daniel, "The Armenian Question and American-Turkish Relations, 1914–1927," *Mississippi Valley Historical Review* 46 (Sept. 1959); 252–75; and John Philip Richardson, "The American Military Mission to Armenia" [Harbord Mission] (Master's thesis, George Washington University, 1964).

21. Harry N. Howard, *An Inquiry in the Middle East: The King-Crane Commission* (Beirut: Khayat's, 1963).

22. Joseph L. Grabill, *Protestant Diplomacy and the Near East: Missionary Influences on American Policy, 1810–1927,* scheduled for spring 1971 publication by the University of Minnesota Press. See also idem, "Missionary Influence on American Relations with the Near East, 1914–1923," *Muslim World* 58 (Jan. and Apr. 1968): 43–56, 141–58.

23. Boothe will examine the tenure of Ambassador Henry Morgenthau in Constantinople and then treat the Near Eastern problem on a geographical or racial-ethnic basis, following this pattern: the Turks proper; the Arabs; Egypt; the Palestine problem and the Zionists; and the Armenians. A concluding chapter will analyze the influence (or lack of it) of these groups on United States foreign policy between 1913 and 1921.

24. Lawrence Evans, *United States Policy and the Partition of Turkey* (Baltimore: Johns Hopkins Press, 1965). Covering the same decade more comprehensively is Howard M. Sachar's scholarly and readable *The Emergence of the Middle East: 1914–1924* (New York: Alfred A. Knopf, 1969).

25. Lenoir C. Wright, "President Wilson and the Egyptian Nationalists." Leon Boothe has a similar article in progress.

26. The book will be published by the University of Minnesota Press in 1971. Among Trask's articles are Roger R. Trask, "The United States and Turkish Nationalism: Investments and Technical Aid during the Atatürk Era," *Business History Review* 38 (Spring 1964): 58–77; idem, " 'Unnamed Christianity' in Turkey during the Atatürk Era," *Muslim World* 55 (Jan. and Apr. 1965): 66–76, 101–11; idem, "Joseph C. Grew and Turco-American Rapprochement, 1927–1932," in *Studies on Asia, 1967,* ed. Sidney D. Brown (Lincoln, Neb., 1968), pp. 139–70; and idem, "The 'Terrible Turk' and Turkish-American Relations in the Interwar Period," scheduled for publication in the *Historian,* late 1970 or 1971. See also Robert L. Daniel, "The United States and the Turkish Republic before World War II: The Cultural Dimension," *Middle East Journal* 21 (Winter 1967): 52–63.

27. See note 9 and also John S. Salapatas, "The Open Door in the Middle East: The Anglo-American Oil Agreements" (Master's thesis, University of Wisconsin, 1965).

28. See also Ben Halpern, *The Idea of the Jewish State* (Cambridge: Harvard University Press, 1961); Samuel Halperin, *The Political World of American Zionism* (Detroit: Wayne State University Press, 1961); Leonard Stein, *The Balfour Declaration* (New York: Simon & Schuster, 1961); and Richard P. Stevens, *American Zionism and United States Foreign Policy, 1942–1947* (New York: Pageant Press, 1962). See also note 7.

29. After completing a volume on the years from 1939 to 1945, I plan another for the Truman years.

30. Stephen Xydis, *Greece and the Great Powers, 1944–1947: Prelude to the "Truman Doctrine"* (Thessalonica: Institute for Balkan Studies, 1963). Among Xydis's helpful articles are idem, "The Genesis of the Sixth Fleet," *United States Naval Institute Proceedings* 85 (1958): 41–50; idem, "The USSR and the Creation of the Commission of Investigation concerning Greek Frontier Incidents," *Balkan Studies* 4 (1963): 1–14; and idem, "America, Britain, and the USSR in the Greek Arena, 1944–1947," *Political Science Quarterly* 78 (Dec. 1963): 581-96. John O. Iatrides has under way a study of the Greek problem in United States foreign policy during the 1940s. See also Harry N. Howard, "The Entry of Turkey into World War II," *Belleten* [Ankara, Turkey] 31 (Apr. 1967): 221–75.

31. See also Michael K. Sheehan, *Iran: The Impact of United States Interests and Policies, 1941–1954* (Brooklyn, N.Y.: Theo. Gaus' Sons, 1968).

32. Georgiana G. Stevens, ed., *The United States and the Middle East* (Englewood Cliffs, N.J.: Prentice-Hall, 1964). Chapter 6 is Richard H. Nolte's "United States Policy and the Middle East."

33. Nadav Safran, *The United States and Israel* (Cambridge: Harvard University Press, 1963); William R. Polk, *The United States and the Arab World* (Cambridge: Harvard University Press, 1965; rev. ed. 1969).

34. John S. Badeau; *The American Approach to the Arab World* (New York: Harper & Row, 1968). See also George Lenczowski, ed., *United States Interests in the Middle East* (Washington, D.C.: American Enterprise Institute for Public Policy Research, 1968).

35. In addition to the references in note 28, see Alfred Lilienthal, *What Price Israel* (Chicago: Henry Regnery Co., 1953) for an anti-Zionist interpretation.

36. Joseph L. Grabill has called my attention to the "underused resources" of the Missionary Research Library, now part of Union Theological Seminary, New York City. See *Dictionary Catalog of the Missionary Research Library,* 17 vols. (Boston: G. K. Hall, 1968).

37. Drawing on his deep knowledge of the Far East, but obviously worrying about Vietnam, Prof. John K. Fairbank has pointed to some baneful side effects of the missionary tradition: "Plainly the missionary impulse has contributed both to the American swelled head and to its recent crown of thorns." Fairbank, "Assignment for the '70's," *American Historical Review* 74 (Feb. 1969): 879.

38. For a suggestive introduction to the opium trade with China via Turkey, see Jacques M. Downs, "American Merchants and the China Opium Trade,

1800–1840," *Business History Review* 42 (Winter 1968): 418–26, 432–33, 436–37. One can imagine some future scholar writing under such a title as "From Opium to Oil: American Economic Enterprise in the Middle East."

39. An example of what can be done is John A. Wilson, *Signs and Wonders upon Pharaoh: A History of American Egyptology* (Chicago: University of Chicago Press, 1964).

40. Stephen B. L. Penrose, Jr., *That They May Have Life: The Story of the American University of Beirut, 1866–1941* (New York: Trustees of the American University of Beirut, 1941). See also the shorter account carrying the university into the middle 1950s: Bayard Dodge, *The American University of Beirut: A Brief History of the University and the Lands Which It Serves* (Beirut: Khayat's, 1958). See also Joseph R. Rosenbloom, "A Profile of Robert College Graduates," *Muslim World* 59 (Apr. 1969): 153–57. For the early years of Robert, there is Keith M. Greenwood's "Robert College: The American Founders" (Ph.D. diss., Johns Hopkins University, 1965).

41. Francis X. Sutton, vice-president of the International Division of the Ford Foundation, has offered this insight into the function of foundations: "The programs of American foundations are naturally shaped to express broad concerns with human welfare and not simply with American national interests. The foundations can do things that, while ultimately fostering American interests through a better international environment, need not be constrained by as sharp tests of serving the national interest as may be required for public funds. A presumption thus exists that we should keep our eyes open for good things to do that may not immediately relate to this country's image or interests. And if we do, the greater will be the need for public funds to do the things we cannot do." "American Foundations and U.S. Public Diplomacy," Address before the Symposium on Future of U.S. Public Diplomacy, Sub-Committee on International Organization and Movements, House Committee on Foreign Affairs, July 22, 1968 (Ford Foundation reprint, p. 12).

42. Raleigh, "Influence of American Democracy on the Arab Middle East," incorporates the results of a questionnaire eliciting responses from Arab students about their education in the United States during the 1950s.

43. A handy guide to the regulations of foreign governments pertaining to their official records is U.S., Department of State, Historical Office, "Public Availability of Diplomatic Archives," mimeographed (Washington, D.C., May 1968). Harry N. Howard has begun a file of data on Americans who have had connections with the Middle East for the Middle East Institute, Washington, D.C. This project is part of a larger cooperative effort supervised by Elizabeth Monroe, Saint Anthony's College, Oxford University, looking toward preparation of an index or guide to private papers on the Middle East. For private papers in England, the Historical Manuscripts Commission in London can answer inquiries about specific collections that are part of the National Register of Archives.

44. At this writing, the 1946 volume on the Near East has appeared. Better understood should be the monumental frustrations experienced by the Historical Office of the Department of State in editing these volumes. A staff

smaller in 1967 than in 1947 combed through the much heavier documentation to prepare the increased number of annual volumes. See "Report of the
Thirteenth Meeting of the Advisory Committee on 'Foreign Relations of
the United States,'" American Historical Association, *AHA Newsletter* 8
(Apr. 1970): 2–10.
45. U.S., Department of State, Division of Communications and Records, *Classification of Correspondence* (adopted Aug. 29, 1910), 4th ed. (Washington,
D.C.: Government Printing Office, 1939).
46. U.S., National Archives and Records Service, *Materials in the National
Archives Relating to the Middle East,* Reference Information Paper no.
44, by Elizabeth Buck (Washington, D.C., 1955).
47. One example is designated "Lot 60-D 224" and contains documents pertaining to postwar foreign policy planning. Some documents from lot files
have been printed in recent volumes of the *Foreign Relations* series.
48. See U.S., National Archives and Records Service, *List of Foreign Service
Post Records in the National Archives,* Special List no. 9, comp. Mark G.
Eckhoff and Alexander P. Mavro (Washington, D.C., 1958). The National
Archives has informed me that they have draft inventories for selected
posts, both diplomatic and consular.
49. See U.S., National Archives and Records Service, "Preliminary Inventory
of the Records of the United States Consulate General in Constantinople
(Istanbul)," comp. Laddie J. Stewart, processed (Washington, D.C., 1955).
For a recent example of the utilization of the valuable material in consular
post records, see Edward H. McKinley, "American Relations with Tropical
Africa, 1919–1939" (Ph.D. diss., University of Wisconsin, 1970).
50. Invaluable are the many fine official monographs exploiting the military
archives in the so-called Green Series, published under the title, *The United
States Army in World War II.* There is obviously a large military aspect
to the post–World War II period with such components as the United States
Sixth Fleet in the Mediterranean, American forces in Turkey, missiles,
radars, U-2 bases, and the like. Probably some worthwhile studies of these
matters will be possible now, but it will be years before all the required
documents are available to scholars.
51. Extremely helpful, even if formidable, are U.S., National Archives and
Records Service, *Federal Records of World War II,* vol. 1, *Civilian Agencies,* and vol. 2, *Military Agencies,* ed. Philip Hamer (Washington, D.C.:
Government Printing Office, 1950–51). See also idem, *Materials in the
National Archives Relating to the Historical Programs of Civilian Government Agencies during World War II,* Reference Information Paper no. 43,
(Washington, D.C., 1952); idem, *Records of the Foreign Economic Administration,* Preliminary Inventory no. 29, comp. H. Stephen Helton
(Washington, D.C., 1951); and idem, *Records of the Office of War Information,* Preliminary Inventory no. 56, comp. H. Stephen Helton (Washington, D.C., 1953).
52. Walter Rundell, Jr., "Restricted Records: Suggestions from the Survey"
[the Survey on the Use of Original Sources in Graduate History Training,
sponsored by the National Historical Publications Commission], *AHA*

*Newsletter* 7 (June 1969): 39–43. "There should be a central agency in Washington to handle researchers' inquiries concerning access to all government records. Such an agency, if located high within the executive department and invested with adequate authority, could greatly simplify and facilitate research in official documents. One would hope that it could promote uniform and liberal policies of access to those records and that it could standardize security clearances." Ibid., pp. 42–43. See also James MacGregor Burns, "The Historian's Right to See," *New York Times Book Review,* Nov. 8, 1970, pp. 2, 42–44.

53. See DeNovo, "Unfinished Business," p. 80, for my views on this problem more than a decade ago.

54. Ernest R. May, "Emergence to World Power," in *The Reconstruction of American History,* ed. John Higham (New York: Harper & Row, 1962), p. 180.

55. James A. Field, Jr., "Transnationalism and the New Tribe," unpublished paper (courtesy of the author), p. 6.

56. James A. Field offered an interesting comment on an earlier version of this paper: "Clearly all we have are 'impressions'; but what else is history made of? We know that Greeks, Turks, and Persians asked for naval support, that some Armenians were converted, that Ismail wanted soldiers and the Persians solicited advice, that the colleges survived and grew, that the Saudi Arabians drive Cadillacs." He also observed that "to go beyond the present level of impressions . . . [requires that] the right questions have to be asked and the right people found to answer them." Memorandum, Field to DeNovo, Nov. 10, 1970.

57. My plea echoes that made by Thomas J. McCormick, "The State of American Diplomatic History," in *The State of American History,* ed. Herbert J. Bass (Chicago: Quadrangle Books, 1970). See especially pages 139–40, where McCormick develops his argument "for a conception of diplomatic history . . . as the study of the *total impact* of societies upon other societies."

58. Roderic H. Davison, *Reform in the Ottoman Empire, 1856–1876* (Princeton: Princeton University Press, 1963), pp. 74–75; idem, "Turkish Attitudes concerning Christian-Muslim Equality in the Nineteenth Century," *American Historical Review* 59 (1954): 855–56, 859–60; John Joseph, *The Nestorians and Their Muslim Neighbors: A Study of Western Influence on Their Relations* (Princeton: Princeton University Press, 1961), pp. 124, 221–25.

59. Kemal H. Karpat, *Turkey's Politics: The Transition to a Multi-Party System* (Princeton: Princeton University Press, 1959), pp. 324–25, 337. Idem, "The Military and Politics in Turkey, 1960–1964: A Socio-Cultural Analysis of a Revolution," *American Historical Review* 75 (Oct. 1970): 1662.

60. David Hirst, *Oil and Public Opinion in the Middle East* (New York: Frederick A. Praeger, 1966); Kamal S. Sayegh, *Oil and Arab Regional Development* (New York: Frederick A. Praeger, 1968).

61. I am proposing that we emulate the approach being devised for American–East Asian relations, described in the *AHA Newsletter* 8 (Oct. 1969): 21–25, especially p. 21. For announcements about the American Institute

for Iranian Studies, the American Research Center in Egypt, and the American Research Institute in Turkey, see *Middle Eastern Studies Association Bulletin* 2 (Oct. 15, 1968): 44–46. See also Rouhollah K. Ramazani, "Research Facilities in Iran," ibid. 3 (Oct. 15, 1969): 53–61; idem, "Research Facilities in Iran: Postscript," ibid. 4 (Feb. 15, 1970): 51. John A. Williams, "Research Facilities in the U.A.R.," ibid. (May 15, 1970): 47–54.

# Sources in the National Archives Bearing on the History of African–American Relations

## MORRIS RIEGER

The holdings of the National Archives bearing on the history of African-American relations are very rich—so much so that in the brief time available it is possible to attempt only an overview.

From the very nature of archival sources it should be clear that the National Archives contains no separate collection of materials on Africa; rather, such materials are located among the records of federal departments and agencies. The State Department, of course, takes first place among such agencies.

## STATE DEPARTMENT RECORDS

Department of State records pertaining to relations with Africa are to be found in five major groupings. The first of these, the treaty series, covers the period from 1778 to 1962 and includes treaties with African states or with European states dealing with African territories or Africa-related matters, together with associated documentation and maps. There are several major categories of Africa-related treaties: (1) "peace and friendship" treaties (all with the various Barbary States between 1786 and 1836); (2) commercial treaties (with Muscat and Zanzibar, 1833; Madagascar, 1867 and 1881; Orange Free State, 1871; Egypt, 1884; Congo Free State, 1891, and Ethiopia, 1903 and 1914); (3) antislave trade treaties (two with Great Britain, in 1842—the Webster-Ashburton Treaty—and in 1870; and one in 1890 with the European powers multilaterally—the Statute of Brussels); and (4) treaties defining United States rights in the post–World War I African mandates (seven between 1923 and 1925 with the mandatory powers:

England, France, and Belgium). Other important treaties include that of 1884 recognizing the flag of the International Congo Association (which soon afterwards became the Congo Free State), the Algeciras Convention of 1906 regarding Morocco, and the 1919 Versailles multilateral agreement regulating the liquor traffic in Africa.

The second major group consists of the basic headquarters records of the department which break down into two major segments: first, the 1789–1906 records, which consist of separate series, arranged geographically and thereunder chronologically, of instructions to and despatches from American diplomatic and consular representatives and special agents abroad, notes to and from foreign missions and consuls in the United States, and miscellaneous outgoing and incoming correspondence. The second segment consists of materials of the same kind organized into two series of central files: the numerical file, 1906–10, and the subject-classified decimal file, 1910–44.

Distributed through these records is a great volume and variety of documentation concerning American relations with the various African territories and/or their European metropoles during the century and a half following the establishment of the federal government. *All* aspects of these relations are documented, in particular the following principal themes:

(1) the series of Barbary Wars;

(2) the transatlantic slave trade and the long history of nineteenth century efforts to eliminate it (including such milestones as the Webster-Ashburton Treaty of 1842 with Britain, the operations of the United States Navy's African Squadron during the 1840s and 1850s, and the Brussels Conference of 1890);

(3) the "colonization" movement that brought about the mid-nineteenth century settlement in Liberia of freed American slaves and of Africans liberated from slave ships seized by the United States African Squadron;

(4) the special quasi-protectorate relationship of Liberia to the United States since the 1820s and the United States military, diplomatic, financial, and economic support this often necessitated;

(5) the development of "legitimate" (i.e., nonslave) trade with the coastal regions of subsaharan Africa, beginning in southern Africa soon after the Revolution as an outgrowth of our commerce with the Orient and in association with our offshore whaling operations in the region, expanding to dominant proportions in east Africa and to very substantial ones in west Africa during the middle third of the nineteenth century, and reaching its peak at the beginning of the Civil War;

(6) the decline in our African trade during the last decades of the nineteenth century and the efforts to revive it, which bore fruit only in the twentieth century;

(7) the American missionary movement in subsaharan Africa, its origin in Liberia and southern Africa before the Civil War, and its constant growth and expansion since;

(8) the United States effort to preserve the commercial Open Door in tropical Africa during the period of its partition amongst the European powers, particularly through support of the establishment of the Congo Free State before and during the Berlin African Conference in 1884–85;

(9) the growth of American capital investment in subsaharan Africa— in mineral and forest resources especially—beginning in southern Africa in the late nineteenth century and expanding to central and west Africa during the twentieth (as, for example, gold and diamonds in South Africa, copper in northern Rhodesia and the Congo, rubber and iron ore in Liberia, etc.);

(10) the participation of Americans in the struggle between Great Britain and the Boer Republics leading to the Boer War, and the pro-Boer popular sentiment in the United States during the war;

(11) the Congo scandals during the first decade of this century and American involvement in the international campaign for reform;

(12) the American role in the establishment of the mandate system in Africa at the Versailles Peace Conference;

(13) United States military operations and subsequent occupation responsiblities in North Africa during World War II.

These themes and others associated with them are documented in considerable detail among the headquarters records of the State Department.

The third major group consists of the field records of the department, which provide the same kinds of information concerning American relations with Africa as do the headquarters records. They often contain additional documentation of research value that had not been transmitted to Washington with the despatches to which they relate. The information on Africa, scattered among the records of the diplomatic posts in European metropole capitals, is to be found in concentrated form in the records of our legations in independent African countries and in those of our consular posts throughout the continent. The National Archives now has in custody records of diplomatic posts in the metropoles as follows: Belgium, 1832–1935; France, 1789–1935; Germany, 1835–1913; Great Britain, 1826–1935; Italy, 1839–1939; Portugal, 1824–1935; and Spain, 1801–1935. Also available are records of our legations in Egypt, 1873–1935; Ethiopia,

1908–36; Liberia, 1870–1935; Morocco, 1903–17; and the Union of South Africa, 1921–35; as well as the files of some sixty consulates in every part of Africa. The dates of these consular records range from the late eighteenth and the early nineteenth century to the mid-1930s: those of Tunis, for example, begin in 1795, of Zanzibar in 1834, of Capetown in 1835, and of Monrovia in 1856.

There is an unusual collection that should also be mentioned: the microfilm copy of originals in Belgium of the private papers of a Marylander, R. Dorsey Mohun, who served as United States commercial agent at Boma, the port of the Congo Free State, from 1892 to 1895 and as United States consul at Zanzibar from 1895 to 1897, and who was employed thereafter as the agent of various private investors in the Congo and southern Africa until 1911. Of special interest are the papers in this collection relating to Mohun's service, while an American official, in the Free State's military campaign against Arab slavers in the eastern Congo.

The fourth major group of State Department records relates to United States participation in international conferences, commissions, and expositions. It contains the formal documentation of the Berlin Conference on West African Affairs, 1884–85, which ratified the establishment of the Congo Free State under Leopold II's control and agreed on the ground rules for the partition of tropical Africa. This formal documentation consists of printed copies of the proposals and projects, protocols, reports of commissions and the culminating General Act of the conference. The State Department's own record of the major American role at the conference—where the United States was represented by men in the employ of Leopold II—are to be found among the records of, or relating to, our Berlin legation. Also in this group are general records concerning the Capitulations Conference of 1937 at Montreux, which dealt with the termination of extraterritorial rights in Egypt.

The fifth major group consists of the records of the American Commission to Negotiate Peace, which document United States participation in the Versailles Conference of 1919. The central files of the United States delegation contain—among the minutes and reports of the Conference Commissions on Colonies, German Colonies, Colonial Mandates, Morocco, and Revision of the General Acts of Berlin and of Brussels, as well as elsewhere in the series—materials relating to the partition of the German Empire in Africa, the rival claims of Britain, France, Italy, and Belgium, the origins of the mandate system, and the American role in these negotiations and developments. Related to these records are those of the Inquiry, a predecessor of the American Commission established under Colonel Edward House in 1917 at President Wilson's instigation to make background studies of subjects likely to arise at the peace conference. The files of the Inquiry include many reports, studies, notes, and other papers pertaining to geographical, demographic, ethnological, religious, diplomatic, political, administrative, military, economic, and social problems of the various regions and territories of Africa. Among them are two lengthy studies by G. L. Beer on international controls in Middle Africa and on Germany's African colonies which were later published posthumously in Beer's 1923 volume entitled *African Questions at the Paris Peace Conference.*

## MILITARY AND NAVAL RECORDS

The United States Navy has long played a major role in American-African relations, and its records reflect this fact. Chief among the records are those in the Naval Records Collection of the Office of Naval Records and Library, which contains virtually all of the records of the secretary of the navy predating 1886.

Of the relevant correspondence series of the Office of the Secretary, the earliest is a volume of letters, 1803–8, relating to official efforts to procure certain naval supplies and to deliver them to the dey of Algiers and the bashaw of Tripoli during the period of the Barbary Wars. There is also a considerable body of correspondence, 1819–44, of the secretary, mainly with United States agents stationed in Sierra Leone and later Liberia for the reception of Africans liberated from seized slave ships, but also with federal executive and judicial officials, the American Colonization Society, and private individuals and firms—all in relation to the capture and condemnation in United States district courts of American slave ships, arrangements for the shipment of liberated Africans to reception centers, first in Sierra Leone and then in Liberia, the establishment, maintenance, and supply of these centers, the role of United States naval vessels in combatting the traffic in slaves and in facilitating African and American Negro colonization in Liberia, and the activities in connection therewith of the American Colonization Society and the several state societies.

A related series comprises the extensive correspondence, 1843–61, between the secretary of the navy and the successive commandants of the African Squadron established under the Webster-Ashburton Treaty of 1842 to help suppress the slave trade. Apart from reporting on the state of that trade and the squadron's operations with respect to it, the commanders commented on the geographic, demographic, ethnographic, and economic features and problems of west Africa, the often restrictive commercial policies of the European powers active in the region, the conditions of legitimate trade there and particularly the American share of it (which the squadron was instructed to protect and promote), and the squadron's relations, formal and informal, with local authorities along the coast. Letter books of the first commander of the squadron, Commo. Matthew C. Perry, 1843–45, and of a successor, Commo. William C. Bolton, 1847–49, deal with the same subject matter, but contain much supporting documentation not transmitted to the secretary with their reports.

The secretary's post–Civil War correspondence with the commanders of squadrons and individual vessels in African waters contains significant material on occasion; as, for example, that relating to Commo. Robert W. Shufeldt's tour of the coasts of subsaharan Africa during 1879, undertaken primarily to stimulate American trade with the area but also to attempt to settle a dispute between Britain and Liberia over the latter's boundary with Sierra Leone; or that relating to the readiness of the European Squadron, in accordance with instructions from Washington, to protect American interests in Egypt during the 1882 nationalist revolt there; or that concerning the 1884–85 expedition of Rear Adm. Early English to the mouth of the Congo to obtain a suitable "commercial resort" there for American use and to cooperate with United States Commercial Agent Willard P. Tisdel's mission to explore the commercial possibilities of the lower Congo valley.

The general files of the Office of the Secretary, 1885–1940, contain a scattering of correspondence relating to the intermittent movements of American naval vessels along the African coasts and to the state of, and facilities in, various ports there. Among the records of squadrons and fleets, 1865–1940, are materials relating to visits to African ports by United States naval vessels, while the records of Naval Districts and Shore Establishments contain operational records of advanced amphibious training bases in Morocco and Algeria in 1943–44. These bases were used for the training and servicing of amphibious squadrons during the World War II North African and Sicilian campaigns.

The extensive series of logbooks of naval vessels, 1801–1946, contains detailed information—substantive as well as technical—on the activities of vessels that visited African waters and on the ports they entered. To illustrate, the series includes the logs of the U.S.S. *Peacock* on its 1832 voyage that led to the establishment of official relations with Zanzibar; of the *Susquehanna* on its 1851 mission to bomb Zanzibar; of the *Macedonian, Decatur, Saratoga,* and *Porpoise* during their tours of duty in the mid-1840s as the first ships composing the antislave trade African Squadron; and of the *Ticonderoga,* Commodore Shufeldt's flagship during his commerce-promoting mission to subsaharan Africa in 1878–79.

The United States Army had no significant contact with Africa before World War II, and hence few records of consequence for the period. For the period of the war, however, there is considerable material among War Department records pertaining to United States military and supporting operations in the African—particularly the North African—theaters, and to the United States subsequent military occupation and government there. This documentation concerns every aspect of the American relationship with the area—political, administrative, judicial, economic, and social, as well as the predominantly military one.


## RECORDS OF OTHER CIVIL DEPARTMENTS AND AGENCIES

Other World War I and World War II temporary agencies such as the War Trade Board, the Foreign Economic Administration, the War Production Board, and the War Shipping Administration have dealt with affairs in Africa within the specific framework of their own functions. Their records reflect this. Similarly the records of many of the continuing old-line agencies and bureaus such as the Public Health Service, the Weather Bureau, the Bureau of Reclamation, the Bureau of Foreign and Domestic Commerce, the Bureau of Agricultural Economics, and others will contain Africa data within their own areas of competence.

The propaganda agency of the United States during World War II was the Office of War Information. Its Mediterranean-Africa Region Informational File contains OWI "outpost," monitoring, intelligence, and research reports from and about the region. There is also on file documentation of OWI policies with respect to Africa and copies of news stories and recordings of broadcasts directed there.

The attorney general's letter books, 1817–71, contain correspondence relating to the slave trade (particularly to court cases arising from the trade), and to the transportation of freed slaves to Africa. Among letters of the secretary of the interior dating from the early 1860s concerning judiciary expenses is correspondence on enforcement of the laws prohibiting the slave trade and on payments to the American Colonization Society. The records of various United States attorneys for the pre-1865 period, particularly those of the Southern District of New York, contain scattered correspondence concerning enforcement of legislation prohibiting the import of slaves.

With the transfer from the navy to the Interior Department in 1861 of responsibility for administering the antislave trade laws and those providing for the colonization of free and liberated Negroes in Liberia and other tropical countries, the secretary of the interior accumulated considerable correspondence on these and related subjects. Included in this correspondence are letters from the president, Congress, and various executive departments, 1858–72, and from the United States agent for liberated Africans in Liberia, 1860–65. Some of the correspondence concerns the proceedings of mixed prize arbitration courts in New York, Capetown, and Freetown, Sierra Leone, 1861–70. (The prizes, of course, were the seized slave ships.)

Also, among the records of the Bureau of Mines, there is a Point IV program file, 1950–52, containing correspondence and some substantial reports on mining conditions and requirements and American technical assistance activities in several African countries, particularly Egypt, Ethiopia, Liberia, and Libya.

The records of the Congress fall into two groups: those of the Senate and those of the House of Representatives. The principal records of the Senate, most of which for the period 1789–1970 are now in the custody of the National Archives, consist of journals and minutes of legislative proceedings, bills and resolutions, committee reports and files, reports and communications from the president and executive agencies (including papers relating to treaties), petitions and memorials, and voting records. These records are rich in Africa-related materials. The files of the Committee on Foreign Affairs primarily, but most of the other categories I have mentioned as well, reflect to a greater or lesser degree all of the major and many of the minor themes of America's diplomatic, military, economic and other relationships with the various territories of Africa and their metropoles since 1789.

The House records (most of which for the period 1789–1968 are now in Archives custody) fall into essentially the same categories as those of the Senate and cover similar ground with respect to American-African relations. However, it should be noted that constitutionally and traditionally the role of the House in foreign affairs, and hence its record of them, is secondary compared with that of the Senate.

There remain two groups of federal court records to be considered: those for the Supreme Court, and those for the district courts. Both levels, especially the latter, were concerned with African slave-trade cases until the end of the Civil War. The files of the district and circuit courts for the Southern District of New York and the Eastern District of Pennsylvania contain many admiralty and criminal cases pertaining to the slave trade. (The admiralty cases relate to the seizure, condemnation, and sale of ships engaged in the slave trade, while the criminal cases revolve around charges of outfitting slave ships and serving aboard them.) A very famous slave-trade case adjudicated by the Supreme Court and included among its records is the *Amistad* case of 1841.

So, on the somber note of the slave trade, I end this survey where it began. I hope that I have succeeded in making the point intended—that existing sources here in the National Archives will support a very wide range of researches on the history of African-American relations.

# History and Foreign Policy

# Reflections of a Professional Diplomat

## FOY D. KOHLER

My colleague and one-time mentor, George F. Kennan, dug up a Confucius story that seems to me to present some justification for my present professorial appointment and for my participation in a scholarly conference. It seems that some twenty-four hundred years ago Confucius's disciple Tse-Kung asked his master, "What kind of a person do you think can properly be called a scholar?" Confucius replied, and I quote him: "A person who shows a sense of honor in his personal conduct and who can be relied upon to carry out a diplomatic mission in a foreign country with competence and dignity can properly be called a scholar." I do not want to overstate my presentation of credentials, but I was a professional diplomat for thirty-six years, and I suppose it inevitable that my remarks will reflect that experience.

The older practitioners of diplomacy tend to yearn for the good old days when diplomacy was a Machiavellian pursuit and to resent the publicity and the public pressures and the congressional scrutiny that attend diplomacy these days. But the modern Foreign Service officer knows, I think, that if the United States is to have a meaningful and effective foreign policy, then it must be a policy that has the basic understanding and support of the Congress and of the general public; and despite the abuses—and we have suffered some—of the extremists and the self-servers, I think no foreign service officer of today would have it otherwise.

## HISTORY AND THE DIPLOMAT

Diplomacy is no longer a matter of dealing with a handful of courtiers or of influencing a sovereign. It bears only a remote resemblance to the picture of personal intrigue that emerges from old histories and romantic novels and

277

exciting whodunits. Modern diplomacy is, rather, a continuing and exhaustive study of whole societies and of their interrelationships. It requires a knowledge of the history and culture, of the political, economic, technological, and social forces at work in the society in which the diplomat resides; and it requires a careful evaluation of the direction in which these forces will move within that society and of the effect they will have on relations between that society and other societies—in particular the diplomat's own.

If this definition is correct, then it is clear that the practicing diplomat must have a profound knowledge of history—not just diplomatic history, but history in its broadest sense—of his own country and of the world.

In the Foreign Service we try to assure that the candidate has this knowledge in a basic way when he enters our ranks. After the modern American Foreign Service was created by the Rogers Act of 1924, the department had the foresight to recruit a perfectionist from the academic world—Prof. Joseph Coy Green of Princeton—to direct the process of creating a merit system through examinations. These examinations, since the days of Joe Green, have by all odds been the highest in standards in the United States government, and they continue to be so to this day. When I read the sample exams from year to year, I confess I would not want to have to take them again.

So, upon entry a Foreign Service officer must have a good sense of world history and of the role of his own country in the world. He knows that the basic goals that he is pledged to serve are set forth in the Declaration of Independence—man's "unalienable right to life, liberty, and the pursuit of happiness"—and also in the more prosaic prescriptions of the Constitution—"to form a more perfect union, establish justice, insure domestic tranquillity, provide for the common defense, promote the general welfare, and secure the blessings of liberty to ourselves and our posterity." The young Foreign Service officer will have studied the history of the active and the effective United States diplomacy during the Revolution and the postrevolutionary period, as the United States was winning and establishing its independence. He will realize that in the founding days there were established certain basic and continuing principles of American foreign policy that we still follow today—self-determination and self-government and nonintervention—exactly the things we fought for in those days. This young officer will also have studied and have a sense of the application of these principles in such forms as the Monroe Doctrine and the Open Door policy.

The young Foreign Service officer will probably also have some appreciation of the fact that after we were firmly established as a nation we turned inward, devoting the next century and a half to the settlement and development of the continent; and that we were able to do so thanks only to the unacknowledged and unappreciated security afforded us by Britannia's rule of the waves. If he does not then appreciate it, he will soon learn that further study of American diplomatic history has mainly a negative value, telling him what *not* to do: from the violation of our own basic principles in the Mexican and Spanish-American wars, to the rejection of the League of Nations, to the pious folly of the Kellogg-Briand Pact, to the neutrality legislation in the 1930s. If this young officer had any illusions about the nature of the life of an American diplomat, he will soon find out that all he read before changed on the day that Hitler's forces moved into Poland in September 1939. He will find that the pleasant and social and—may I say?—academic existence that he may have associated with diplomacy from some of his earlier reading has changed to a life of hard work around the clock, of very considerable responsibility, and of occasional danger.

After he gets into active duty, the Foreign Service officer's excursions into history tend to focus on the country of his assignment. He delves deeply into its past—political, diplomatic, cultural, ethnic, economic, spiritual, literary—and its interrelations with his own country. This in turn leads him back again to American history and to the interpenetration of influences both ways: to State Department volumes on foreign relations that are pertinent; to cases in international law that involve both countries; to the memoirs of his predecessors; to diplomatic histories. As he moves from one post to another, the officer finds himself bemused by the comparative development of the various civilizations of which he becomes a part. In my case, my early posts were in the Balkans, in the Near East, in England, and in Russia; and then I had shorter assignments as an evaluator of our aid programs in Southeast Asia and on the Indian subcontinent and in Latin America. I found myself repeatedly being drawn into making my own comparative chronologies, and all this drove home a great many lessons: above all, that out of the past—only out of the past—can one have a full understanding of the present.

The most striking example in my own experience, of course, was Russia, because no one can hope to understand Russia who does not appreciate the fact that the beginning of constitutional government in the West (with the granting of the Magna Charta in the thirteenth century) roughly coincided with the Mongol-Tatar conquest of the fledgling Russian state in Kiev and the subsequent occupation and the despoliation of the Russian lands by these invaders for the next three centuries. Thereafter, the isolation of the Russians from the world—under these Tatar khans and a succession of Tatar-influenced czars—while the West was progressing under the stimuli of the Renaissance and the Reformation and the Age of Exploration and Discovery, goes far to explain to the Foreign Service officer the Russian mentality and its prejudices and the difference in views, on a multitude of subjects, between the Russian and himself. It also enables him to understand the fundamental antipathy that continues between the Russians and the Chinese after those seven centuries—because the Mongol-Tatar invaders were Chinese to the Russians. An appreciation of this kind of background leads the diplomatic practitioner to one of the fundamental conclusions that he must reach if he is going to be any good in dealing with Soviet affairs: that is, that the greatest mistake you can make is to think that the Russian civilization or country began fifty years ago.

For this kind of deep knowledge and background impression the diplomat depends mainly on the printed historical record. For more current impressions and a basis for his judgments, the diplomat relies on more primary sources. Taking Russia and myself again as an example, I would say that during the twenty-five years that I have dealt, off and on, with Soviet affairs, my primary sources have included the following: my personal observations during nearly seven years of residence and travel in the Soviet Union; thousands of hours of conversation with Soviet citizens, ranging from the Kremlin leadership and the university rectors in Moscow and elsewhere to a factory manager in Sverdlovsk, to a port captain in the Soviet Far East port of Nakhodka, and to an aging peasant woman who was waiting along with us for a ferry across the Volga River; hundreds of hours of participating in negotiations with Soviet officials, both bilaterally and multilaterally, in diverse forums; endless discussions with my own American diplomatic colleagues and with outside experts on Russia and the Soviet Union; similar exchanges of views and opinions with countless officials and diplomats of other countries; reading of the Soviet press and other publications for this quarter century; listening for thousands of hours to Soviet radio and television; seeing and hearing hundreds of Russian plays and operas and ballets and concerts; going through the general readers of the seven-year Soviet primary school (they're comparable to the old McGuffey readers in our own elementary school curriculum); and then, the acquisition of my own very eclectic library in the languages I know (English, French, and Russian), ranging from serious studies to the Russian classics, modern Soviet novels, and scores of local guidebooks about Soviet places.

## THE DIPLOMAT AND HISTORY

So much for history and the diplomat: now some reflections on the diplomat and history. In cables and despatches from his posts and in memorandums and oral briefings to his superiors in the department or the White House, as he moves into what we call desk officer or regional or functional, working-level jobs, the Foreign Service officer calls not only on the background of the printed record but also on the growing store of knowledge and experience that he has acquired firsthand. He does the same when he is called upon to testify before congressional committees or, more rarely, to give background briefings to the press. As the professional moves into policy-making positions at the levels of assistant secretary or above, he relies increasingly on this storehouse and on the personal information retrieval system in his own mind.

More often than not—but not always—the professional will either write, or ask a subordinate to write, an explanatory memorandum for the record to support or justify any decision. This means that many elements of a given decision are not a matter of public record—and that the reason for that decision could only be understood and reconstructed by the individual in question or by a researcher with a good knowledge of the mental formation of that individual. Indeed, as I have found out recently in connection with some of these popular oral history projects, even the individual himself finds it very difficult to recall the exact conjuncture of circumstances at a given moment in the past. This has been even more true since the introduction of security regulations, especially after the days of the Joe McCarthy witch-hunts; and the sheer pressure of work in the higher echelons of the State Department and the Foreign Service make it both undesirable and impractical (if not downright unhealthy!) to keep a daily record of events of the kind that served as a basis for diplomatic memoirs in the past.

I note that some political appointees in the White House or the State Department are now trying to fill that void, but I think I would have to sound a certain note of caution on the works of such political in-and-outers. To the extent that I have delved into them, I have found that the tendency is to create the impression that the author played a role well beyond what I have reason to believe he played. I have read some rather lengthy and learned memorandums on foreign policy, or what foreign policy should be, which so far as I know never entered into the decision-making process.

At best, records of decisions and actions and conversations are something less than complete. Even so, as the United States has assumed its present position in the world, the sheer bulk of such records is overwhelming for the policy maker and, later, for the historical researcher.

In view of the traditional practice of anonymity—of all documents being in the name of the president or the secretary of state or the chief of mission (who in fact may have seen only a small fraction of these papers)—it is of some importance for the researcher to note who the drafting officer actually was. We try to train a Foreign Service officer to be accurate and never to yield to the temptation to record as *said* what he only thought afterwards he *should have said*. We try to impress on him that his record should be exactly the same as that of the man he talked with, or what that man's own record would be if he reported accurately himself.

Contrary to the popular myth about diplomats, the longer one is in the Foreign Service the more one comes to realize that the greatest asset one can develop, not only inside his own government and with his own colleagues but with the foreigners with whom he has dealt or may have to deal with in the future, is a reputation for absolutely unquestionable honesty and integrity. He does not have to have a reputation for telling *all* the truth, but he does have to have the reputation for never, never saying an *untruth*. Senior professionals, as a matter of fact, prefer to have the records of their conversations with foreign colleagues prepared by junior officers who were present in order that they can have a kind of objective account of what they actually communicated. But this cannot be counted on with an untrained official. I remember a very distinguished, high-level political appointee who was dealing with a critical event, coming late to a meeting and explaining that he had been working on a memorandum of a conversation he had had with a foreign diplomat. It was an important talk, he said, and everything had to be just right. Well, I am afraid that some of us commented that if it had not been *said* just right, there was not much purpose in making the record show that it was.

Sometimes top officials get carried away by what they consider dangers of leaks or notions of personal diplomacy. The most annoying case, of course, was the era of FDR when the State Department was more likely than not to get copies of the president's correspondence with Churchill, or perhaps even with Stalin, not from the White House but from the British Embassy! (This not only hampered the conduct of current foreign relations but it greatly confused the record keeping.) Others occasionally tend to corner a foreign diplomat for a "private talk"—and only too often this top officer may forget, or be too busy, to make a record of this conversation. Since one can be sure that the foreign diplomat reports such conversations fully, the net result is that the foreign government has a good record, but the United States government does not.

I may surprise you by saying that a professional diplomat is nearly as frustrated as a historian about the problem of access to relatively current records. During my career, the filing system in the State Department was a nightmare of disorder and inefficiency amounting to almost total inaccessibility. Sen. Henry M. Jackson asked me a few years ago, when I was testifying before his Government Operations Subcommittee, what could be done to enable the State Department and the missions to do a better job. I had no hesitation or trouble in replying—and I quote myself: "I think we should modernize . . . should have better communications . . . should have IBM systems that give us access to information more quickly and to quotations from people we have talked with. . . . We have modern techniques now that ought to be applied to the diplomatic process."

During my last year in the department, after I came back from Moscow, there were a couple of striking examples to illustrate this problem. I had occasion to want to review a paper on the Near East that I had written in 1953 when I was in the Bureau of Near Eastern Affairs. After a search of the informal files of the State Department revealed no trace, I was told that the paper had probably been shipped off to storage in Saint Louis or somewhere in the Middle West and that it would take two or three weeks to locate it. It struck me as a little preposterous, and it still does, that records of a function that has the continuity of foreign affairs should be buried like the gold in Fort Knox, but I ordered the search to be made. Well, to make a long story short, it was not two or three weeks—the paper was just never found.

At this same time (this was, as you may have suspected, at the time of the Arab-Israeli war in June 1967), the researchers prepared documents for all of us on the seventh floor relating to previous United States actions and to the commitments on both sides. But when the Israeli foreign minister came to visit us in the State Department, he presented us with the original record of an important commitment that Secretary Dulles had made to him at the time of the Suez crisis ten years earlier and that was not included in our own papers. There was not any question about the authenticity of this paper; it was properly signed and initialed. A search was launched, but as I recall, we never did find our own copy.

William M. Franklin at this conference has given us an account of the problems of the Historical Office in this respect, and I am supplementing that a bit with an account of my own experience. Due to the inadequacy of the central filing system, the country desk officers and area and functional researchers have generally developed the practice of maintaining copies of important documents in their own unofficial files, covering roughly the period between the latest *Foreign Relations* volumes and the present time. I thought we were careful to keep only copies, not originals, but I suppose I have to accept Dr. Franklin's testimony that these "lots," as I think he referred to them, did sometimes contain unique copies.

In any case, these informal files tend to be the working files of the State Department, and they are in constant use. In the last year or so, some progress has been made in computerizing the decoding, the distribution, the filing, and, as I understand, the retrieval, of cable traffic. However, it is an awesome comment that the best retrieval system in the State Department today is the memory of individual officers. This will inevitably be true for some years to come, even if we start tomorrow to index and to program a modern retrieval system that goes back into years past.

In place of keeping diaries these days—these post-McCarthy days—individual Foreign Service officers keep personal files of published or unclassified materials and chronologies of events, hoping that these will recall some still classified discussions, actions, and decisions behind those developments in foreign policy in which he has played a role.

I would like to join those who urge that files be opened earlier and that the schedule for publication of *Foreign Relations* volumes be pushed up from the present lag of twenty-two years. It would help the professional diplomat as well as the historian. I do have to admit, however, that there are some problems. In his letter inviting me to this conference, Dr. Gustafson told me that in the files there were certain documents, which it was decided could not be printed in the 1944 volume, that were, specifically, memorandums of conversations prepared by me personally and apparently relating to the situation in Lebanon. Frankly, I do not remember what these documents are. I suppose they are related to some still-living personality playing a political role in Lebanon, or to some actions by General de Gaulle, who was at that time trying to reimpose the French influence; or perhaps the government of Lebanon itself opposed publication of the material. In any case, *I* did not make that negative decision. This responsibility was that of the assistant secretary in charge of Near Eastern affairs at the time it was decided to publish. I will say that I probably made some similar decisions respecting other documents, which I myself did not prepare, when I was assistant secretary for European affairs.

There will always be some materials that it will be injudicious to publish for a long time, and I thought Dr. Franklin, in talking about the Chamizal documents, gave us a dramatic case. So, what is better? Is it better to publish at shorter intervals, with deletions? Many deletions probably would not mislead or falsify the record and would not be crucial to a basic understanding. Perhaps the reasons really relate to purely transitory problems connected with personalities. But how is the historian to know? If, for his information, he were shown what has been omitted, could he be depended on not to publish these spectacular and attention-getting tidbits?—or if the information were critical to understanding, would he be satisfied to be guided by, but not to use, the sensitive parts? These specific questions raise a more basic question as to whether selection and discrimination in granting access would be either possible or desirable. You must remember that not everyone wanting earlier access to files is an objective historian: there are sensation seekers and those with political axes to grind. How do you eliminate them? Ideally, I would say, a historian should have access to information current up to the day before yesterday, at least for his guidance in using public sources, if not for his direct use; but would the historical community accept the kind of restrictive and censored arrangements that would be necessary for this? Would historians be willing to undergo security checks, to submit their work for review in return for early access to the records?

I think only the historical community itself could answer such questions. If any of these answers were in the affirmative, then I think perhaps they would strengthen Dr. Franklin's hand in the continuing battle he has to wage to make these records available at the earliest possible date. I do know from experience that in this respect you can depend on the Historical Office to push the political officers hard; and we could all help Dr. Franklin and the National Archives by asking our congressmen to give them more money and more employees.

## THE HISTORIAN AND HISTORY

Finally, I am going to be bold enough to make a few remarks, not about diplomats and history, but about historians and history. Even if the problem of access to United States government records were solved, it seems to me that this would not be enough for the writer of diplomatic history since all international questions involve two sides, if not more; and the diplomatic historian must understand both sides. It is true that foreign archives are even less accessible than American archives, especially in the Communist-ruled countries. On the other hand, it would be an understatement to say that the publicly available sources are sufficient to give a basic understanding of the motivations and aims of the Communist leaders.

Since I came back to the United States at the end of 1966 I have been bothered by this rash of "revisionist" histories of the so-called cold war. I confess I have only read a couple of these, but I have also examined a number of very scholarly analyses that highlight the principal revisionist propositions, which are, notably—

that Russia's weakness dictated postwar cooperation with the West, but that the Western leaders' hostility to communism prevented them from seeing this fact, an understanding of which might have prevented the cold war;

that abrupt termination of lend-lease in August 1945 and the United States failure to lend the Soviet Union $2 billion for postwar reconstruction left Stalin little choice but to act as he did;

that the cold war cannot be understood simply as the American response to Soviet challenge; rather, it must be recognized as the insidious interaction of mutual suspicions, the blame for which must be shared by all;

that after the United States acquired the atomic bomb, American diplomats tried to recoup what they had implicitly conceded at Yalta with respect to Eastern Europe; and, finally,

that American policy in the early years of the cold war must be seen as part of a larger pattern of American globalism dating as far back as 1898.

Before such an informed and learned gathering as this, I do not want or need to debate or attempt to rebut these propositions in detail: to examine the dreary record of the Soviet take-overs in Eastern Europe, or their attempt to partition Iran, or the territorial demands they made on Turkey, or their support of the guerrillas in Greece, or their blockade of Berlin, or their first rape of Czechoslovakia, or their attack in Korea. Neither do I need to review the measures that were taken inside the Soviet Union in these years to "tighten the screws" on the Soviet peoples themselves. Nor do I need to stress that the historical tragedy of the first forty years of this century was not a continuation of the adolescent aberrations of 1898, but rather the American retreat into isolationism and neutrality and our consequent failure to make even a "good college try" at helping to prevent World War II.

What I do want to stress, though, is my view that the basic fallacy of these revisionist theories is their authors' ignorance of the other half of the equation. Anyone who can read would understand that Stalin's so-called election speech of February 9, 1946, renouncing the wartime alliance and proclaiming a return to what we then called Marxism-Leninism-Stalinism, was an official declaration of what we came to know as the cold war between communism and capitalism. It is true that Stalin's official recognition only belatedly confirmed a line that had already started to develop in action both internationally and inside the Soviet Union. This is really beside the point, however, because anyone professing to be a student of political systems should understand why Stalin both acted and spoke as he did. He should know that the answer lies primarily in the question of legitimacy. It is important always to remember that Bolshevik rule in the Soviet Union constitutes a minority's monopoly of political power, by their own definition. Even today, membership in the Communist party is only about fourteen million people, or roughly 5 percent of the population. After the war, and despite the wartime inflation of membership, it was even lower.

We know the Bolsheviks are just as sensitive as any other sovereign—perhaps more sensitive—to the need to justify their right to rule. Lacking the accepted doctrine of the divine right of kings or the constitutional systems of our Western democracies, the Communist countries seek—and must seek—their legitimacy on the basis of the Marxist-Leninist doctrine (we have now dropped Stalin) that justifies the dictatorship of the proletariat in the name of the inevitable world revolution against capitalism and imperialism. If the capitalist and imperialist states were no longer the mortal enemy to be struggled against and to be overthrown, then there would be no justification for the continued maintenance of the single Communist party system and for depriving the Soviet peoples of the right to freely choose their own leaders.

Perhaps it was unnecessary for me to go into this much detail to justify my reaction to the revisionists. I might simply have suggested to them that if they want an accurate description of the continuing cold war they really have only to read the Soviet definition of what they call "peaceful coexistence." There are many sources for this—the Declaration of the Moscow Conference of the Communist Parties in 1960 or many, many other declarations of the Kremlin leaders. I will select just one of these by the man who is the titular president of the Soviet Union, the chairman of the Supreme Soviet, Mr. Podgorny. At the Twenty-third Party Congress, he explained: "The principle of peaceful coexistence is the principle of relations among states with different social systems. It is absolutely inapplicable in the class struggle between exploiters and those exploited, in the struggle between colonialists and oppressed peoples, in the struggle between socialists and bourgeois ideologies. Under present conditions, the implementation of this principle facilitates victories by socialism in economic competition with capitalism and favors the successful struggle of all detachments of the world workers and national liberation movements."

# History and Foreign Policy

DISCUSSION

*Brian L. Villa, United States Military Academy:* Ambassador Kohler mentioned his reaction to revisionists and some of his objections to them. I wonder if he could cite someone whom he tends to approve of as giving a fairly accurate picture of the origins of the cold war. Does General Deane [John R. Deane, *The Strange Alliance* (New York: Viking Press, 1947)] or someone else he might name seem in his view to come rather closer to explaining the origins of the cold war?

*Ambassador Kohler:* Oh, I think I would start with Stalin and Khrushchev. [*Laughter.*]

*Robert E. Beitzell, University of Maine:* I am editing the Soviet protocols of the Tehran, Yalta, and Potsdam Conferences. I had initially wanted to support the State Department in terms of those three little dots indicating excised material. In the Soviet protocols a great deal of the material is removed; in the American protocols, very little. I would also like to say that what is removed in the American State Department publications can, for the most part, be found by additional research.

However, I would also like to address myself to the remarks made here by the ambassador. The Soviet Union in the Second World War lost approximately twenty-five million people, of which over eleven million were lost in its armed forces. The Soviet Union in the Second World War fielded a force of almost three hundred divisions. The Soviet Union was promised a second front in 1942; it was not delivered. I realize that this promise was not made by the Department of the Army—in fact, General Marshall specifically took exception to President Roosevelt's offering of that second front; nevertheless, the promise was made. The promise was repeated at the Casablanca Conference by Prime Minister Churchill for the spring of 1943. It was repeated in the fall of 1943; it was not delivered. I know why it was not delivered—there were particular reasons of logistics; but I would nevertheless like to say that the Soviet Union won the Second World War. It won it single-handedly. It won it by defeating the German army in the Battle of the Kursk Salient, which, as you must know, was the greatest armored battle ever fought. I think it is very inappropriate for us who did not face those casualties, who did not face that risk, to make some of the comments that have been made.

*Ambassador Kohler:* I think this topic is of some importance. Anybody who thinks that I do not appreciate the sacrifices of the Soviet people, that I do not have a great feeling of sympathy for the Soviet people, and that I have not spent my life trying to find ways to get through to them is quite wrong. But I do not think that it is relevant. I think what you have said was packed with emotion. I was being objective about why Stalin did what he did. I will not debate the promises; I do not know the answers to that— maybe Dr. Franklin does or others do—I just do not know. Anyway, what is the relationship of that with the attempt to take over in Iran or to promote guerrilla warfare in Greece, and various other things? I do not see the relationship, as a matter of objective study of that period.

*Leon E. Boothe, University of Mississippi:* Anyone who has studied the record has seen that in 1941–42 the Soviets were really very candid about saying that when the war was over there was going to have to be a readjustment in Eastern Europe. I think somehow there is a sinisterness attached to Soviet motivations, as interpreted by some people of the postwar world, when the Soviets were really very candid about their motivations during the war. Another viewpoint that I wonder if you might comment on is this: Maybe the cold war really began in 1941 with the Atlantic Charter. Did the United States make the same mistake it made in World War I? In its zealousness to make people rise to the occasion, it overcommitted itself.

*Ambassador Kohler:* Please understand that I am saying that from our point of view we *opposed* certain things that Stalin did. I do not mean by that to say that we do not *understand* why he did it. I cited only the factor of legitimacy, but if one recalls the history of the repeated invasions of the Russian lands and their despoliation, not only by the Tatar-Mongol hordes seven centuries ago but by repeated incursions of Lithuanians, Swedes, Poles, and Germans, and if one considers the geography and the environment of this vast, open plain, then one understands why there is a sense of feeling that the only security lies in extending outward and outward and creating buffer zones. It is understandable, but that is not a good reason we need to accept it; we need, on the contrary, to oppose it.

Now specifically, we are very naive, really. Aside from Roosevelt's illusions that his own great personality could deal with our international problems with Uncle Joe, it is in us, as Americans, to want to love anybody that we have to cooperate with. The ridiculous extremes to which propaganda went inside our own country, not just to cooperate with the Russians but to *love* them, were really fantastic. I am not claiming that there were not many faults on our side, but on this specific question it is a part of this naiveté, in a sense, to get the Russians to subscribe to the noble preamble of the United Nations Charter—and you know damn well they are not going to observe the principles. They do not see their interests that way.

On the other hand, as a worker long in this field, even I have some feeling, just as I have some feeling about the Soviet constitution that is on the books. The Soviets are going through the process of elections—"secret elections"—one reads that in *Pravda*. One gets a feeling that, maybe in the long run, the Russian people will demand that some content be put into these lovely containers.

*Bradford Perkins, University of Michigan:* I consider myself an anti–New Left historian, but I am troubled by the ease with which you fall into what I would have to call the cold war stereotypes in your discussion of the origins of the cold war, specifically in your mention of World War II diplomacy. The thing that caused me to ask for the microphone was, for example, your statement (as I understood it) that the Russians were largely responsible for the uprisings in Greece in 1944 and 1945—for which, I think, there is very, very slim evidence, if any.

*Ambassador Kohler:* I said *support,* did I not?

*Perkins:* There is very slim evidence about the role of the Russians in the uprising that the British put down when they moved into Greece. In fact, I think most evidence suggests that in 1944 and 1945 the Russians were trying to restrain the uprising rather than encourage it. But this is what caused me to rise to my feet; and I would like to go on to something broader. The Russian system is to us less desirable than our own, no doubt, but we have to try to understand that system in 1944 and 1945. We have to try to understand why Stalin perhaps felt betrayed by the implicit promises of the second front—they were not explicit. We have to understand why, to him, free elections meant something different from what it meant to us. It does not do any good to talk about democracy or free enterprise as the thing that makes the world go good and communism as something that makes the world go bad. We must try to understand them and not simply condemn them; and I think, Mr. Ambassador, that you seem to try to impose our values upon the history of that period without making a significant enough effort to understand the values that motivate people who may be evil men.

*Ambassador Kohler:* I really do not have much quarrel with you, except I think you misinterpret me a little bit. I thought I went to some lengths to say that one has to understand *why* they acted as they did. All I was really saying in my previous remarks is that one *has* to understand why they did it and what motivates them and that there is not much excuse for *not* understanding, even though one does not have access to the inner files of the Kremlin.

*Geoffrey Smith, Macalester College:* Mr. Ambassador, in your view, would the best diplomatic historian to be a practicing diplomat?

*Ambassador Kohler:* I doubt that, because I think there would necessarily be a lot of built-in subjective experience. On the other hand, I have been a little struck by this failure of some diplomatic historians to really analyze the other side of the question when they go into these American records and to understand what the motivations are and what the issue is between the two governments.

When we put in the foreign service legislation of 1946, what I greatly hoped for was that the thing we at that time called the Foreign Service Reserve would have worked in the way that it was intended to work—which was to get outsiders (academicians and diplomatic historians in particular) to spend a couple of years in the service, just on an in-and-out basis, and then to return to their universities. Somewhat to my surprise, it did not work. A lot of these people did not apply because they were afraid that the two years would make a break in their seniority and tenure and that somebody would get ahead of them and so forth; the ones who did come in tended either not to be able to return to their universities or not to want to, so we were stuck with them forever. It is too bad it did not work because I do think a few years of that kind of experience would introduce an element of realism that is occasionally missing.

*John Gaddis, Ohio University:* We had a session this afternoon on domestic influences on foreign policy, and I was wondering if you could give us the benefit of your practical experience in this area. What limitations, if any, did you find that domestic influences imposed upon the conduct of foreign policy in your experience?

*Ambassador Kohler:* I regret to say that I missed that particular session. I referred to this issue somewhat in passing, of course, when I said that I think any modern Foreign Service officer is very conscious of domestic influences. He is willing to deal with these influences in terms of (the only terms that they can be dealt with in a democracy) publicity and public pressures and congressional scrutiny and inquiry, even though they go to extremes sometimes. Heaven knows they did in my experience in Joe McCarthy's day. I think it is very good for Foreign Service officers, either when they are back from posts abroad or when they are in posts in the department, to have to go up to Capitol Hill. I would also second the motion I heard someone make in this afternoon's session that congressional hearings provide a lot of information one cannot otherwise obtain—because Congress does have a way of pulling a lot of information out. On the whole I believe it is the right system—I think in the long term it gives us strength.

I came from Ohio and went to Ohio State University. When I was starting to prepare for Foreign Service examinations forty years ago, it was hard to find just the courses one needed to take to pass the examinations. We were very isolationist, and it was not long before I took the Foreign Service exams that Bill Thompson—a famous Chicago mayor who ran on a program of keeping King George out of Chicago—won a whole election on just that platform. When I look back at that and look back at the general acceptance, in my home state of Ohio, of going from a position against entangling alliances to the kind of role we play in the world today, with relatively little flare-up about it—just accepting it as a natural condition that our nation has bound itself in—and when I realize the role that Arthur Vandenberg played in changing the whole mood and tenor of this country, then I think on the whole that public pressures and public opinion have a healthy influence. In spite of having tangled with a few members of Congress during many, many, long hours of testifying before them, I emerged with a healthy respect for most of them. They learn their lessons, and I think that government servants who study *their* lessons do not have to fear congressmen. I think, instead, they can have a very good meeting with them and that it is useful to them. There is a tendency, I think, for a diplomat to become ingrown, to "go native," and so forth.

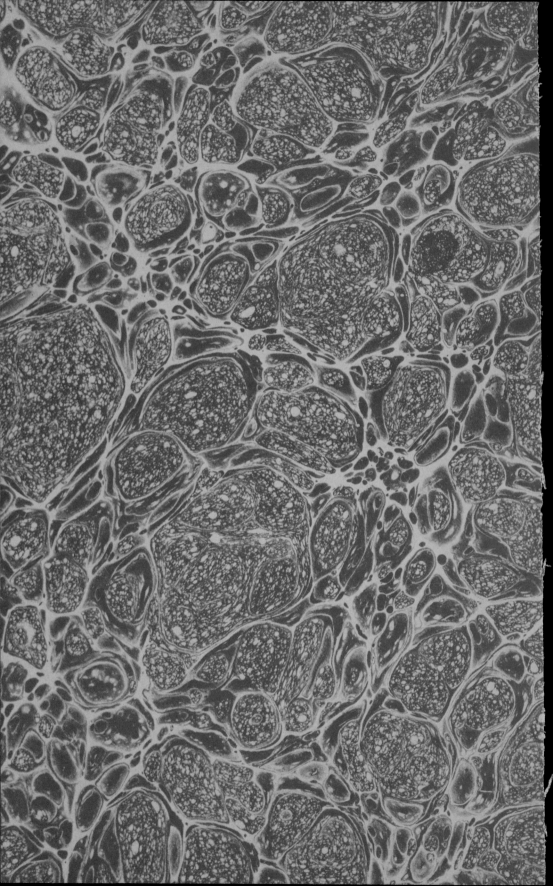